WHY SOCIAL WORK IS IMPORTANT

Malcolm Payne

P

First published in Great Britain in 2024 by

Policy Press, an imprint of
Bristol University Press
University of Bristol
1–9 Old Park Hill
Bristol
BS2 8BB
UK
+44 (0)117 374 6645
bup-info@bristol.ac.uk

Details of international sales and distribution partners are available at
policy.bristoluniversitypress.co.uk

British Library Cataloguing in Publication Data
A catalogue record for this book is available from the British Library

ISBN 978-1-4473-3079-0 hardcover
ISBN 978-1-4473-3081-3 paperback
ISBN 978-1-4473-3082-0 ePub
ISBN 978-1-4473-3080-6 ePDF

Cover design: Robin Hawes
Cover image: iStock/wacomka

Contents

Contents

List of figures and tables

Figures

Tables

Acknowledgements

I am grateful for the many discussions with colleagues, particularly Emma Reith Hall, De Montfort University, on co-production. Some of the material in this book was first developed for conferences, where people present also influenced my thinking. The ones that I can identify and therefore acknowledge are as follows.

'Why social work is still important' at the International Federation of Social Workers (IFSW) European Conference, Prague, 2023. Related variously titled presentations were given at the IFSW European conference online, Serbia, 2021, and a post-graduate seminar at Jan Masaryk University, Brno, Czech Republic, 2017.

'Critical eco practice: a sustainable social work for sustainable social relations?' at Hradec Days of Social Work 2022 international conference, Hradec Králové, Czech Republic, influenced material in Chapters 1 and 12. A revised version of this presentation is published as: Payne, M. (2023) Critical eco practice: how should it develop in social work practice thinking? *Czech and Slovak Social Work*, 23(4): 4–17.

'How social work values are essential to practice' at the 2nd International Conference on Social Work and Sustainable Social Development 2022 (online), Shahjalal University of Science and Technology, Sylhet, Bangladesh; and at 'The essentials of social work', the 14th National Social Work Congress and 2nd IberoAmerican Social Work Congress, May 2022, in Ciudad Real, Spain, and published as: Payne, M. (2022) Por qué los valores del trabajo social son esenciales para la practica. Madrid: Consejo General del Trabajo Social. These papers influenced material in Chapters 7, 9 and 11.

'Social work theory for practice' at Tata Institute of Social Sciences, Mumbai. Online course on History and Perspectives on Social Work, 2021. This course led to the preparation of the analysis in Chapter 5 of 'Social work's streams of thinking', which develops a format used in my various previous publications on social work practice theory.

'Older people's citizenship: social work co-production and participation' at the 1st International Congress in Ageing Communities and Development Challenges, Castelo Branco, Portugal, 2019. This conference stimulated material in Chapters 8 and 12.

'European social works and their identities' at the 7th International Conference of the European Research Institute for Social Work, University of Trnava, Slovakia, 2013. This conference led to the preparation of some of the analysis in Chapter 2, and a revised version of the presentation was previously published as: Payne, M. (2014a) European social works and their identities. *ERIS Web Journal*. 2/2014: 2–14.

★

The case studies are anonymised through omission of identifying details and by changes to information that do not affect the real circumstances discussed.

PART I

Why social work?

Why is there a social work profession throughout the world? To represent the reality that people want and need to secure expertise to deal with complex issues in their lives and complex change in their societies. What are that profession's aims? To develop expertise that focuses on developing human flourishing and social capital in people's lives and in social institutions.

1

Social work: human and social

Introduction: the argument

Social work is important because it represents in any society the organised and professional contribution to improving both human flourishing and the social aspects of wellbeing. Human beings are social beings: all societies consist of social connections among human beings. Being human therefore means that connections always exist, which inevitably leads to societies being sites of cooperation, mutuality and solidarity. Improving any society means that people, as part of natural social behaviour, strive to improve their lives as individuals. In doing so, they also strive to work together to improve collectively the society that is the context of their lives. Any successful society organises to have a social work profession to, where it becomes necessary, co-produce that collective and individual striving for social improvement. That is, the profession works alongside people to achieve collective and individual social progress.

Do you think social work is important?

All social workers, and all people concerned about society, will have their answer to this question. My answer is 'yes' because having social work as part of any society represents that society's commitment to the importance of improving itself.

If we lived in a utopia, a perfect society, would it include social work?

My answer again is 'yes' because human beings are social animals. Cooperation, helping and solidarity with others are an essential part of being human. These actions need to be organised throughout society, as well as being an individual aspiration. Since social work is about organised cooperation in achieving better wellbeing, it would be valued even in a perfect society.

Some people say 'no' because, they argue, in a perfect society, people would have perfect lives, which could not be any better and would not need help from others.

But there are assumptions hidden in the questions and the answers. Human beings are never perfect, and change happens all the time. I cannot imagine people in any society without changes to deal with, difficulties to respond to and improvements to make, so people and their society must arrange to improve. Individuals never achieve that wholly on their own, so social improvement must be collective. Social work is a set of ideas and a participant in social institutions or organisations in the societies where it operates. It is present in most societies across the world. Of course, it varies depending on the ideas and social structures that make up any particular society and the needs for social improvement present in each society.

Also, we don't agree on what 'society' and 'social work' are. People think differently. The yes-people like me think it's human nature to improve help and support for each other, so a perfect society will be organised to include social work to reflect that. The no-people think a perfect society reflects ideal people, who in that perfection will not need to change social relations: perfect individualism within perfect relations. But humanity is always social, so a human society will always contain social work.

Social work's unique contribution

The three parts of the book

In this book, I explore how social work improves people's wellbeing in society. It is divided into three sections. Part I is about aims. Chapter 1 introduces the aims and arguments that the book puts forward: social work is concerned with human flourishing which can only be achieved in social relations. Chapter 2 looks at the aims social work has fashioned to guide its contribution to societies. It does this as part of social agencies managing and organising social provision and policy initiatives, alongside other professions and services.

Part II explores the 'how'. Chapters 3–5 discuss how social work practice contributes uniquely to improving the societies in which it works. The main theme of these chapters is to explore how different practice actions, service strategies and ways of thinking interact to provide a professional service. How that service is organised in societies where it operates is explored in Chapters 6–8. Chapter 6 explains how social work is always practised within the context of social agencies. Chapter 7 explores how it operates in the context of a group of professions contributing to education, health and social care. Chapter 8 brings together the theme of 'co-production', the idea that social care and social work cannot be practised except in concert with the people who are using the service.

What is unique about social work's contribution is its focus on 'the social' aspects of human flourishing and social wellbeing. There is a doing element, a strategic element and a thinking element. The doing element is the focus of Chapter 3 as it looks at actions that respond to people with social needs in their society. That has led to a psycho- and socio-therapeutic approach for parts of its practice. The strategic element is covered in Chapter 4, which explores how social workers direct those actions to achieve personal and social wellbeing. Chapter 5 examines five streams of thought that flow from the cultural traditions of different societies and guide the actions and strategies used in social work. Other professions that are part of social work's practice territory make their own characteristic contributions.

The practice actions, strategies and streams of thought combine to make social work practice what it is. Actions and strategies are the universal part of social work. Combined with the streams of thought, they form social work's distinctive contributions to the different cultural traditions of the societies in which it works.

Chapters 6–8 explore the organisational and social contexts in which social work's unique contribution is made. Because social work is always practised in social agencies, Chapter 6 looks at the impact of those agencies' social aims and roles. Chapter 7 explores how social work's partnerships, relationships and tensions with other professions are worked out. Chapter 8 argues that co-production creates partnerships between social work, its clients and service users, and its agencies. This makes possible a wide range of social provision that social work contributes to.

Part II explores what this special thing called social work is, what it does and how it does so within the social contexts in which it operates. This is how social work contributes to the social aspects of any society.

In Part III, Chapters 9–12 explore economic, political and public understandings of social work and its future. They consider how social work practice and its social contexts interact with wider social forces and how this might play out in the future.

The starting point: experiences of being asked to contribute to wellbeing

My starting point is a recent experience of being asked to help Iulia and Karim. This experience led me to ask the 'utopia' question. The people who asked me to help took for granted that something called 'social work' existed and that I could help make it available to people in difficulties. Reading about this experience, it becomes clear, first, that social difficulties are not wholly caused or wholly owned by the people who experience them and, second, the wish to make social improvements is a natural part of how people respond to distress, but is a tough thing to carry through. This is because we all know that difficulties spring from the less-than-perfect society we live in, and when we come across this reality (again!) we are pushed to do something about it.

Case example: Iulia and Karim, a homeless pregnant migrant couple

Knowing that I have something to do with social work, David, a friend, sent me the following email during a summer hiatus in the then-current COVID-19 coronavirus pandemic. I have edited it slightly and anonymised it; I am grateful that he agreed to my reproducing it here.

> On Sunday, we met a couple outside our church in Norburgh who were asking for help, as they had been sleeping rough. They sat in the same pew as us during the service and then came home with us. We gave them the necessary and somewhere to sleep for a couple of nights, and are now trying to help them keep safe.

They are Iulia and Karim; Iulia is about six months pregnant, and was admitted briefly to Norburgh Hospital. They speak Arabic, but have had very little schooling. Iulia only has basic English. They were in Greenton, but left her father's home after a disagreement. I took them to Norburgh Council asking for temporary housing, but was told that they had been interviewed previously with an interpreter and there was nothing the council could do – they should go to Greenton. We took them to Greenton Council and asked for temporary housing, but were told by an efficient council officer that as they had applied for housing in Norburgh, Greenton could do nothing, Norburgh should have issued them with a letter. We booked them into a hostel in Greenton; I went in and checked that it was reasonably safe. Then we went back to Norburgh Council asking for the letter, but they said no they were not going to issue this.

Councillor Jane Ferber lives next door to us and was displeased with Norburgh's response; she has taken up the matter. We have since then made two further trips to Greenton getting letters signed by Iulia and Karim, giving the council permission to share their details with us and Jane. They are at present living in the Greenton hostel, funded by the church's emergency fund. Iulia has an antenatal appointment on Friday. They need help, but as migrants are not entitled to public funds.

Are they entitled to social work help? If so, how do we point them towards it?

In this distressing story, my friend and his wife, supported by their church, had been most resourceful and energetic in trying to help, far beyond what most people would attempt or expect. Nevertheless, now they were at a loss.

Help is needed in any society for citizens in many social situations

But you might be surprised by the expectation in the last paragraph of the email that there would be social work help in such a situation, available from somewhere, and all they needed was to find where to go for this service. My resourceful friend, a retired high-level international businessman with experience across the world, and his senior healthcare professional wife assume that vulnerable people in difficulties in the UK, perhaps anywhere, would naturally have some sort of *right* to help. Do people like that, in leading roles in our society, routinely take for granted that in such circumstances there is a social worker ready and waiting to step up to help? Is there a *right* to social help? Kathleen Lynch and her colleagues (Lynch, Baker, Lyons et al, 2009) argue that ideas about equality neglect 'affective equality', the right to experience care, love and justice and to offer it to the others that we share our society with. The economic, political and social science thinking, and the law and the social structures expressing that thinking in society, have all failed to prioritise structures like social work that focus on the human and social in our relations. Someone who thinks that a society is only the individuals within it would not agree with

Lynch and her colleagues' (2009) view because individuals don't share in a society. Individualism, the idea that societies comprise only self-reliant individuals, does not provide for affective sharing with others, and therefore neither does it provide for helping behaviour. Arguing that people are on their own and need to stand up for themselves does not understand what it is to be human in a difficult situation. People are citizens, with social rights to participate in society, alongside any other rights they have as human beings. They are autonomous, yes, but only in the decisions they make about how to use their social capital, their participation in social networks and relations.

Both David and his wife are also citizens of humanity, prepared to make a helping contribution when faced with a practical and social difficulty. They are accustomed to making things happen in their own worlds, prepared to take difficulties up, unsurprised that sometimes things go wrong. But they are disconcerted that people with obvious needs and problems do not immediately receive help from the public services or from some kind of profession with a role to help people in such a position.

What is the difficulty? Why cannot they help in the way that they want to and why cannot Iulia and Karim help themselves? David and his wife obviously don't feel fitted for this level of helping: they want someone with a 'helper' label and relevant skills, a social worker, to get personally involved (Lynch, Baker, Lyons et al, 2009 would say 'share affective equality') with Iulia and Karim's difficulties. They think there should be someone to spend time with them, to be alongside them as they negotiate their way through establishing their position in a country that is new to them. In seeing Iulia and Karim are quite reasonably not able to make progress totally on their own, they are expressing an ordinary human response: where's someone who could help? The reaction is: 'there should be a social worker' (or whatever you might call them).

To reflect on this This experience shows that helping with complicated life difficulties, and the failings in organisations and social structures that are supposed to provide helping services to citizens, is not something that even very competent people with available resources feel able to take on. Helping with human complexities and social failings is difficult, and any society needs to have and make available a social structure that includes people and organisations with the expertise to handle such difficulties and failings. Most people, like David and his wife, expect such a structure to exist if they come across a situation that worries them. In twenty-first-century society, that social structure is a profession and a service: social work.

Social work enhances social capital with a relationship, focus and skills

By political policy, the standard local government services in the UK are only minimally available to Iulia and Karim, as migrants, so few public services are expected to respond, as the councillor found in their case. Chapters 6 and 7 show how comprehensive responses to social issues have disappeared in the UK, and in many other countries, with increasing specialisation of formal social care services and retrenchment from having broad support from a welfare state. We have moved to a much more conditional and precarious range of services. The disappearance of comprehensive social help is characteristic of late-twentieth and early-twenty-first-century societies in many parts of the world. Pulling back from social provision by a secure state is an issue for people like David, Iulia and Karim. Their expectations of help as citizens in difficult situations are no longer valid. In many countries, services have never developed to that level of security. But there are one or two good voluntary organisations in our area that could probably help. Provision for good social work requires both the security of an effective state and also the availability of alternative routes to help.

Our local organisations working with refugees don't employ social workers, but I can imagine what a social worker could offer. They could probably help to get some practical services by negotiating with various local organisations and extracting useful help from public services as well (that's the practice strategy element of social work's unique contribution). Iulia and Karim might be too proud and independent to accept this sort of help, but probably by getting to know them a social worker could persuade them to agree to be helped. And then the social worker could do something using the action element of social work's unique contribution.

Once the social worker had a reasonable relationship with them as a result of organising practical help, they would talk through with Iulia and Karim the relationship difficulties with Iulia's father. He is, after all, the future baby's grandfather, and he has been willing to help in the past. Probably some mediation would be possible to resolve whatever difficulty arose between them and get them back with a roof over their head and some family support. Perhaps he could see no end to it, and having a professional who is part of the system working with them, a social worker, would probably help him to accept them back while other ways were found of securing their position. That's an important aspect of secure state social provision, to offer alternatives that provide flexibility. Because personal safeguarding has been so important in recent social work thinking, a social worker would be alert to the possibility that the grandfather has been bullying or misusing them in some way, perhaps using them unacceptably for domestic servitude. One of the important things about social work is that it has built up a breadth of expertise in making effective responses to problem situations that many people inexperienced in these complex interpersonal situations cannot hope to offer. If this is an issue, a social worker could probably get official help to deal with that.

Following up, the social worker would get to know what the possibilities of their receiving public services are. There will be a way of getting access to what bits of provision services are allowed by public policy to supply to migrants. A well-established social worker in the area would already have many of these links and would have responsibilities that would facilitate picking things up quickly. Over time, Iulia and Karim's position could probably be stabilised, and family and other help recruited. They could join in working out how to set them up in the sort of new life they are hoping for. I argue in Chapter 8 that co-production, this drawing the helpstrings together, is crucial for good provision of social work, in Chapter 9 that research shows that this is the approach that service users want, and in Chapter 12 that this is the future of social work. It means that services and people involved in the situation work together to create an involving structure that enhances people's quality of life for the future.

To reflect on this The first thing that training and experience in social work provides is an idea of what to focus on and how to get things moving. One aspect of that is understanding how to go about tackling a set of personal problems entwined with organisational and structural difficulties.

Case example: an unqualified apprentice social worker

Very early in my career as a local authority social work manager, I supervised a colleague who had worked unqualified, without supervision, for another local authority for some years; a bit like the starter in today's apprenticeship qualifying courses. After a while, he said he was confident in the practical element of the unique contribution, but that he had not realised that 'what's first, what's most important' in working with a family, was the strategic foundation of doing something useful in the action aspect of social work. Previously he had just reacted to requests according to the normal routines of his local authority, which he had picked up by being told what to do by his team leader and other colleagues. My view of social work is that it goes beyond simply reacting and following expected routines; this came as a surprise to him. Breaking the boundaries of the everyday by working in alliance through the options to create a strategy is a crucial part of social work when people's starting solutions haven't worked. Strategy for future progress is also important to show people that social work is not nannying people, it's about helping them to get moving in the direction they want to go. He went on to do very well on his qualifying social work education course and no doubt in his social work career, as many of today's social work apprentices do.

In Chapters 2–5, I put forward social work's aims in the territory in which it works, the actions and methods that implement its aims and the streams of thinking that enable social work to make a big impact on people's lives. All of this makes it clear that a society can act successfully with social issues and strengthen its social capital, the networks sustaining the quality of social life that underlies everything a society does to provide wellbeing for its citizens. I argue in Chapters 9 and 10 that social capital is crucial to making the economics and politics of a society work. A successful economic and political system must therefore necessarily pay attention to the quality of the social life lived with it. Social work is an essential element of the quality of that social system when the going gets tough.

The second action element offered by a social worker is that of being human: getting involved, taking time and effort to work on things with Iulia and Karim. This gives them and the people around them confidence that things can be sorted out. Part of this is knowing how to get a trusting relationship going and networking among their social connections and with the people in the organisations and services that might help. Social work is called on when the routine response has failed, so colourless neutrality from officialdom won't cut it; people need to experience through co-production being part of action and engagement on their behalf.

I argue in this book that social work is important because it uses, in actions and strategies, the body of knowledge about how to engage with and tackle serious life difficulties effectively alongside practical help to carry it out. Having such a profession available is one of the ways that a society gives its people the confidence and security to use the practical help available to people in trouble. In this example, Iulia's father is more likely to come round to helping if he can see that there is a way through the problems and there is official help to find the social capital to make it work. In any society, it's the connections and relationships that move difficult things on, not some official system; however, the official system is needed to provide a skilled social work service to secure the connections and the capital.

The social context and its structures

My friend, David, goes beyond the need for practical help and support in a personal relationship. He is clear that the system, the structure for providing the necessary help, is not working properly and maroons people who need help. It has stepped back from being comprehensive, from providing alternative routes to help. Official agencies pass the buck, administration seizes up and documentation for officialdom is the kneejerk requirement. He mobilises political power to get a useful response. More than this, this businessman sees that political choices mean that migrants are left on their own to struggle with difficulties and that economics, social attitudes and structures need to change.

Covert or not-so-hidden racism might be behind some of the poor responses that Iulia and Karim experienced. People might question if they are 'truly' 'in need' or whether public resources should be spent on helping them. Another view might be that their family, or friends and neighbours, even people of goodwill like David and his wife, should help them if they judge that to be right; it should be no business of the government to spend money on helping people who turn up in a country with problems, and we should not be paying for professionals to do this sort of thing either. Good citizens are free to help, and indeed they have, but both Iulia's father and my friends are struggling to work out what to do when there are helping strategies that are obvious to someone with a social worker's experience and training. Or maybe they are not aware of what a social worker might do to help, so it does not occur to people, as it did to David and his wife, to ask for it.

Family and caring volunteers don't have the time and resources to work through the complex byways of helping that a social worker would have the experience and knowledge to pursue reasonably quickly. Social work is an efficiency for society to do its job as a society. But to employ social workers in sufficient quantity and educate and manage a service that would enable them to do this in anything like a comprehensive way is obviously expensive. And wouldn't the offer of it mean that we would find lots of people in need and then it would be even more expensive?

To reflect on this In any society, the political and social choices that a society has made lead to difficulties for the social structures and the people involved, and the choices are integrated into social structures that create the difficulties which are part of less-than-perfect societies. I have argued that any society needs structures that include a profession that aims to improve that society by helping with the difficulties that its choices and structures create. That change-through-helping profession, social work, must have education, methods, skills and organisation to work. You can then argue about how much of it you want and the people or situations it should change through helping.

Human cooperation and competition

The argument for the importance of social work starts from the nature of humanity in the environment on our planet. Because human beings are social animals, wherever they exist, they create societies. And all these societies include helping others, through social relationships. This is because, as social animals, people help each other as a natural part of their humanity. Most spiritual belief systems and secular ideals accept that helping others is a characteristic of being human. Every human society from the beginning of time has had social provision to protect and promote the wellbeing of its people. Social work and today's other social professions are the current expression of that provision, developing and exercising more than a century's creativity in evolving knowledge and skills to carry out helping tasks and providing the social structures for that organised help to be provided. From their origins in the late nineteenth century, these professions have developed to the point where early in the twenty-first century, they are virtually universal, present in almost all countries across the world.

Doubts about social work

Despite this apparent success, some people doubt the value of such social provision and, therefore, social work and other social professions. All professions or services, perhaps especially public services, have their critics and doubters. I want to explain why, despite people's problems with social work, it has an important place in any society.

There are three main arenas of doubt: politics, economics and choice.

Chapter 9 examines policy and political debates about the roles social work should play in society. Politics arises when groups of people in a society oppose or support particular ways of organising social structures. Conflict and debate about those structures are based on beliefs and ideas. Where is social work in the ideas and structures that form the context for society?

Many of these debates connect with economic debates about social work's value, and I examine these issues in Chapter 10. Can, or should, we afford to pay for social work?

Connected with both political and economic issues, there are doubts about whether people want social work and whether they want it to be available in society. I examine these issues in Chapter 11. Do people want their societies to provide help with social wellbeing? The quick answer is yes, they do, but they don't know enough about it to know that they do.

The chapters in Part III connect with the points about social work covered in Parts I and II. Social work's unique contribution, combining human actions into strategies, is important because its presence, field of work and practice assert the value of cooperation and helping as an essential part of any society. It contests the idea that competition for power and resources should dominate social life; this is not the natural human way.

Chapter 12 looks to the future because we can already see changes in the twenty-first century that will both challenge and reinforce social work's importance.

Contesting social Darwinism

One way of thinking that underlies many of these doubts about social work is a view of humanity which gives priority to competition, rather than, as I have done, cooperation. The view says that, like all animals in a natural environment, the biological laws of 'natural selection' mean that people compete with each other and with other animals for the resources to survive. In this view, rather than stretch out a helping hand to others, human animals would naturally snatch away from them the means of flourishing and wellbeing. This view argues that competing is more natural than helping – the 'survival of the fittest'. And it's also effective: doing this enables 'the fittest' to reproduce themselves more successfully than weaker beings. All animals are the same, according to the widely accepted theory about how life evolves from the less complex to more complex proposed by the pioneering biologist Charles Darwin. The social version of this idea is sometimes called 'social Darwinism': implying that human societies are made up of competitive rather than cooperative social animals.

Social Darwinism can be challenged in several ways. The most important point is that, while competition between species of animals is natural, social animals use their cooperation collectively to improve how they compete with other species. Cooperation among human beings – helping each other – is essential to how they compete. A second point is that human beings are more than animals. This is because they can use their rational thinking in cooperation to live their lives successfully and enable them to see their world and society more broadly than its immediate requirements. That's why I emphasise co-production, social work doing its job alongside the people it is involved with. Even in a competitive environment, using rational thinking to operate as social animals, sociality, is more effective than competition. This is because working together by helping increases safety and security and creates social structures that preserve life and the capacity to reproduce the next generation of humans. Part of that is ensuring that the world in which our social structures operate will also flourish. As a result, we have to be concerned about whether it can support our collective life, in its natural environment and in its biodiversity. This analysis of the importance of mutual aid in small-scale communities for the good of humanity and the natural world has been around for centuries, and is well expressed in the ideas of Kropotkin (2022 [1902], p 71, italics in original).

> 'Don't compete! Competition is always injurious to the species, and you have plenty of resources to avoid it!' That is the *tendency* of nature, not always realized in full, but always present. ... 'Therefore combine – practise mutual aid! That is the surest means for giving to each and to all the greatest safety, the best guarantee of existence and progress, bodily, intellectual, and moral.'

There is no clearer statement of the social ethos of social work. And, since all human life depends on biological diversity within our planet's ecological system, solidarity supports cooperation with the whole environment of our lives. It also, therefore, rejects competition where it is damaging. To go further, human diversity also increases the range of possibilities available to use in our cooperative endeavours. That's a biological argument for preserving all sorts of knowledge, skills and thinking, and promoting diversity and inclusion in the solidarity of our societies, including migrants like Iulia and Karim. It's also a biological, ecological argument that social work is important for environmental sustainability. Societies are ultimately not sustainable unless we give priority to solidarity rather than competition.

My agenda for this book

Any society needs to have strong and active social work to do its special combining of action, strategy and specific ways of thinking, alongside other professions, to contribute to the balance between cooperation and competitiveness in human social relations. Social workers need to be able to develop and practise their professional skills, and society needs comprehensive social care services, including public services, to provide a base for social work to make its unique contribution.

Social work is an important part of any society because of its unique potential to contribute to that society's social capital, its collective community and social life and cooperative helping.

Social work is not alone. It is part of a panoply of professions and services, overlapping with or similar to social work. The unique focus and emphasis of social work make clear why social work is importantly different from, and contributes something special to, achieving the work of services that do their work alongside social care and social work. Related professions benefit from making use of social work's contribution.

Finally, I want to show how we should develop social work so that its value to any society in the future is recognised, and its practitioners are able to make their important contribution to helping human societies flourish in all their biodiverse environments.

Taking action on the human and social

Value social capital and social engagement, and the practice actions, strategies and ways of thinking about the social that form social work's contribution to wellbeing. The quality of all human life relies on social cooperation to achieve wellbeing. This therefore requires effective social professions alongside community, family and individual efforts, and other professions.

The next chapters ...

... look at social work's aims and the territory of its work (Chapter 2) and then go on to explore the main elements of its practice (Chapters 3–5).

2

Social work's field of practice

Introduction: understanding social work's field of practice

How does social work bring together the human and the social? Chapter 1 emphasised that human beings are always social. Social work, therefore, is concerned both with individuals improving their wellbeing and flourishing as individuals, and also with improving the wellbeing of their social connections, social institutions and social relationships. This dual focus on both the individual and the social is sometimes a tension for social work: is it possible to improve social wellbeing by individual flourishing? Or does improving the social mean downplaying the individual? Arguing that only individual flourishing is valid, leaving social wellbeing to take care of itself, is inconsistent with social work. It always seeks to do both and, further, claims that individual flourishing can only be achieved in the context of also improving social wellbeing. That is because humanity is always social.

The dual focus, on both the human and the social, is evident in social work's field of practice, the territory that the profession works in. This chapter identifies three aspects which demonstrate this dual focus:

- Four different forms of social work are in use in various parts of the world, forming social professions that all have a dual human and social focus.
- Evidence about the aims of social work establishes its field of practice, which balances the dual focus.
- Evidence about how social workers establish their professional identity shows how they develop the dual focus.

Explaining social work

Imagine you are asked to describe social work and explain what it is to an important group of senior managers or politicians. This doesn't happen often, but some people we work with like to get a full picture. I remember one senior healthcare manager, accustomed to working with people with 'therapist' in their job title, asking me 'Why is it social *work*?' On another occasion, a senior youth work manager, who was untroubled by 'work' because of his own job title, said he thought mine should say who I worked with, since in his view all work with people was 'social'.

Every social worker has at some time to describe or explain social work to others, who have little knowledge of it but may have power over it; professional organisations do this all the time. Or perhaps they're just interested. Explaining professional purposes and roles is part of being accountable, being prepared to justify actions. It also helps social work practice through better alliances and understanding with people who influence it and people who use it. The current way of thinking about such alliances is 'co-production'; more on that in Chapter 8. This chapter aims to think through understanding and representing social work, expressing its accountability and showing our confidence about how important it is.

Different social works

Social professions and their four social works

There are several social works, not just one, carrying on a variety of social professions and practices. I summarise the main points about four of them in Table 2.1. They all contain unique, dual elements, both human and social. Global organisational links exist between these social professions and their practices, but they come from different cultural and national traditions. They also pursue different priorities, because needs around the world vary. Social work, therefore, differs from place to place and from time to time. Limiting our view of social work only to what is relevant here and now, denies that there are wider possibilities than local assumptions. The kind of social work in any society is an economic and political choice. It is important to clarify the choices that any particular society is making and how those choices extend or limit what social work can offer. Knowing about this range of social works also allows us to take on ideas from different traditions and make use of them in new ways.

Social work is a profession in Western welfare states, originating from European states, including the UK, and from the US. The term 'social work' originated as a general term which international social work organisations apply to a wider range of social professions. But 'social work' overemphasises the human aspect of its human/social dual nature. It believes that social issues derived from human relationships are the main source of the problems in any society. Social work therefore aims to help people achieve personal wellbeing and improved capacity to live their lives freely and well within the social structures of the society in which they live. The profession's main practice is to use interpersonal helping relationships to free individuals from personal problems. As well as this, it facilitates broader changes to limit the adverse effects of social problems on people's community, family and individual wellbeing.

Table 2.1 moves on from Western 'social work' to set out other social works that have other ways of using social work's actions to achieve social wellbeing, which may include the interpersonal, problem-based help of Western societies. 'Social care', social assistance or social protection see social work as mainly providing services, emphasising the practical strategies involved in offering help to people and their communities in meeting social and personal needs. This approach lessens the limitations of the 'interpersonal help' form of social

Table 2.1: Four global social works

Type	Derives from	Sees social work aims as	Mode of action	Summary
Social work	Western welfare states, particularly the US	Personal wellbeing and social liberation tackling personal and social problems	Works through relationships between people, develops social capital and resources	Interpersonal action with personal and social problems
Social care, social service	Europe	Service provision and personal help to help deal with social issues	Delivery of social welfare services and personal help	Help through services to meet personal and social needs
Social education, social pedagogy	Mainland Europe	Facilitating informal education and community participation	Strengthens social capital to support personal and social wellbeing	Education to increase community capacity and personal strengths
Social development	Africa, Asia	Social aspects of economic and physical development	Community and group actions to define and pursue social resilience and cohesion	Improve communities' capacity and resilience to resolve shared needs

Source: Developed from Payne (2012, pp 126–7)

work by providing services. 'Social pedagogy' develops informal education to include practice strategies for increasing community resilience and strength to enable people to use their personal capacities and skills. 'Social development' stimulates community activity to improve cohesion and resilience to enhance economic, physical and social resources. It achieves this through the practical strategy of working together on social projects.

The intrusion critique

One criticism of all these social works is intrusion. They involve intervening, that is, cutting across some of the boundaries, in people's lives, and not accepting it if they prefer not to have to change, or not to have someone involved in helping them. On a small scale, this means a professional using social influence on behalf of social institutions to change how people live their lives. If that intervention is on a big scale, that probably means the power of the authorities, the state, is part of that intrusion. Why should our society take that on, and spend effort and resources on it? Why should people accept it? Part of the answer is that human life is social. Chapter 1 proposed that social work is the organised structure of collective participation; however, if the organised and professional contribution to wellbeing is authoritarian and intrusive, people may not connect it with their wish to be involved with others around them. Social work and its practice, therefore, must be designed and organised in ways that make intrusions into the private spheres of people's lives acceptable and understandable. To be accountable, a profession must have an ethics (a value base) to justify intrusion into people's private relationships and social worlds.

All these professional activities aim to improve social wellbeing; however, each social profession, representing each social work, goes about it differently, aiming to achieve slightly different ends. Each type of social work uses a different balance of human methods using educational, interpersonal help and collective action in communities, as well as the practice strategies of doing something people want to achieve. I look at these different balances in more detail in Chapters 3–5.

Critics of social work, and some social workers, are unhappy about the intrusion involved. The main point, though, is that formulations of social work all rely on Chapter 1's 'human is social' assumption. Fostering social wellbeing is a natural part of human flourishing and a society naturally generates action to secure individual wellbeing. In contrast, all the criticisms favour competitive individuality. This critique of the human/social duality claims that societies are more successful when individuals compete for wellbeing, with the total amount of individual gains then resulting in a general improvement in human flourishing. The social work view is that totting up individual gains is not as valuable as improving the feel-good factor that comes from improving social capital by people being involved with others around them.

Naming 'social' and 'work': what does it mean and where does it come from?

Exploring further, these different forms of social work start from the words we use, 'social' and 'work'; where do the variations come from?

'Social' refers to society and to talk about 'the social' assumes that people believe that 'societies' exist, formed of connections among people who share in common their lives in the place they live. And perhaps more than connections: interactions or relationships. These connections, interactions and relationships are 'social capital', the resources that enable people to build better human lives. This also suggests that societies have some degree of continuity in their networks, varying over time, perhaps, which leads to social institutions, patterns of relationships that become established as organisations, and social structures. To talk about the 'social' makes the claim that people's society and the relationships within it are important to them. The word 'social' is attached to the various terms in use globally to describe the forms of social work discussed earlier. The concept of 'social capital' refers to the benefits everyone in a society gets from social connections being expanded and strengthened.

The social aspect of social work is concerned with social relations in social institutions; social work aims to improve those institutions through developing more social capital. The existence of social work expresses a value judgement based on 'idealist' philosophy, which claims that it is both desirable and also possible to improve such a complex phenomenon as a society (Offer, 2006). A society wouldn't have such a profession and service unless it valued those aims and possibilities.

To expand on the practicalities of achieving social improvement through social work involves actions to facilitate, help and improve social relations among people to enhance individual wellbeing. I talk about 'actions' rather than interventions because the idea of intervention accepts the element of intrusion that I discussed in the previous section. Intervention implies that it is acceptable for social institutions and professions to cross personal boundaries to influence individual behaviour in social relations; this is the element that individualist critics find most difficult about social work. Talking about 'actions' emphasises that social work actions are joint. They are co-produced between human beings who join with social workers. This enables them to influence how social work increases the capacity of institutions or organisations they are involved with.

Participation enriches social relations now and for the future. As the International Federation of Social Workers describes it in their constitution: '[social workers] facilitate sustainable social outcomes that enable people and their communities to reach their potential for this and future generations' (IFSW, 2016, Article 4). Although it includes working with people as individuals and their personal potentialities, therefore, social work always does its job within the 'social' aspect of people's lives, their social capital of connections and networks in society. This can contribute to the working of social institutions, in the sense of established aspects of society, such as communities, families and other social groups. It takes place in another kind of social institution, in the sense of settings such as people's homes, faith organisations, leisure facilities, meeting places, schools and workplaces as well as in agencies set up to provide a location for social work. It is this co-production that links the human and social in social work.

The history of the term 'social work' began in the late nineteenth century in the UK and US, at the same time as idealist philosophy developed. It is associated also with 'progressivism' in the US, the idea that societies progress towards a better future. At the time, this inspired political activism trying to achieve that; some people in the US still see themselves as progressivists. People concerned about social issues were thought of as social reformers and social researchers, aiming to improve or understand social conditions in general. Some people were known as social *workers*, because they wanted to do more: something active, to organise or provide help to the people suffering from poor social conditions.

That is why 'action' is such an important element of the human/social duality in social work. Within a wider movement for social improvement, the particular contribution of the first social workers to improving social conditions was to be active in doing something to use the ideas and knowledge that social reformers and researchers were building up. During the early twentieth century, the term began to replace 'charitable' or 'philanthropic' work, particularly as it became a paid job for middle-class women and for organisers in the new services as they began to see that it involved more than administration (Lubove, 1965). This change in terminology was established as a description of this range of activities by the 1930s (Payne, 2005).

An example of how 'social work' was seen in this period, as the broad term for provision for care and social wellbeing, is D'Aeth's (1925) mini-textbook *Social Administration*. Its opening paragraph is 'In this little volume an attempt is made to set out in general what is being done at the present time in England for the care and wellbeing of the human individual, or, in other words, to make a survey of the field of social work' (D'Aeth, 1925, p 9).

This early history of social work reveals an emphasis on active doing. But, the boundary-crossing element of intervention includes intrusion, an image of interfering and busybodying. It has overtones of being moralistic: 'improving' social relations and 'developing' people. Examples of widespread feelings of concern about this aspect of social work appear in some of the quotations, from everyday and specialist literature, supporting the definition of social work in the *Oxford English Dictionary*.

Social assistance, social care, social protection, social service, social professions

While interpersonal problem-based social work is universal, the professional name is not. Varying linguistic usages say something about the range of ways to think about social work. Several variations are used in different countries.

The term is sometimes translated directly from English, where it originated: social work becomes *sozialarbeit* in Germanic or Nordic languages, *travail social* in French, *trabajo social* in Spanish. But there are complications. German- and Spanish-speaking countries also use *sozial assistanz* or *asistencia social* giving significance to 'assistance' by providing services, particularly financial help, rather than 'work'. This is, perhaps, a more standing-aside, helping-hand emphasis rather than the 'take action' through interpersonal relationships approach of social work as English speakers think of it.

To travel beyond Europe and the US, in Türkiye, 'social work' is often translated as *sosyal hizmet*, and sometimes you hear *toplum hizmeti*. Both terms, especially the latter, also carry broader ideas, not of that interpersonal practice to solve problems associated with 'social work', but of 'social service' or 'community service'. Many other languages also refer to broader elements of community or social service, of duty and responsibility. Such usages do not clearly distinguish professional actions from services as some English-language usages of the term 'social work' do; a professional action is a community service in these conceptions.

To describe services like social assistance and social service, the term 'social care' has been adopted in the UK, to make a political link with healthcare. In the 1990s, 'social care' came to replace 'the social services' and 'the personal social services' in UK government terminology, and official documents often refer to an omnibus term: 'health and social care', neglecting those aspects of social work connected with other social services such as education, housing or social security. In most other countries, British 'social care' is called 'social work services', so there is less of a distinction. Talking about 'social care' emphasises that providing effective services is a crucial part of social work, and the official dominance of the term 'social care' seems to subordinate social work to a specific set of service-providing functions within it. Some people have preferred its broad and widely accepted meaning, and the warmth of 'care', compared with a 'social work' seen as more linked to a specific set of, sometimes intrusive, professional activities.

The term 'social care' has been used in the UK since at least 1982, when 'social care planning' was described in the independent but government-inspired Barclay Report (1982, paras 3.2–3) on the 'role and tasks of social work'. It was described as one of social work's two roles, focusing on the practical element of social work's unique contribution; the other was 'counselling', focusing on the human element of that contribution. Social care planning was described in the report as '... to plan, establish, maintain and evaluate the provision of social care'. After the report, people began to use the idea of the 'social care' role to refer to 'indirect' social work in providing services, often primarily with adults, in contrast to direct work in relationships with service users and their families, often primarily concerned with children. Examples of indirect work include organising services or advocating on behalf of service users with other agencies.

Since the 1990s, and in particular after legal changes in the early 2000s, social care, in England and Wales particularly, has often been organisationally divided into 'children's social care' and 'adult social care'. This returns to how services were organised in the period 1948–71. It reflects a long-standing battle between local government education and healthcare services for control of social provision within their services. For example, when the Poor Law was dismantled in the late 1940s, both of the well-established local government education and health administrations were keen that the new children's service should be included within their responsibilities. But public controversy had led to a political imperative to set up a separate department with a clear focus on children.

Similarly, when local government social services departments were established in the early 1970s, medical officers of health again sought to have general social services provision incorporated into health departments. This was fought by social workers, who wanted to achieve a social work-led agency (Hall, 1976; Cooper, 1983). A step further occurred in 1974 when local government and National Health Service reorganisations took place, and social work in hospitals was incorporated into local government social services departments, completing the shift from healthcare control.

Goldberg and Connelly (1982, p 2), in relation to the care of older people, pointed to the value of social work as an emphasis on the social, rather than the economic, in social provision:

The term 'social care', meaning 'the social as distinct from the economic ways in which people look after each other, directly or indirectly' (Barnes & Connelly, 1978), seems to convey more adequately these recent developments in the personal social services. The concept embraces not only social work and other statutory personal social services but also all kinds of voluntary activities as well as self-help and mutual help.

While the logic of the separate categories for adults and children lingers in public perceptions from its history, it rejects this emphasis on the 'social'. This is important because making social work secondary to an emphasis on education (in children's services) or health (in adult services) means that decisions are sometimes taken to accord with the needs of the dominant service and its professional outlook, rather than the social needs in the situation.

Case example: medicalised COVID-19 pandemic reactions failed social care

In early 2020, the response to the COVID-19 global pandemic was led by medical professionals and the need for more treatment beds in hospitals. For a period, the UK government discharged older people from hospitals (healthcare) to care homes (social care) without testing for the disease, leading to increased risk of infection in the care homes. In many other countries, not only in the UK, a lack of understanding led to poor outcomes for older people receiving social care (Payne, 2022).

Another term, 'social protection', is used internationally. It refers to economic and social policies concentrating on the economic wellbeing of people in poverty, so there are connections not only with social work, but also with social assistance and with the UK usage 'social welfare', which since the 1980s mainly refers to economic help, although it retains its broader meaning in some African and Asian countries, notably India. 'Social protection' is used mostly by the social policy arms of multi-national agencies. An example of what it means is the World Bank's brief defining mission statement: 'Social protection systems help poor and vulnerable people cope with crises and shocks, find jobs, invest in the health and education of their children, and protect the aging population' (World Bank, 2022). Services to provide for some of these aims might include social work, but the main focus is on employment and social security policy interventions at national and global levels.

Summarising, there are variations in the implications of the terms used to refer to social work and what it does. Understanding social work becomes more complicated when we think about different social professions, that is, occupational groups that have aims similar to social work in the UK and in English-speaking countries, but classify it differently or do it in a different context. Social pedagogy and social development are the two most important social professions that do not use the term 'social work' to describe their actions, and I discuss these in the next two subsections.

Social education and social pedagogy

The distinction between 'social education', 'social pedagogy' and 'social work' is salient in Europe. Social pedagogy is the most widely used term for this view of social work, deriving from German and Polish practice theories of *sozialpaedagogik*, but the related idea and term 'social education' is used in countries such as France and the Netherlands, with the latter also using 'social cultural' work.

In Germany, there has been an institutional distinction. This is because *sozialpaedagogik* is historically associated with traditional universities connected with teacher education while *sozialarbeit* was once regarded as a more practical subject concerned with providing social assistance, taught in less-prestigious vocational colleges. These differences are disappearing as status differences between the institutions come under pressure from moves to rationalise professional education on a Europe-wide basis through, for example, the Bologna process (Lorenz, 2005). There are also different traditions and interpretations within social pedagogy, just as there are within social work. For example, one Nordic tradition strong in Denmark is informal education in the widely available after-school services, providing informal care and education for children whose parents go out to work. Another Danish tradition is to use social pedagogy as a theoretical base for therapeutic work with children in public care. Awareness of this tradition means that attempts have been made to interpret one or more of these ideas in UK social work, and a number of UK professional training courses as a result (Jones, 1994; Cameron, Petrie, Wigfall et al, 2011; Hatton, 2013; Charfe & Gardner, 2019).

Social pedagogy, as its name implies, builds social learning. In some countries this is part of universal community social provision; elsewhere it values organising social learning as part of making progress in community and life relationships. This conception contests the understanding of social work in English-speaking countries, where it is often seen as working on something social that has gone wrong, as a service for people who are problematic in some way or who are experiencing troubles. It may be therapeutic, helping people move on or recover from those troubles, or it may be controlling, managing or ordering society. It includes a therapeutic idea dominated by the US conception of social work as a form of interpersonal and often individualistic help, particularly with mental health troubles. Also, more present in social work than in social pedagogy is a social cohesion aspect more associated with social work in public services in the European welfare states, such as adult and child protection or safeguarding, and assessment for and delivery of social services, such as care provision for disabled or older people.

Social development

Social development is a significant form of social work in many resource-poor countries of the Global South. It brings together people who share a common interest or location in participative groups to plan and activate social progress as part of economic development, where economic development takes political priority. Although this meant an important priority was to work with people living in poverty, increasingly social development has focused on the interests of groups that are oppressed and discriminated against because of shared but devalued identities, such as disabled people or women. Exchanges of ideas and personnel between colonies and colonial powers in the 1940s and 1950s developed community interventions in a locality or neighbourhood. This often involved work to increase facilities for children, improve housing and living conditions and reduce health and other consequences of poverty. Similar methods of practice in both Western and former colonial countries encouraged participation in combating oppression and co-producing local services responding to identified needs in both contexts, both poverty in resource-poor countries and also deprived communities in richer countries. Sanders (1982) in a classic early presentation of 'developmental social work' proposed five elements: a focus on social change rather than social control; engaging with a wide range of sectors of the economy; institutional and structural change; concern for cultural factors; and participation from a range of interests aiming for social justice.

United Nations programmes for community development during the last half of the twentieth century moved towards the concept of social development (Midgley, 1995; Midgley & Conley, 2010). This was increasingly taken up by social work professional literature in Africa (for example, Patel, 2015) and Asia (Desai, 2014, 2015; Tan, Chan, Mehta et al, 2017).

To show how Sanders' (1982) professionalised conceptualisation has been enhanced, I have edited Patel's (2015, pp 124–5) brief statement on present-day multisectoral and multidisciplinary social development. This identifies its key dimensions to illustrate its focus as follows:

- A vision of an empowered just and humane society, aiming for pro-poor policies and challenging inequality.
- A goal of promoting social and economic development inclusive of socially excluded people.
- Principles of social and economic justice, empowerment, collective action to promote public benefit and values seeking more equal distribution of resources and liberation.
- Programmes focused on supporting vulnerable people and groups to build assets through local development, including productive employment for excluded people and strengthening social capital, good governance and democracy.

- Its auspices are pluralist, involving public, private and civil society sectors of the economy.
- Participants and change agents include both providers and beneficiaries.
- Local, national and global governments are active participants, with roles also in protecting rights.

Patel distinguishes this approach from institutional approaches to social welfare, which are more characteristic of English-speaking social work, focused on providing help and services for people experiencing oppression or troubles in their lives and relationships. She also separates the ideals of social development from residual services, providing the minimum necessary when people are unable to finance economic and social survival.

Summary: social work globally

Looking across the globe, over the twentieth and twenty-first centuries, a notion of social work has arisen which describes professional activity that focuses on social aspects of human life. There are various conceptions of it and there are variations in emphasis and interpretation in how it conceives of its nature. Four important variations in emphasis are:

- Social work: mainly interpersonal actions to respond to social problems.
- Social care, social services: services to improve social wellbeing.
- Social education, social pedagogy: actions to strengthen people's capacity, learning and resilience in their communities.
- Social development: facilitating equality and social change to strengthen the capacity of social institutions in responding to social needs, particularly among excluded or poor people.

Different types of service provision, such as social assistance, social care and social protection are present in these interpretations of social work as a form of action on a variety of concerns for social wellbeing.

Defining social work's field of work

What does it mean to define something?

Moving on from this broad account of social work as an institutional presence across the globe, this section deals with attempts at defining it more closely. Definitions are brief statements offering an overall grasp of the meaning of a concept. They help to identify a field of work, territory, the area of activity and concern. But they cannot express fully, in one brief statement, social work's identity, because that is complex, it varies across the globe and there might be many legitimate disagreements about what it does or should consist of. Many attempts at definition exist and they are never comprehensive, or forever.

When I reviewed the nature of dictionary and professional definitions of social work over the twentieth century (in Payne, 2006, ch 2; see also 2009), I found that dictionaries aim to interpret common understandings of an unfamiliar term. Their succinct characterisation of social work is a starting point for inquiring minds, rather than a final disposition. Formal professional definitions, I found, were often made at important turning points for international or national social work organisations to clarify and express the meaning of the term. They are what Castells (1997, p 8) calls 'project identities', attempts by social actors such as governments or professional bodies to define or redefine their position in a society and transform it to their advantage. They reflect the purposes for which the definition was devised and the historical, political and social context in which it was created, drawing, as Castells says, on the cultural traditions available to them.

The varying definitions and understandings inevitably reflect the cultural sources of social work in each country or region and how people involved want to change that. An example is the analysis of definitions of social work practice issued by the regulatory authorities in each of the fifty-one US states (Hill, Fogel, Plitt Donaldson et al, 2017). They found that, while both interpersonal practice with individuals and practice with communities aimed at broader social objectives were covered, there was a wide variety in how the profession was characterised, even in just one country. The same is true for the official reports and studies everywhere, which inevitably define social work to help meet their aims within the cultural and national expectations within which they were created.

There are three main ways of creating definitions:

- Expressing the essence of the concept. The aim is to describe specific things that have to be present for an activity to be social work. If they are absent, it is clear that it is not social work.
- Listing the elements that make something up, where an essence cannot be easily expressed, but can be observed by looking at the sorts of things that social work consists of.
- Giving a range of examples, so you can say 'If what you're looking at is like these, then there's a good chance it's social work.'

Next, I look at two examples offered by professional bodies in social work about the field of work. These definitions help in understanding social work's aims and values.

Example 1: The global definition of social work

The two main international social work organisations offer an agreed definition, the 'global definition of social work', to represent a broad view of social work to decision makers and policy makers. Table 2.2 sets out the definition approved in 2000, alongside the revision approved in 2014. I select this example because they are widely referred to, including by governments and official bodies,

Table 2.2: Global definition of social work

2000	2014
The social work profession promotes social change, problem solving in human relationships and the empowerment and liberation of people to enhance wellbeing. Utilising theories of human behaviour and social systems, social work intervenes at the points where people interact with their environments. Principles of human rights and social justice are fundamental to social work.	Social work is a practice-based profession and an academic discipline that promotes social change and development, social cohesion, and the empowerment and liberation of people. Principles of social justice, human rights, collective responsibility and respect for diversities are central to social work. Underpinned by theories of social work, social sciences, humanities and indigenous knowledges, social work engages people and structures to address life challenges and enhance wellbeing.

Source: IFSW (2014)

applicable internationally, agreed by representative bodies of social workers and cover a range of issues about the nature of social work. There were previous such definitions, but the twenty-first-century format created in 2000 has been retained in the 2014 revision, so comparing the two allows us to consider recent shifts in thinking about the nature of the global profession. The format combines different sorts of definitions: it presents elements of social work's essence, and, particularly in the 2014 revision, seems also to add examples to extend a reader's understanding of the points being made.

Differences between the 2000 and 2014 global definitions

The broad content of the definition remains the same, describing:

- three objectives
- value principles
- knowledge or theoretical bases
- social work actions

The definitions, therefore, imply that to understand social work requires exploring its objectives, principles, knowledge or theoretical bases and actions, and I follow this in Chapters 3–5.

The 2014 definition is longer, words have been added and some language and the positioning of some concepts have changed. The main changes are as follows:

- Inclusion of an emphasis on practice as the basis of the profession, that this is important in understanding it. I have followed this point in Chapter 3, highlighting that understanding practice actions is essential to expressing social work's role in the world.
- Inclusion of a statement that social work is also an academic discipline, that it is not just practical.

- One of the three objectives is changed, from 'problem solving in human relationships' to 'social cohesion'.
- Value principles are moved from being a bit of an afterthought to the second point in the definition, and thus given greater prominence.
- The priority given to the two principles is reversed, with social justice coming first in the 2014 revision.
- Two value principles are added to the 2000 definition: collective responsibility and respect for diversities and they become 'central' rather than 'fundamental'.
- Theory has become an 'underpinning' rather than being 'utilised', and the two theories of 'human behaviour'; and 'social systems' are replaced by a different formulation of 'social work, social sciences, humanities and indigenous knowledges'.
- Social work actions shift from intervention, towards 'engagement to address', reflecting concern about the issue of intrusion, discussed earlier in this chapter. The focus is shifted from the 'point where people interact with their environments' to 'engaging people and structures to address life challenges and enhance wellbeing'.
- Because values are moved forward, actions come at the end. By starting Part II of this book with social work actions in Chapter 3, I am showing that I think this downgrading in importance does not help to understand social work.
- 'Problem solving in human relationships' becomes 'address life challenges' and shifts from an objective to being an action, its position shifting from near the beginning to near the end.
- 'Enhance wellbeing' is shifted from applying to all the objectives towards being something that the actions address, and therefore from early to late in the definition.

Everyone can make their interpretation of how to regard these changes, and the associations provide a more detailed commentary. I would make the following points.

Understanding the differences

A significant aspect of the 2014 revision is the increased material on theory and practice: first, it asserts at the outset the importance of practice, then it extends the description of social work's knowledge base. It puts first in the list a claim that theories of social work are valid and important, rather than, as in 2000, behavioural and social theories from outside social work, and signals the breadth of knowledge sources used by social workers, not just the social sciences but also the humanities and indigenous knowledges. This displaces from the 2000 definition a long-standing formulation that social work uses knowledge from both psychological and social sources, representing a traditional formulation of the human/social duality discussed in this chapter. It also dispenses with systems theory terminology, which is mainly influential in Germany and the

US. This better represents the global view. In this way, the 2014 revision claims the importance of social work understanding before other knowledges.

The change of one of the three objectives from 'problem solving in human relationships' to 'social cohesion' does two things. First, it broadens objectives out from the long-standing theorisation of social work in Europe and the US as concerned with people's problems and social problems, which may be intuitive to many people who have been influenced by that tradition. There are both social and psychological objections to it. For one thing, recent developments in psychology and social work practice argue that focusing on problems starts from a negative, and it is better to help people identify goals, opportunities, solutions and strengths in their lives rather than look for negatives in their present situation. The shift also solidifies a move from a medical model of diagnosing and correcting problems towards a more open-minded social model of practice. This perhaps reflects a shift in assumptions about the role of social work in society. More broadly, 'problem solving' might see the people that social work helps as troubled or problematic, accepting the stigma that goes with seeing people in that way, or see working with troubled individuals as a way of resolving social and structural issues in society. All of these views are at least questionable.

Connected with such a view is the shift from talking about problems to discussing challenges. In a way, this may be just an update to twenty-first-century conventional managerial terminology, but it also reflects a practice assumption. Perhaps such views might be criticised as unrealistic idealism. Another possible reason for this change is the perception that the previous formulation, problem solving, is of a different, rather practical, kind from the other objectives that the definition sets out: social change and empowerment. Cohesion presents a similar broad conceptual objective, so that change makes the definition more consistent. It also reflects a shift from emphasising the Western view of social work as problem based, to a more open conception of accepting the social cohesion emphases of other social professions around the world.

Second, the change from problem solving to a cohesion objective asserts the role of social work in contributing to ideas such as cohesion, cooperation, participation and solidarity in society. The social cohesion role might be seen in two ways. First, it presents a social work role as beneficent and possibly to be valued by society and by the powerful within society. On the other hand, second, it hints at a well-known critique of social work that it serves to control or maintain the present social order rather than seek improvements in society. Including 'social cohesion' among the three objectives points to a tension between this objective and the social change and empowerment objectives, supporters of which sometimes have their doubts about cohesion.

The extension of the list of principles incorporates two new issues: 'collective responsibility' and 'respect for diversities'. Both, as with the cohesion objective, emphasise solidarity as an important aspect of the definition. Collective responsibility implies a mode of social work action, working through getting people to work together through the issues they face, mutual aid, participation, and including co-production. Perhaps this includes the social worker as well as people using the services. While these two issues might be covered by social justice and human rights, they give a stronger clarity to collectivity, diversities and respect. Including respect makes a connection to the value of 'respect for persons' or 'for others' frequently included in discussions of social work values and important in other similar professions (Downie & Telfer, 1969).

A final comment: the switch in priority of human rights and social justice, together with the other points I have made here, suggests a greater importance of the collective and the social in the 2014 revision compared with the more individualist rights-based account of the 2000 definition. It thus reflects a political choice made by the framers of the definition.

The aims of social work establish its territory

The global definition's three aims help to identify a territory for social work, a field of work in which it makes its unique contribution. I first set this out in Payne (1996), using political and sociological ideas. Later, I revised it using the global definitions as they were created and then amended. I present it in Figure 2.1.

I represent these objectives in Figure 2.1 as the corners of a triangle, which forms the boundary of social work practice. The space in the triangle depicts the territory within that boundary claimed by the social work profession. Its aims are debated and fulfilled within that territory and so it represents the different emphases we found earlier when looking at the different social professions. These social work objectives connect with different political views about how

Figure 2.1: Three social work objectives and their underlying political philosophies

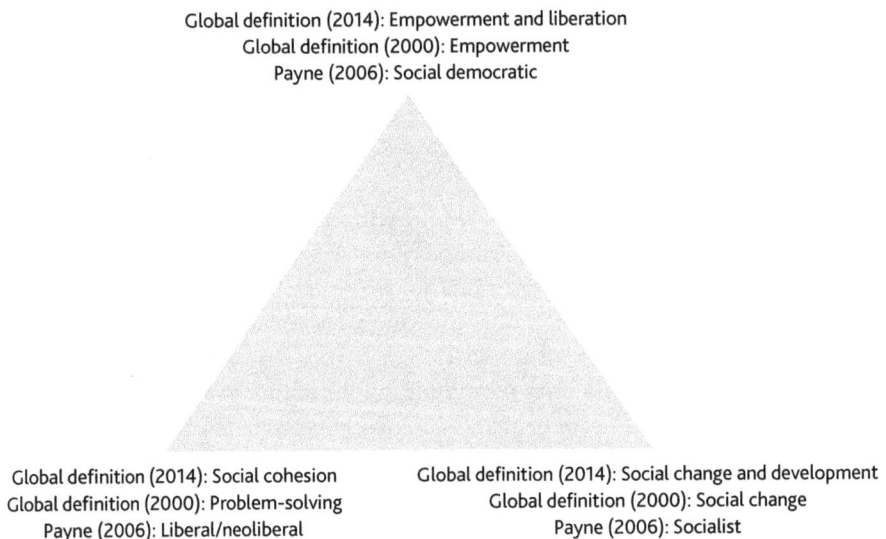

Global definition (2014): Empowerment and liberation
Global definition (2000): Empowerment
Payne (2006): Social democratic

Global definition (2014): Social cohesion
Global definition (2000): Problem-solving
Payne (2006): Liberal/neoliberal

Global definition (2014): Social change and development
Global definition (2000): Social change
Payne (2006): Socialist

welfare should be provided, which I look at in more detail in Chapter 9. Each objective represents a political position in social work, connected with a political philosophy that would be recognised more widely in society, socialist, liberal or neoliberal and social democratic political philosophies (Payne, 2006). Social workers operate within this territory, and their practice balances these three objectives. For example, if they mainly look at social cohesion objectives in their practice, they may limit their emphasis on social change or empowerment in their work; however, those objectives are unlikely to be completely absent from what they do. The balance of what they do may shift over time or in particular aspects of their tasks.

Case example: doing interpersonal problem solving and social development together

An example of the kind of balance I'm talking about is when I worked in local government children's safeguarding, mainly on a public housing estate, and therefore doing mainly social cohesion work. The everyday aim was interpersonal problem solving. I also represented the local authority on the committee of a community advice project in the area, providing information services mainly about poverty. In this way, I included social change in my overall practice. Both social work aims also included different aspects of both the human actions and practice strategies of social work's unique contribution. All social work was there.

Example 2: Social Work Reform Board public description of social work

Table 2.3 sets out the 'Public description of social work' created during the work of the Social Work Reform Board for England, set up by the British government. The reason for doing this is stated in the board's report, as follows:

> The Task Force has developed a new description of social work as a first step towards a much stronger common understanding of the role and purpose of the profession. It has been developed in plain English to help the profession meet the challenge of explaining what it does to service users and the public. (Social Work Task Force, 2009, p 66)

This 'description' specifically does not set out to be a 'definition', and presents it in everyday language to help social workers explain themselves to others. Its approach is largely descriptive; it uses the kind of definition that gives examples to indicate what social work is, but without trying to be exhaustive. In tone, it seeks to be reassuring to people who have doubts about whether social work might be useful to them, or worry that it's an intrusive form of control or management of their lives.

Compared with the global definitions, it does not try to set out broad principles or objectives; in particular human rights, social justice and diversities are absent,

Table 2.3: Public description of social work

Social work helps adults and children to be safe so they can cope and take control of their lives again.

Social workers make life better for people in crisis who are struggling to cope, feel alone and cannot sort out their problems unaided.

How social workers do this depends on the circumstances. Usually, they work in partnership with the people they are supporting – check out what they need, find what will help them, build their confidence, and open doors to other services. Sometimes, in extreme situations such as where people are at risk of harm or in danger of hurting others, social workers have to take stronger action – and they have the legal powers and duties to do this.

You may think you already do this for your friends and family, but social workers have specialist training in fully analysing problems and unmet needs, in how people develop and relate to each other, in understanding the challenging circumstances some people face, and in how best to help them cope and make progress. They are qualified to tell when people are in danger of being harmed or harming others and know when and how to use their legal powers and responsibilities in these situations.

You may think that you'll never need a social worker, but there is a wide range of situations where you or your family might need one, such as:

- caring for family members;
- having problems with family relationships and conflict;
- struggling with the challenges of growing old;
- suffering serious personal troubles and mental distress;
- having drug and alcohol problems;
- facing difficulties as a result of disability;
- being isolated within the community;
- having practical problems with money or housing.

Source: Social Work Task Force (2009, p 67)

and there is a strong emphasis on safety, risk of harm and social workers' legal powers and responsibilities. Hidden in the text, however, are some of the same principles in the global definitions. For example:

- 'make life better' is another way of saying the global definition of 'enhance wellbeing';
- 'take control of their lives' is the global definition of 'empowerment and liberation';
- 'partnership' connects with the collective responsibility element of the global definitions;
- 'understanding challenging circumstances' connects with 'address life challenges' in the 2014 global definition;
- the emphasis on training and qualification connects with the global definition's concern to promote social work's academic discipline and knowledge base. And the practical examples of when social work might intervene and the issues that it deals with also pick up the 'practice-based profession' of the global definition.

Summary: social work's aims and field of work

Accounts by social work professionals of their field of work, objectives, values, and knowledge and practice approaches help us to understand the boundaries of its claimed territory. We can say: this is the area in which it operates. But it does not say much about what social work consists of. An eminent Swiss social worker, Staub-Bernasconi (2017), for example, comments that the global definition only offers vague generalities, such as 'life challenges' and proposes a 'moral overload' of contradictory professional values. Similarly, she argues that its formulation of human rights and social justice as important professional values simply lists value ideas without articulating how they may be applied specifically in social work. Consequently, she says, they dispossess clients of their distress and fail to provide an explicit mandate for professional roles.

Social work's identity

Why social work's professional identity is important

Creating Castells-style 'project identities' (1997), as these definitions do, seeks to gain authoritative legitimation of social work's role and status. Identity is about what the social factors included in the definition say about a profession, what makes a professional similar to or distinct from others. It connects with the idea of identification because strong similarity factors lead people within a social group to identify with other members of the group. This is important because social factors create solidarity. For example, shared commitment to the kind of objectives set out in the global definition and 'public explanation' of social work creates values that seem to contrast with dominant economic and political values in society, which are sometimes inimical to social work practice (see Chapters 9 and 10). Thus, Hyslop (2018) argues that identification with a set of values associated with the identity of social work generates a robust resistance to impractical economic and political demands. It allows social workers to evaluate whether their agency is supporting the full possibilities of social work, or only pursuing a limited conception of it; more on this in Chapter 6.

But the fact that the social work organisations think that the definition is needed suggests that social work's claims about its identity have not achieved legitimacy; it still seems uncertain, perhaps threatened, needing to be asserted and clarified. Looking at the debate within the social work profession about its identity, therefore, helps to understand the issues that it sees as important in representing itself to colleagues. It also helps in making explanations to people such as politicians and policy makers with influence in determining their professional role and to actual and potential clients. This is because thinking about identity shows us how it is built up from personal factors in social workers' make-up, from group membership or sets of social connections. It also develops from formal memberships in collectives where social workers practise, such as teams and organisations, which may be multiprofessional (Sullivan, 2000, pp 2–3; Webb, 2017, p 1).

Research on social work professional identities, reviewed in the next subsection, shows how these multiple identities present conflicts and difficulties. Webb (2017, p 2) suggests that identity has consequently become a significant area of debate within social work since the millennium as an alternative way of clarifying social work's field of work and role.

Are social workers overconcerned about their uncertain professional identity? Many professionals have concerns about their professional identity and threats to it (Breakwell, 1983, 1986). There is a constant process of negotiation and reconstruction of identities as occupational groups and professions adapt to change and their need to control their work (Navrátil & Bajer, 2018). González (2018) discusses how people's obligations spring from threats to their identity. To resist threats to their identity, groups need to create a 'practical identity' that works for them in their relationships with others to help them respond to others' attacks on the worth of what they are doing. Defending their identity in everyday interactions with colleagues in other professions and with the public helps professionals, and all social groups, to clarify their practice and their role in society for themselves.

That the anxiety about professional identity is wider than social work is obvious in studies of other professions. Ten Hoeve, Jansen & Roodbol's (2014, p 295) literature review of studies about nursing identity, for example, might surprise social workers and others who view nursing from the outside. It seemed to nurses that their identity was 'diverse and incongruous' because of the profession's 'invisibility and their lack of public discourse'. Yet public discourse seems to have a very positive view of the value of nursing.

Another example is Zhang's (2013) study of midwives, an immensely valued group you would think, which focuses on their concern about being devalued by colleagues in healthcare settings and explores how they managed their work to build control of their practice, negotiating with other professionals in their setting who might influence how they do their job. Leah (2017) studied the professional identities of nurses, social workers and occupational therapists who became 'approved mental health professionals', a professional and legal role in England previously undertaken only by social workers. Through dialogue, they created images of differing professional perspectives, both with each other and other colleagues in their service, seeking to span professional boundaries by creating hybrid roles. What these studies, and many others, tell us is that social groups and professionals often perceive uncertainties about their social identities and may see their roles as threatened or devalued; social work is not alone in this. These studies also suggest that professional identity is often subject to change because of changes in the organisations and social structures that surround a profession, such as employing agencies and other professions.

Establishing social work's professional identity

Important aspects of the process of establishing and then enacting social work's professional identity are:

- Professional socialisation, particularly through social work education and other ways in which professionals prepare for practice.
- Professional practices which create patterns of accountability and discretion within and between cognate professions, that is, other occupational groups whose work connects with social work actions.
- Workplace relationships within organisations in which social work and other professional activities are practised, which create boundaries and establish jurisdiction and territory in relation to other organisations and professions.
- Class, gender and other social divisions which generate differences in status and power, alliances, conflicts and inequalities. (Hudson, 2002; Webb, 2017)

Professional identity derives from formative life experiences and attitudes. Daly's (2018) study of twenty Scottish social workers found that a variety of life experiences brought people into social work: lived experience, that is, what had happened to them during their lives; family and community values; religious and church experiences; political and social awareness; and experience of volunteering. For most, a common motivation was a sense of wanting greater fairness and justice, a wish to help people and a wish to do something practical in their work, all of which were present in earlier studies, such as Hindmarsh's (1992) study of New Zealand students, and in the professional representation of social work discussed earlier in this chapter. A Czech study (Navrátil & Bajer, 2018) also found that identity formation drew on such established perspectives in social work's literature and the policies and political perspectives of social work agencies.

Studies of social work education find that, in the early stages of their professional career, students struggle with establishing their professional identity, combining a mix of the desired traits of their profession, a growing understanding of collective views of its identity, and working through a process to gain a subjective sense of what helped them to perform confidently as a social worker with both colleagues and people they served (Wiles, 2013).

Daly and Kettle's (2017) study identified the importance of 'fateful moments', when significant events in the student's experience led to an opportunity to pause, reflect and reconsider existing thinking to redirect the creation of important aspects of identity. Tamm's (2010) study of 122 Estonian social work students identified positive features of their self-concept as being professional in their work, including being innovative in practice, achieving results, cooperating with others, being able to build empathy with service users, being able to take risks, and to be self-confident in their practice. Their professional identity incorporated a commitment to the work, being innovative, gaining autonomy and influence as they developed, being seen as professional in their behaviour, approval from colleagues and managers, self-confident in taking action, being able to cooperate with others, and motivated to grow as practitioners.

Roscoe and Pithouse's (2018) study of seven social work students carrying out assessments of older people for care services in the UK found that in building their professional identity, they incorporated discourses in the theoretical literature (for example, one-to-one work, assessment) and in the agency context (for example, legal powers, bureaucratic decision-making processes) to form accounts of their practice aims and actions.

Wheeler (2017a, 2017b) studied how social workers developed their professional identity, internalising this to support effective actions when working with clients and colleagues. She identified four important areas in which this occurred:

- During personal experiences of being helped or helping prior to beginning professional education.
- Discussing professional identity informally with peers during their professional education.
- Establishing a reciprocal personal relationship with their practice educator during practice placements within their professional education. Practice educators are often called practice teachers or fieldwork or student supervisors in older literature or in countries other than the UK.
- An agency environment which was concerned about and supported professional socialisation during practice education placements. An Italian study (Bruno & Dell'Aversana, 2018) found that explicit planning to integrate the work in practice education with an academic understanding of social work is required to help students develop ideas about their professional identities.

Mackay & Zufferey's (2015) study of how social work educators in two Australian universities helped students to construct their professional identity found that they drew on a range of professional discourses regarding helping and caring, emancipatory aims and social control discourses; the sorts of discourses about social work actions discussed in Chapter 3. Practitioners were led to present themselves to other professions and clients, by explaining their perspectives on the task that they were to carry out.

This struggle seems widespread in education and socialisation as social workers gain experience and become increasingly confident in practice after qualification. Leigh (2017) found a confident sense of self as a social worker grew from actions during practice to establish credibility with both clients and colleagues. She saw these as performances, actively demonstrating competence through 'credibility work' in practice actions and in paperwork. Fargion's (2006) Italian study of how social workers used theory in their practice found that, rather than seeing theory as a source of practical ideas for implementation, they saw instead a series of world views which helped them to understand and explain the situation as a whole. The theory helped them clarify with clients and colleagues the duties, powers and responsibilities that they were implementing, or the relationship factors that they were working on. Fargion's later (2008) study of 91 Italian social workers' self-identities found that this was formed through a struggle to create a balance between the psychological and social in their work, which connects with the human/social duality discussed in this book. They were also troubled by difficulties in practising with a scientific perspective, as against a humanistic perspective emphasising helping relationships in their practice, and the balance between using existing theories of practice against theory-creating practice. She argues that the process of understanding these balances is characteristic of social work internationally.

Similarly, a study of 34 Estonian social workers in local government and 13 social work policy makers and educators (Mitendorf & van Ewijk, 2018; Mitendorf, 2020) identified a negotiation between internal and external 'norms' about social work. The negotiations were around discourses on the aims and content of social work, especially the idea of helping people to help themselves, structural changes in social services, demands and complaints by powerful or concerned people, and the ambiguous relationship between social work and social policy. Social workers identified an impact of neoliberal policy ideas, which shifted social service provision from institutionalised social provision towards family- and community-based alternatives. This included substituting service provision with ideas of active citizenship, mutual assistance and service users meeting their own needs.

Beddoe (2017) suggests that, while healthcare settings offer many opportunities for demonstrating credibility and identity, multi-professional engagement often diminishes the clarity of particular professions' fields of practice. Nevertheless, medical dominance has declined, leaving space for other professions to build successful professional capital. Lévesque, Negura, Gaucher et al (2019) studied thirty Canadian healthcare social workers and identified four elements organising their social representation of social work: counselling for support; empowerment and respect; social justice; and compassionate vocation. There were three families of concepts in their thinking:

- The first was social work's social context. Issues here included the profession's definition, its field of practice, and filling gaps in essential areas of service provision. Practice ideas such as empathic listening, empowerment and social justice and mitigating burnout were significant. Working together was also important, including shared perspectives of the work among colleagues, the bond among social workers and developing a professional identity that could be recognised in the service.
- The second area was the personal identity factors such as commitment to pursuing social work, meeting needs relevant to particular populations or specialisations and practice areas, the desire to help others, incorporating personal life experiences, commitment to advocacy on behalf of service users and thinking about users in the person–in–environment approach typical of North American social work.

- The third area was external influences on identity, including awareness of broad societal pressures, including maintaining political awareness about the impacts of the organisation's policy and public policy on social work and the service. The responsibility to build professional capacity in individual, team and agency networks was also an issue for them.

Studies of practice in various forms of childcare social work also suggest that building a shared identity takes time, as organisational changes disrupt practice settings (Harlow, 2017), raise conflicts between positive practice and the focus on risk management according to managerial demands based on economic and policy issues (Keddell & Stanley, 2017), and rationalistic assumptions from research clash with practitioners' embodied experience (Hardesty, 2017).

Summary: social work's identity

Social work's identity, like that of many social groups and professions, cannot be legitimised by claims from the profession. Understanding how its identity is created within professional socialisation, professional practices and workplace interactions can help us understand what is important in establishing social workers' and others' perceptions of its roles and status within society.

Its professional identity starts from the attitudes, life experiences and values of people who come to be social workers: importantly, a belief in the need for greater fairness and justice, a wish to help others and to do something practical. Social workers build on those personal foundations by incorporating established professional values and political and social policies that have constructed the services where they work. As practitioners, they do this collectively with colleagues, differentiating them from other professions they are involved with. Practical learning, in particular, is also important, helped by practice educators and supervisors, contributions from the professional literature and understanding the requirements of the agency in keeping records and making decisions. This enables them to build a sense of confidence in their credibility as practitioners.

As they move into workplaces as independent practitioners, social workers enter negotiations with colleagues about the roles they take on. They also take part in discourse about the aspects of their workplace requirements that impair their ideals of good practice and find ways of balancing these with opportunities for positive practice. By being part of teams and workplaces that develop shared perspectives on their work, they build a bond with colleagues about the nature of social work, demonstrating their credibility and identity within that team perspective.

Conclusion

Social work takes action within social relationships and structures and engages with people to enhance social capital. It values greater human social planning and understanding through policy making and research, but it prioritises practice action. Its four basic models of practice are:

- Interpersonal help to resolve social problems and promote individual flourishing.
- Service provision that protects and supports individual wellbeing in families and communities.
- Informal community education to strengthen social relationships and resources.
- Enabling organised collective change in response to social needs.

Social work's field of practice, its territory of action, is the social aspect of people's lives. Its practice aims to balance:

- Social cohesion, solidarity and cooperation among people.
- Social change to achieve social contexts that enable human flourishing.
- Collective and individual freedom for people to take control of their lives and wellbeing.

Social work students come into the profession committed to fairness and social justice, and this connects with the priorities set out in social work's values.

Taking action on social work's field of practice

Balance the various aspects of social work, that is, interpersonal help, service provision, informal education and organised collective change, and practise aiming for social cohesion, social change and social wellbeing, enabling people to take control of their lives.

In the next chapters ...

Chapters 3–5 set out the distinctive nature of social work's practice and Chapters 6–8 explain how the agency and professional context requires co-production as a secure social context of that practice.

PART II

How social work works

Social work practice is the way social workers act as they contribute to the human striving to improve social capital, that is, the value of social connections to wellbeing. To understand why social work is important, we must understand how its practice is distinctive and therefore special in its contribution to human wellbeing. People and their social relationships in all their diversity are complicated, so this is not easy.

Chapters 3–5 explain what that special contribution of social work practice is. Chapter 3 proposes seven actions which are ingredients in the recipes that social workers use in doing their work. Chapter 4 describes five strategies which connect those recipes with social work's focus on the human/social duality, its unique contribution to its territory. Chapter 5 sets out five streams of thought that illuminate the culture and traditions which influence the different social works identified in Chapter 2.

Social work practice is affected by the contexts in which it takes place. Chapter 6 examines the impact of social work agencies, the organisations that transfer cultural, moral and social expectations through political and social policy into practice. Chapter 7 looks at the influence of economic thinking on social work practice. Because humanity is social, these political, policy and economic contexts must provide for the humanistic values inherent in the human/social duality of social work, and Chapter 8 discusses co-production, the contemporary understanding of how human cooperation, mutuality and solidarity is achieved by social work within these contexts.

3

Social work's practice actions

Social work practice: actions–strategies–thinking

Social work practice is the actions social workers take. They are formed into strategies whereby their actions contribute to human flourishing and social wellbeing. All of this is influenced by ways of thinking, drawing on their cultural and social traditions. To explain further, Chapters 3–5 explore actions, strategies and thinking in turn:

- Seven important social work actions discussed in this chapter organise ideas about what social workers do to achieve the human flourishing aspect of social work's unique contribution. These actions are the ingredients in the recipe of practice; social workers do them in various combinations. A reminder from Chapter 2: I start with actions because acting, 'doing something practical', was the historic distinction between social work and surrounding groups of people with social concerns. Social work, then, classically and forever, is taking action.
- Practice strategies: social workers don't just act; they take actions to achieve a result, so the actions are combined into practice strategies, which I discuss in Chapter 4. These organise how the actions are directed so that they meet social purposes, the result that they are trying to achieve. There are five broad strategies, and social workers take aspects of these strategies to resolve tensions inherent in the human/social duality in each set of circumstances they are dealing with.
- Thinking: the actions and strategies are based on one, or more likely a combination, of five streams of thinking about how to do social work. Chapter 5 focuses on these streams of thinking. Social workers gather actions and strategies into broad themes to create alternative practice styles. These alternative styles are expressed in the differences between the social works discussed in Chapter 2.

So, actions, strategies and streams of thinking interact. Figure 3.1 sets out patterns of constraint, influence and interaction graphically.

These different ways of looking at social work practice start from human actions, because, (Chapter 2 again), social work is about acting, doing something. The idea of action is better than 'intervention', which communicates

Figure 3.1: Contributions to structures of practice

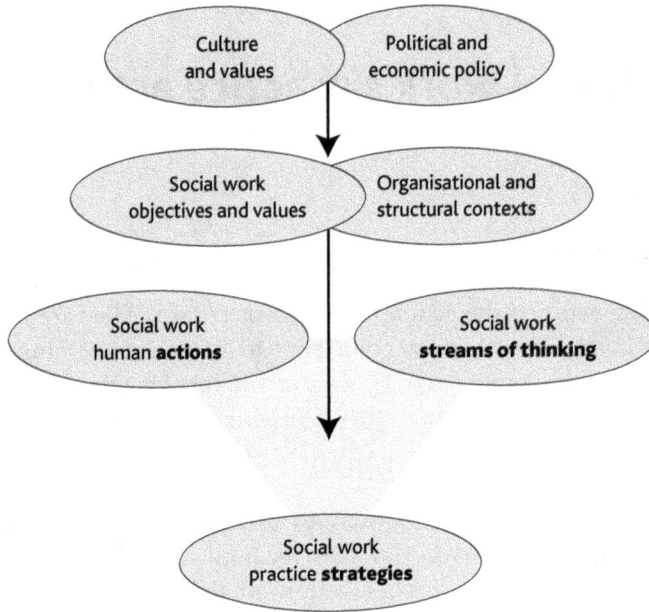

intrusion, cutting across boundaries, busybodying, which a lot of people find an unhappy aspect of social work. Action, on the other hand, can participate in co-production. I argue in Chapter 8 that this is an increasingly important approach to organising practice. It is valuable because it works in alliance and solidarity with clients, communities and service users, rather than intervening in the exercise of their freedoms. Social work actions influence and are influenced by historical streams of thinking. Human actions and thinking interact with social work's practice strategies in a triangle of social work practices.

Actions, thinking and strategies come from two sources within social work. One is the underlying humanistic values of social work discussed in Chapter 1. These propose that fostering social capital through collective, mutual helping is natural to people's flourishing as human beings. Second, these ideas articulate the objectives and values expressed in the identities of the different social works, the social professions explored in Chapter 2.

These practice structures are constrained and influenced by external contexts of two kinds. The first is the organisational, professional and social structures within which social work is practised; I explore these in Chapters 6–8, positioning co-production as a positive strategy for mutuality in organising practice. The values and objectives of social work, the practice explored in Chapters 3–5 and the context explored in Chapters 6–8 are also constrained and influenced by the second external context. This is the economic and political ideas discussed in Chapters 9 and 10. These ideas can be damaging to social work if they corrode the human social values necessary for social wellbeing.

░ *Case example: Mrs Mooney's dying mother*

Practice actions, thinking and strategies, and the constraints and influences on them, are present in the work done with the Mooney family. I was responsible for adult safeguarding in the hospice where I worked, and I was asked to look into the Mooney family in which Janet Mooney had taken on, in her own home, the care of her dying mother, Colette. Soon, colleagues were hearing allegations from other members of the family that Janet was neglecting and physically abusing her mother and stealing her money.

The family's social worker and I interviewed the various family members involved. There were practical worries about the arrangements, but a complicated picture emerged that changed our understanding of what was going on. The stresses that often go with a family member's impending death reactivated long-standing rivalries among family members. Some family members experienced guilt about not being able to do enough for their mother, not just now but throughout her life. We arranged for the mother's (as it happened, very senior) doctor to talk things through privately with her. She agreed that her daughter was rough with her. As in many such situations, however, she wanted to continue with the present care arrangements. We arranged for a physiotherapist to give Janet 'manual handling' training, to help her lift and move her increasingly disabled mother more easily and safely. Following the agreed procedures, we convened a strategy meeting with social workers from the local adult social care department to plan what we would do. This led to the coordination of, and regular communication about, community nurse, hospice and social care visits which, combined, would allow for a daily check on the mother's situation. The social worker discussed the unplanned money management arrangements with Janet, the caring daughter. She organised a welfare rights worker to advise about applications for financial help, and for a nurse to reinforce guidance about feeding and physical care. The social worker also spent time with other family members talking about their lifetime involvement with their mother and the help that they could give now.

A couple of weeks later the doctor paused as he passed me in the corridor. He said that having had this experience, he now realised how the safeguarding procedures had fitted together as part of the care for his patient. Previously, he admitted, he had seen them as mere bureaucracies. His reaction was a gain for the valuation of social work in our agency (because of his influence in his profession), and probably more widely for an awareness of the value of safeguarding work in all care. Colette died a few weeks later, and the feedback from the Mooneys about her care was positive.

What social workers do is often not obvious to people, including our professional colleagues. Some professions working alongside social workers have a more programmed approach to their tasks, and members of the public and policy makers sometimes expect a similar approach in social work. The openness of social work to a practical 'finding a way' through difficult situations is often valued by the people it helps (see Chapter 11) but makes it hard to explain actions in an organised way. The actions–strategies–streams of thinking framework seeks to set out a holistic view of how social workers organise their interventions.

Social work human actions

One of the difficulties of demonstrating how practice is organised is the broad, often taken-for-granted labels, such as 'caring' or 'helping', for social work human actions. Social workers have struggled to find a way to express with greater clarity why they act as they do. One late-twentieth-century attempt to achieve this was the 'functional analysis' of social work roles and tasks (Barker & Briggs, 1969; Briggs, 1973; British Association of Social Workers, 1977; Lonsdale, Webb & Briggs, 1980).

This approach sought to specify actions that articulated the nature of social work practice and underlie the distinctions between social work and social care tasks. It also enabled practitioners to think through different ingredients that, combined, contribute to mixtures of skills in work teams. Asquith, Clark and Waterhouse's (2005) review, summarising the twentieth-century literature, identified advocacy, agent of social control, assessor of need or risk, care manager, counselling, and partner with disadvantaged people and groups as well-established social work roles that describe social work's characteristics. Drawing on these analyses, seven human actions are characteristic ingredients of social work. They are often used together but they sometimes do not mix well because there are tensions between them. Each concept is debated, and just one of these labels does not clarify social work practice. To account for and explain each piece of social work practice, social workers need to explain how they understand the permutations and tensions within the social work human actions that make up their recipes for practice.

Care and caring

Care and social care

One way of understanding social work is as a caring profession. Previous chapters discussed the humanistic view of caring as part of human nature, and social care as part of, and sometimes an extension of, social work. Social work, then, takes in a range of direct caring and service provision for working with people affected by long-term care needs, alongside social work's interpersonal behavioural or social change roles. Understanding social work's importance, therefore, necessarily means grasping how caring fits into it. Limiting social work to a more practical 'social care' in UK social provision separates caring from social work, which also contains actions aimed at human flourishing. This separation emerged partly from the creation in the 1990s of a for-profit sector of the economy and consequently of marketisation and privatisation in services. In its turn, this is an aspect of changes in economic and political thinking. I discuss these trends further in Chapters 9 and 10.

It may seem obvious that social work involves care: social workers arrange foster care for children or care in children's homes. At one time, UK social workers doing this work in local government were called 'child care officers'.

Social workers also organise 'care homes', 'daycare' or 'domiciliary (home) care' for disabled, mentally ill or older people, who are provided with care by 'care workers' who are much more numerous than social workers. Designating a social care sector that emphasises non-professional social care workers in this way potentially expresses the deprofessionalisation of social care practice. This is because it excludes or separates caring as a form of service provision from professional social work, somehow different from and perhaps lesser than, or more valuable than, a broader understanding of social work. An alternative critique suggests that it is developing another profession, rejecting how social work has developed.

But 'social' and 'care' are in some respects inconsistent concepts (Payne, 2014b, pp 398–9). Caring is personal, often involving the emotions, intimate actions with a person's body and mind carried out in an interpersonal relationship. Many people's images of care see it as individualised, private and concerned with personal relationships, for example as mothers caring for children, or health and social care workers caring for disabled, older and sick people. The 'social' is almost the opposite, and certainly contests thinking about caring as always individualised, because it refers to human lives in societies, groups, institutions and organisations. There are, then, legitimate alternatives to individualisation in how people often think of organised social care.

Interpersonal and collective caring

Since the seismic change in the social order associated with the Enlightenment in Western societies, McBeath and Webb (1997) argue that virtuous citizens have been seen to have a moral responsibility for caring both for others and for important ethical and political principles. This has been seen individualistically, as a moral duty to care. But it is also collective because if a cared-for person has rights as a human being – human rights, in this historic turn in Western thinking – they require others to act altruistically to reduce suffering and benefit the interests of the cared-for person rather than the carer (Mayeroff, 1971). Everyone, potentially, has the capacity to care, building on their life experience of caring; for example, between parents and children and in other intimate relationships (Hollway, 2006). Policy thinking relying on interpersonal relations therefore often treats care as a residual issue, a matter of family, human and personal relationships, without seeing this as part of collective responsibility and ultimately part of the duties of the state (Lynch, Kalaitzake & Crean, 2020). Feminist thinking, however, notes that caring has mostly been undertaken by women, minority ethnic workers and servants, slaves and working-class people, who are badly paid (or unpaid), exploited, poorly educated and inadequately supported, isolated in and lacking respect for their caring roles. So, it is valued in principle but marginalised in reality because the mutuality of the relationship lies unrecognised (Tronto, 1993, pp 111–17).

And there are critics of calling social work 'caring' (Garrett, 2018b, pp 155–75). People who think social work should be rational and organised argue that caring is a vague notion, involving hard-to-specify actions. 'Caring' is a positive-sounding 'warm bath' word, but without clarity about what is being offered. Describing social work as a 'caring profession' does not distinguish it from the physical caring associated with medicine or nursing, where care of the body is more prominent than in social work. The idea of 'social caring', caring as part of collective social connectivity, is not intuitive to many people. Also, it does not clarify social work's difference from the highly valued, practical but non-nursing caring done, for example, by staff in care homes for older people, or a cousin doing an older relative's shopping thus demonstrating family concern. Social work needs to qualify what care means in its context, describe the type of caring involved, and how caring combines with other actions. It might include caring and controlling, or caring and counselling actions, for example.

Care is not only interpersonal but also social; any society naturally includes care as part of the human condition. Caring requires cultural and social judgements about complex reactions to social obligations and cultural expectations. This comes about because, when caring, people often reciprocate past care or meet other social expectations, which they negotiate between the parties involved (Finch, 1989; Finch & Mason, 1993). An older person may resist caring behaviour if they think it is not motivated by past relationships, for example. Also, people may care for ideas, for populations, for animals and for non-human and non-living aspects of the world, such as the environment, which is becoming increasingly important in many people's minds (Puig de la Bellacasa, 2017). Thus, Fisher and Tronto's (1991, p 40) widely cited definition of care is '... a species activity that includes everything that we do to maintain, continue and repair our "world" so that we can live in it as well as possible ...'. 'World' here includes our bodies, ourselves and our environment, and part of caring is our attempt to weave all these things into a 'complex, life-sustaining web'. Even though people mostly do not think about that complexity, care must therefore inevitably be social as well as concerning the individual person. Its availability raises issues of social justice, since care may be less available to some groups than others because of their patterns of relationships (Barnes, 2012; Payne, 2014b), and Lynch, Baker, Lyons et al (2009) argue that 'affective equality', giving everyone the right to care and be cared for, is an important human right.

This leads to ideas such as:

- Altruism: having regard for others' needs in deciding how to act.
- Beneficence: being willing to help others simply because they need help.
- Duty or obligation: helping others as a taken-for-granted way of thinking.
- Tradition: caring to comply with expected behaviour in societies, because understanding and responding to expectations leads to certainty and efficiency.
- Reciprocity: returning care that others have given to us, or more broadly returning to society the care we have received through social relationships. (Bulmer, 1987, ch 5)

The ethics of care

The idea that a society providing for human nature must include mutual caring connects with the feminist concept of the ethics of care. This view argues that all caring, even when it is done for individual, personal reasons, comes from connections between people, and is therefore inevitably social. What is moral, considered good, is not a matter for distant considerations of duties and rights, but a matter of what concerns us, what we pay attention to. Such perspectives and values inform Fisher and Tronto's (1991) definition of caring.

Health and social care, and social work , therefore, are valued as the collective expression of both the moral duty and the personal responsibility. But health and social care also have general and public benefit, preventing the spread of disease, mental ill-health and social stress arising from care needs interfering with the economy and social life. Care is, therefore, both actually and potentially political, and social care is just as relevant as healthcare to that collective expression of public responsibility. A central aspect of these services is intense personal care of the body. Examples are nursing the body, bathing the body, injecting medicine into or carrying out surgery on the body (Fine, 2007, pp 171–98), and in the case of social work, safeguarding and security of the body and its mental health and social relationships within the family and community. Touch as part of care and avoiding touch as part of safeguarding therefore also become important issues. Analysis of UK public perceptions of care activities suggests that intimate, personal and physical help may for most people only be provided by a spouse, a female relative or a paid care worker. Other kinds of help, such as fetching the shopping or organising finances, might be provided by men or by neighbours (Parker & Lawton, 1994).

Pursuing an ethics of care, in Tronto's (1993) view, therefore requires four elements:

- Attentiveness: paying attention to the world and making efforts to identify and know about matters that might require our care; staying ignorant is not an option.
- Responsibility: looking beyond formally defined duties, becoming aware of the consequences if we do not trouble ourselves to care.
- Competence: providing good care, as soon as, by paying attention, we realise that we have responsibility. Because of this, it is a professional's responsibility to say, 'I am not competent to provide that service.' For example, the inexperienced surgeon does not agree to carry out major innovative surgery; teachers do not agree to teach subjects they know nothing about; the new social worker does not agree to make the decision in a complex child-safeguarding case. They share the responsibility and make it clear when they cannot act because it is beyond their present ability.
- Responsiveness: accepting interdependence and the duty to become involved with, rather than demanding total autonomy of, vulnerable people.

Caring requires active participation in a care process (Tronto, 1993, pp 137–55), engaging everyone potentially involved in it; it is, therefore, holistic not individualistic. A classification approach – such as comparing the present situation with formal statements of criteria in a detached way that we sometimes see in criteria for service provision – is not caring and we should make that understanding clear in what we say and what we do. Sevenhuijsen (1998, pp 55–68), applying feminist ideas to caring processes, emphasises the importance of moral subjectivity, not separating thinking from feeling, evaluating what feels right, and therefore the importance of exploring the stories and contexts of the people involved, which created the need for this particular care. Issues such as people's interdependence, the interaction of different aspects and needs in their lives, reciprocity, how people in different contexts think about what's important in care, and the cultural assumptions and policies that support or constrain caring are also important (Barnes, Brannelly, Ward et al, 2015).

Tronto (1993, pp 105–8) identifies this process as comprising four integrated, two-way phases of caring:

- 'Caring about', the starting point, involves recognising that caring is necessary. For caring to take place this requires the political decision to resource care or caring services. But it is also needed in a particular situation, for example at the outset noticing that someone needs care or a particular kind of care, and then assessing the situation to decide what to provide and how to do it; this is an important role of social work, which I examine later in this chapter.
- 'Taking care of' is taking responsibility for that caring and deciding how to respond to the need.
- 'Caregiving' involves the direct work of meeting needs for care. Usually, this involves contact between the carer and the person cared for, but increasingly care is provided technologically. Social work may therefore need to offer interpersonal help so that care through an internet link or television screen is acceptable (Puig de la Bellacasa, 2017).
- 'Care receiving' involves responses by care receivers and the people around them to caregiving. Such responses affect the extent to which care needs are met and the quality of the caring experience, for example whether caregivers are respected and care receivers can preserve their dignity.

Summary: care and caring

Social work caring, to sum up, is personal and individual but not only that; it is also part of building collective social capital as well as personal actions. This means it must also include other actions within the social work arsenal of processes that develop the sociality that always underlies social relationships.

Change

Interpersonal and social change

Important ideas about social work focus on change, but Chapter 1 identified the tension between social work's commitment to both individual change and social change that improves social capital. Behavioural and environmental change is individualised, mainly achieved by interpersonal caring and help, while social change emphasises interpersonal actions to achieve broader change, in policy and its implementation, and in the social structures, all of which affect individuals indirectly. Thus, as with helping, change focused on the individual can only be achieved within social connections, so that change must always be part of a developing social capital and therefore of any social work.

Because social change affecting the many is broad, connects with political change and uses collective methods, it seems more impactful and important than individual change. But while it stimulates the high-profile interest of journalists and politicians, it is only achieved in interpersonal actions, carried out below the radar. Community, family, personal and small group change moving towards social change is just as important to the people involved. Making that available to people is not worthless and may add up over time to significant shifts in the social fabric of societies. The advantage of such models of practice is the participation of service users in equal relationships with practitioners through co-production and similar mutualities (see Chapter 8) because they facilitate the participants' objectives. Often these apparently insignificant actions build on and connect to global social movements, alliances of activist groups and people seeking widespread social change on a global scale using broad ideological concepts, such as environmental sustainability and women's equality.

Behavioural change and change in the social environment of individuals, groups and communities is probably the main form of practice across the world, influenced by extensive streams of thinking (see Chapter 5).

Social change through community work and social pedagogy involves practitioners in focusing on networks and organisations, often in a small locality or reflecting particular interests, for example people recovering from domestic abuse, parents of young children or people who share a common disability or health condition. This kind of work has a long history in social work, for example in the settlements where middle-class helpers representing middle-class institutions such as private schools and universities 'settled' their help in deprived working-class communities. The aim to provide resources to assist people with specific difficulties while attending to organisations also helps to build and sustain a good general social infrastructure benefiting others. Professional contributions in early analyses of community work practice include organisational and policy analysis and development; community problem solving by helping people in localities or with shared interests to build organisations to identify problems and work towards solutions; being a change agent on behalf of the government or the community; and managing social conflict (Kramer & Specht, 1969, 1975,

1983; Popple, 2015). Feminist practice has introduced the idea of dialogic practice as a means of engaging people with particular concerns and interests in broader social change. All of this practice is, therefore, both human and social.

Rational and other change processes

The rationalistic view of change in social work assumes, for both individualised and social change, that targets, processes and outcomes of change can be defined in advance and addressed rationally; you can think through the changes that you want to see and plan and work with people to achieve them. I suggested in Chapter 1, though, that one of social work's assets is its preparedness to tackle a complex problem and find a way through. Postmodern thinking contests the rationalistic approach by proposing that society and its relations are ambiguous, that social relations shift and diversify; they cannot always be seen and understood or specified. In this conception of social work, communities, practitioners and service users participate jointly in discourses, processes and relationships that aim to shift their direction and power in people's lives in ways that help them achieve their interpersonal and personal choices within the social movements that we all participate in. This seems to offer greater freedom and influence for communities and service users, while the rational view implies that the change is needed because the service user is not being rational and needs help with this. Chaos theory also contests the traditional view of social work change, suggesting that there are patterns in individual and social change that may be perceived but may not be susceptible to planned, rational intervention (Hudson, 2010). Even if it is, evidence from the transtheoretical model of change (Prochaska & DiClemente, 1983; Prochaska, DiClemente & Norcross, 1994), and motivational interviewing based on it (Miller & Rollnick, 2013; Hohman, 2016) propose that it is a difficult process for many people and requires careful preparation.

While the idea of change may be intuitive, it is, as with caring and helping, ambiguous and complex. It connects people, in that practitioners work with them in their social environment and with policy makers and observers. Thinking about change, therefore, means that people can come to social work, or if they are policy makers develop a social work service, with the idea that they want change. Evaluation, looking back on the social work process and seeing the change achieved wholly, partly or not at all, provides clarity. By doing this, people can follow the logic of what is going on, and see the steps that move towards the change they seek. The idea of social work as achieving change is therefore accountable to others. Change is also motivational, even inspiring, an achievement or a possibility.

Summary: change and social cohesion

Connected with the positives about change, Chapter 2 pointed out that acting to achieve cohesion can give preserving the present social order a higher priority than change. Focusing on change as part of social work actions, therefore, emphasises an important foundation of social work, that it aims at social improvement. Improvement implies change, and social work will always build on change. On the other hand, change might involve changing the pattern or stream of events affecting an individual, group or society. Social work could change that pattern or stream to preserve existing positive strengths, and that might be both a change and a social improvement, but a different point of view might see it as maintaining the present situation; not all change is progressive.

Change, therefore, can involve balancing attitudes to movements and pressures on communities, people and societies to prevent disruption, or shifting towards improvements. Constant churning in people's lives and their social context is not always good and other practice actions may be needed to balance change actions.

Counselling

Counselling traditions in social work

Looking at the origins of the term 'social care' in Chapter 2, I noted that the Barclay Report (1982) on the role and tasks of social work distinguished two main roles of social work: social care planning and counselling. This second role reflected a practice tradition which emerged in the early twentieth century to be incorporated in the interpersonal practice of social work in the European/US problem-solving, individualised form of social work outlined in Chapter 2.

It came from the adoption of psychology into social work in mental health services for adults and children. This innovation, particularly in the US in the 1930s, drew on the psychodynamic theory and treatment methods of the psychoanalyst Freud and his followers, in which mental energy was seen as driving social behaviour (Payne, 2021, ch 4). It enabled social workers, when dealing with practical problems (such as poverty or poor housing), to extend advice, guidance and moral exhortation towards intervention with the behavioural and psychological issues affecting people's lives. As a wider range of psychological ideas and research became available, further psychological interventions were introduced, some of which were also picked up in social work. By the mid-twentieth century, social workers used psychological knowledge to provide counselling services as part of their wider work, and used counselling skills, particularly where they were involved in mental health provision or working with children; this continues in many countries. Halmos's (1965) study of social change claimed that the influence of medicine and religion had declined, in favour of professions, such as social work, which responded to an increased concern in many Western societies to achieve psychological and social self-actualisation.

Towards the end of the twentieth century, in many countries, clinical psychology professions established structured interventions supported by empirical research. In addition, counselling professionals developed practice using psychological techniques to facilitate people's decision making, insight into and understanding of concerns in their lives and personal planning to overcome them. Both these professions and their interventions, where they exist, are separate from social work, but their techniques inform the interpersonal aspects of social work practice. Some social workers gain additional qualifications to incorporate these professional practices into their social work actions.

Summary: separating counselling and social work

A weakness of counselling is that it concentrates on helping a focal client non-directively to manage issues of psychological concern to them. This may be done as part of wider social care or helping provision. Examples include assistance to parents experiencing difficulties in managing their children's behaviour, relationship problems in families or marriages, grief and loss, overcoming anxiety and depression, or managing the pressures of caring responsibilities (Riggall, 2012). In contrast, because social work incorporates the social, it takes action and works with the agencies, community and family members involved. With the Mooney family, social work was less concerned with helping people think through how they wanted to resolve their problems, instead making practical arrangements, and organising social care services and visits to observe and take action in the home, school, work and other community settings affecting them.

In this way, we can see that social work, in seeking to develop social capital as well as human flourishing, often includes counselling as part of caring and helping within its practice strategies (see Chapter 4). Counselling and psychotherapy professions do not usually offer a similar range of actions in their practice strategies. Social work is needed in the mix of professions to make such contributions.

Help

Natural and formalised helping

Helping sometimes contests caring as a way of understanding social work's identity, seeing it as a 'helping profession'. Natural, even instinctive, human helping behaviour becomes an institutionalised service involving professionalised actions. These services often draw on a psychologisation of helping behaviour, which focuses on using interpersonal processes and skills to achieve behavioural change in rationalistic ways. Examples are Carkhuff with Benoit's (2019) model of helping, or Miller and Rollnick's (2013) motivational interviewing.

And there is a tension: formalising help seems to disconnect it from showing humanity, which is so important in caring. It emphasises the ability of a helper to overcome the sense of intrusion into people's private troubles and relationships. Bower (2005) argued that for much social work, people not being able to accept help is part, or all, of the problem. Examples are parents working towards having their children in compulsory care returned to them, or independently minded older people having to accept checks by social carers or technology on their wellbeing. Jordan (1979) argues that social workers provide help because of their life experiences of helping and being helped, part of the process of achieving a social work identity (see Chapter 2). Empathy, in using the experiences of reverses in practitioners' lives, allows practitioners to affirm and respond to clients' experiences of oppression. Practitioners experience the truth of clients' realities, and clients experience the truth of practitioners' commitment to helping and engagement with them. Social work helping thus emphasises the importance of coming alongside people's living reality through empathy in interpersonal relationships. Helping requires openness and a process of engaging in relationships by clients and practitioners in an alliance.

Being an acceptable helper

Keith-Lucas's (1972) classic account of social work helping also accepts that most people do not want to be helped. Being an acceptable helper, therefore, requires giving help by upholding a client's choice to use it actively and willingly, even if they are demanding or insistent. Helping, therefore, contains the following factors:

- A connection with the reality of the situation that the helped person faces.
- Empathy that the situation must be faced.
- Support in facing and dealing with the situation.

In this view, help is something tangible or intangible given by one person to another or one group to another. It must be done, therefore, in ways that allow the other to increase their choices in improving self-fulfilment in their experience of life. This analysis is similar to Mayeroff's (1971) account of caring that I discussed earlier; it requires acting only to achieve things that the client wants.

Shakespeare's (2000) account of helping, focusing on his own experience of disability, looks at these critiques of helping from the other side, seeing where you can go wrong with helping actions, by identifying four unhelpful aspects of help:

- Polarisation involves over-emphasising a client's problems in comparison with what people would see as a 'normal' situation. If you do this, you create a stronger distinction between the problem, such as disability or criminality, and other similar people who don't have that problem. Rather than exaggerating or affirming the problems, social workers should emphasise the opportunities or strengths. Rather than emphasising difficulties in people's lives, we should see them as challenges to be overcome.
- 'Burden' means seeing problems as a burden on others or on society, creating dependence on community, family or public services such as housing or social security. Social workers can work with people to value the positives of needing help and encourage them to use it as part of building relationships, connections and networks.
- Preventing clients from having the opportunity to have voice, speaking for themselves to define the issues that they face and the help that they need. As well as contesting the kind of helping that has a menu of services that are

routinely provided, failing to facilitate clients' voice may be a failing with a social work that focuses on advocacy on behalf of clients.

- Infantilisation, seeing someone who needs help with everything, rather as we see infants needing care for everything. Instead, social work should help people identify specific needs and preferred ways of providing for them, building on opportunities and strengths.

Summary: helping is social

Jordan's (1979) account of helping places these issues in the context of the helping services of large public agencies. He emphasises access to services that mitigate inequalities and oppression. Jordan's (1979) and Shakespeare's (2000) accounts of helping emphasise the social contexts and outcomes of helping rather than individualistic personal change, as with modern accounts of care and change.

Social control, social order and surveillance

Social cohesion and social control

The discussion in Chapter 2 about social change raised a critique of social cohesion as a social work objective: it might be or might become conservative in wanting to sustain existing social stability and the present social order. Some people, including practitioners, might prefer this to seeking human and social flourishing. This critique also affected the problem–solving aim in many European/US accounts of social work, because social problems are constructed in the social relationships created by existing social forces; they are problems of the present social order, but may be defeated by more suitable future orders.

If social work aims for social order and stability, this critique suggests that it is violating its underlying objective of positive change. Aiming for social cohesion in the care and parenting of children, and helping mentally ill people and offenders are all open to the possibility that social workers seek control of individuals or society rather than caring, counselling or helping. This is particularly so if the social worker is acting on behalf of or employed by the government or the state. Penketh and Pratt (2000, p 122) argue that it is a common characteristic of governments to respond to disruption and protest with attempts to promote stability by incorporating dissenting ideas tentatively into social structures and services. Governments also use social institutions such as social work to exert social control in favour of the present social order by oppressing disruptors. Davies (1985, pp 28–46), contesting this analysis, points out the value of maintaining the present social order if it is deteriorating because of social problems that social work might prevent or ameliorate. To go further, social order and stability might be an important base for successful positive social change.

The critique of aiming for social cohesion and social order in social work emerged most strongly in the 1970s. The social sciences stepped back from a structural-functional analysis which suggested that structures in society had functions in creating and maintaining a stable ordered society. Twenty-first-century sociological scholarship has been influential in raising the need to scrutinise governmentality and surveillance. Garrett (2018a, pp 179–80) refers to Donzelot's (1979) Foucauldian exploration of the art of government as a form of social policing, particularly of families and people in poverty. Powell (2013, pp 54–6) shows how Foucault's thinking views social work as observing its clients from a position of hierarchical power, normalising conventional judgements of behaviour within assessments required for bureaucratic decision making.

Social control in social work thinking

The issue has always been present in social work. For example, the earliest social work practices of the charity organisation societies were seen as replacements in the new urban industrialised Europe of the moral power of the Christian churches as arbiters of behaviour in medieval times (Payne, 2005). Weber's (Gerth & Mills, 1948) analysis of bureaucratic power in the early twentieth century influenced the social sciences to be concerned about sources of influence and power and their impact on social relations. The 1950s was a period when social work sought to distance itself from the use of power by focusing on authority and by developing a professional model of practice in which clients had self-determination in deciding the direction and approach of the help they received (Foren & Bailey, 1968; Yelaja, 1971; Biestek & Gehrig, 1978). The focus on non-directive counselling and helping interventions pursued the interests of the client. This value system continues to influence ideas about social work practice.

Early critiques of this problem-solving social work were couched as being about social control. Epstein's (1975) discussion of psychological practice models, for example, argues that the organisational influences of social work agencies, in focusing on the behavioural specifics of individuals, means that social workers 'cool out' the behavioural consequences of poverty and distress rather than seeking wider social change to alleviate or eradicate that distress. Weinstein's (2011, pp 15–16) account of the radical social work movement of the 1970s notes a concern about control of clients, but also, with the increasing size and importance of large government social work agencies in this period, an increased emphasis on management in agencies. Enlarged managerial structures led to less autonomy for practitioners and a more significant workforce concerned with behaviour management. A striking polemic by a renowned UK campaigner about homelessness in this period describes buck-passing up hierarchies of management: are social workers 'pawns, police or agitators?', he asked (Bailey, 1980, p 215). Dominelli (2004, p 89) pointed to movements to extend government agencies' involvement in social work education to seek influence over the objectives and values of social work.

This critical analysis extended to many client groups. Satyamurti (1979) argued that care and control were integral to the compulsory powers exercised by child protection social workers in the UK. Both children's behaviour and their parenting were controlled. The state, through its social workers, guided and supported but also managed cultural and social expectations of parents, in ways that might impose middle-class mores on parents from minority ethnic groups and working-class communities. Ferguson (2000) argued that emphasising social control of mentally ill people because of myths about their dangerousness distracts attention from the lack of resources for treatment and care.

More generally, Fook (2016, pp 78–9) argued that care, counselling and help as part of social work provision is incorporated into a system of thought alarmed about working-class and ethnically and culturally diverse social groups disrupting an existing conception of social life. Their distinct ways of life are devalued in favour of dominant ideas about appropriate education, family, work and other social structures. Social work brings these dominant ideas into its practice to form a social order that engages with controlling expected behaviour in minority or oppressed groups; in this way social work manages people's behaviour. 'Hegemony', creating and using dominant ideas in society as part of a process of regulating societies, is an important concept deriving from the political sociology of Gramsci (Garrett, 2018a, pp 109–11), and Habermas's ideas about communicative action proposes that powerful communications regulate social structures (Houston, 2013).

Summary: social control and social order

The risk that social work, in its communicational, people-working form, becomes social control, is tempered by an acceptance that social order is a legitimate aspect of any society and stability is valued by both rich and poor. Fook (2016, p 7) acknowledges that it is important to incorporate the critique of social control into practice thinking to enable us to think critically about how we use other aspects of practice that seem helpful to the people we work with. Pritchard and Taylor's (1978) account of radical ideas in social work saw control as interacting with change, conflict and comfort, all legitimate elements of practice. Irvine (1978) argued, in the same period, that social control achieved through social work was of a different order from oppressive social control in authoritarian political regimes, or even overt control exercised occasionally by police forces. Beckett and Horner (2016, pp 56–8) usefully distinguish between explicit and implicit uses of 'coercive powers'. It is explicit when legal powers are used, for example in the UK and many other countries, to remove children from their parents or admit patients compulsorily to psychiatric hospitals, as against using social power implicit in professional or therapeutic relationships to influence behaviour. It is also important to distinguish between using powers to protect clients and using powers to leverage behaviour in clients. Another important aspect of control is the wish of communities and clients to be in control of their lives, both generally and at difficult times, such as illness or during the dying process.

Social justice and human rights

Social work and social justice

The global definitions of social work (Table 2.2) signalled that social justice and human rights are important social work values in achieving or at least improving social justice, which motivates many practitioners to take up social work. Pursuing social justice is controversial for some liberal or neoliberal critics of social work, who see arguments for social justice as only about the redistribution of wealth from the rich to people in poverty. They see this as interfering with necessary economic inequalities in society, with adverse consequences for social relations; I consider this issue in Chapters 9 and 10. It connects with the Marxist or socialist view that social justice requires reducing or removing social class differences, for example by achieving social mobility. Critics of such views of social change see arguing for social justice as trying to smuggle unrealistic changes in social structure into debates about fairness in helping people. A 'materialist tradition' of thinking (Lynch & Lyons, 2009, p. 54) which monetises everything and assumes social justice refers only to financial redistribution, whereas it may equally be about changing other power relations. This makes clear that there are different political positions hidden in debates about social justice. In this case, the critics fail to acknowledge other forms of social justice, such as people participating or having a voice in decisions that affect them.

Watts and Hodgson (2019) clarify these hidden views by identifying four perspectives on social justice:

- Critical perspectives challenge, criticise and transform relations of domination and oppression in existing political and economic structures.
- Distributive perspectives aim for an equal and fair distribution of benefits, opportunities and resources in society's publicly accountable institutions.
- Autonomy and rights perspectives want social relations in which people can act as moral agents with dignity and worth, being recognised as possessing rights as human beings with personal and social identities. Those rights are expressed in the economic, political and social rights of citizenship participation in their communities, families and society (see Chapter 5).
- Participation and democratic perspectives aim to achieve participation and voice in decision making, both in people's personal lives and in democratic processes and public discourse.

Individual human rights and social justice

These perspectives incorporate two aspects of social justice. The first is different kinds of fairness, such as not dominating, redistributing resources, valuing people and their voice, and encouraging participation. The second is the social context in which this is done. As with caring, counselling and helping, if justice is to be social rather than individual it has to include appropriate social institutions and structures within which justice and human rights may be pursued. Watts and Hodgson (2019) suggest that fairness between individuals is not enough; social institutions in which people interact also have to achieve appropriately fair structures for relationships. The consequence for social work is that it must achieve social justice in the institutions of social work, for example in the impact of social work agencies on both individuals and society, and in its actions must aim for just social structures, as well as just relations between people.

The global definition (see Table 2.2) distinguishes between human rights and social justice. The reason for making this distinction is unclear. It may be to differentiate between the structural requirements of social justice and perhaps more individual and interpersonal requirements of professionals to respect human rights. Watts and Hodgson, however, include human rights, respect for other people and their worth within autonomy and rights and participation perspectives.

Staub-Bernasconi (2016) links two aspects of human rights work in social work. The first is the focus on vulnerable individuals and peoples; this is crucial for the human element of the unique contribution of social work implementing the specific aims of its values. The second is the focus on social as opposed to other aspects of justice, ensuring that social work remains practical when tackling issues and does not spread its concerns too thinly into policy activism in areas which should be the focus of other professions. Staub-Bernasconi (2011) also points out the need to bring together Western interpretation of human rights (as a range of broad freedoms) with Asian and other cultural interpretations of rights which do not allow for freedom to reject dominant religious and social ideologies in particular regimes.

Ife's (2012) account of human rights social work practice distinguishes three traditions of practice:

- Advocacy on behalf of individuals and groups.
- Direct practice with clients, organisations and policy advocacy to support rights.
- Community development to promote a social context that appropriately supports rights.

Summary: balancing rights and justice

Practice to achieve these various aspects of human rights requires balancing public and individuals' private rights, with culturally important human rights. Social work practice should also respect rights as part of professional needs assessment. Working in this way, practitioners align ethical social work practice with human rights objectives. It also enables support for clients' and service users' engagement with human rights practice in a co-productive way, so that rights work is shared and not seen as only a professional responsibility.

Case example: human rights practice and social work ethics

Leilani was working with a mentally ill man, who had for some years, supported by his wife, been managing his depression derived from chemical imbalances in his brain of genetic origins, with complex medication which maintained his equilibrium. Concerns about his medication were raised by his doctor, as new research had indicated physical risks of long-term use of some of these drugs. But changing the prescription led to severe reactions, with his disturbed and difficult behaviour affecting neighbours and people in the community and the police becoming involved on several occasions. This was very distressing for the man's wife, who had lost the pleasing personality she had become used to. Leilani negotiated with doctors and nurses about the management of the medication, an advocacy approach to human rights work. She also got him involved with a local mental health day centre, which engaged him with peer support from two other men whose lived experience of similar mental health problems helped them both; this was a direct practice approach to enabling him and local mental health services to respond to his needs. As a result of this experience, as he became stable once again, Leilani helped the three men to get a charitable grant to form a support group for people with medication issues in mental health, a community development approach to the issue, which helped to provide much wider information resources benefiting the community more widely.

Support

Support and social work

Support is another interpretation of social work actions, often present where social work is part of other services, for example, in criminal or other legal proceedings, education or healthcare. It implies helping people find a way to bear the weight of their troubles. Because it does not specify clear objectives, however, focusing on support often devalues social work's contribution, with other professionals seeing it as a nice extra to more rigorous actions.

Support is theorised in a variety of ways. Hollis and Woods' (1981, pp 109–16) psychosocial practice conceptualised sustainment as reducing feelings of anxiety and lack of self-esteem or self-confidence. The practitioner demonstrates interest in the client, acceptance of them and a desire to help, thus showing that the client may repose faith and trust in the worker's knowledge and goodwill. Calm consideration, encouragement, reaching out to suggest options and being actively involved in thinking through clients' concerns help to sustain them. Ego psychology, a form of psychodynamic practice, proposed that responsibility for support differentiated social work from traditional psychoanalytic practice, which is focused on bringing internal psychological difficulties to the surface and reducing their impact by giving people insight into them (Bandler, 1963).

Four types of support were distinguished during the late twentieth century (Compton, Galaway & Cournoyer, 2005, p 259):

- Affiliational: enabling people to feel bound to and valued by another person or group.
- Informational: providing information about resources and training in skills to deal with current challenges.
- Emotional: enabling people to express feelings and reflect on emotionally difficult events in one or more relationships.
- Instrumental: providing financial aid or practical services.

Similar forms of support are identified as useful within agencies, organisations and in teamwork. Support needs, once they are defined through social work assessment, might be provided by the social worker directly, or through arrangements for care workers and other services to carry out tasks in people's homes, care homes or daycare settings.

Another strategy is to enable clients to improve supportive links in their existing social networks or to build new links. A significant stream of practice grew from the preventive psychiatry of Caplan (1974; Caplan & Killilea, 1976) to develop support networks, either for specific clients or more commonly as projects for groups of clients experiencing similar difficulties through mutual support.

Summary: support as social

Helpful concepts from the intellectual and physical disabilities and mental health fields include 'supported living' and 'active support' deriving from the disabled living, ordinary housing and ordinary living movements seeking to sustain valued lifestyles for various groups. Supported living (deriving from mental health services) provides an independent lifestyle, but with wraparound services that check up on clients, helping them feel safe because someone reacts when they experience difficulty. Person-centred active support (deriving from work with people with intellectual disabilities) emphasises a social pedagogy approach, in which every moment has the potential to achieve a better quality of life: little-and-often interventions providing graded assistance, and maximising choice and control are all supportive (Beadle-Brown, Murphy & Bradshaw, 2017).

Conclusion

This chapter explored seven modes of social work action, identifying their ambiguities, complexities and interactions as ingredients in social work. While they address one part of social work's unique contribution to society – actions that facilitate human flourishing – analysis always suggests how this is closely tied to the other aspect of social work's unique contribution: developing the social capital which forms the only basis for human flourishing. Social work always integrates both in its actions; a focus on the individual is doomed to fail without the social resources to contextualise and enable it.

Taking action in human flourishing

Social workers always examine and explain which actions form the ingredients of a particular piece of work that they are undertaking, and consider whether other actions should also be included in their recipe for practice.

In the next chapter ...

... practice strategies are explored. These move the combination of actions that form the ingredients of social work practice into tackling the human/social duality. Practice strategies make sure that individualised actions are also social actions.

4

Social work's practice strategies

Why strategies are important

This second aspect of social work practice focuses on how social workers direct the human actions discussed in Chapter 3 so that they contribute to creating social capital as well as human flourishing. The five strategies characteristic of social work are art and science, assessment, home visiting, making arrangements, and networks and relationships. By thinking through and then using such strategies, social workers clarify their knowledge about 'how to go on', as Kearney (2004, pp 163–80) puts it. This helps to show others involved that this is how they mean to go about making their actions move towards their social aims. It helps them to take into account the organisational and professional contexts they practise in (more in Chapters 6–8).

Art and science

Social work is always both artistic and scientific. Practitioners therefore have to arrive at and express a position that balances these two aspects of practice. In doing so, they pay attention to an underlying debate. One position is rational technical thinking, such as evidence-based practice. These views claim that social work knowledge and action can only rely on empirical rational understanding of the social, and that this has priority over other forms of understanding. But combining artistic and empirical understanding is typical of all caring, health and helping professions. Medicine, nursing, occupational therapy and physiotherapy, and psychology: all use scientific knowledge drawn from empirical and observational research and logical, rational analysis. They also engage with the arts and humanities, for example in art and music therapy and the community arts. Other artistic aspects of practice are the use of human discretion, judgement and relationships with the people they serve. My experience of using creative arts in (rationalist, medicalised) palliative care is that you can use both empirical research and rational analysis to evaluate artistic practice (Payne, 2008a). Social work can do this too.

This duality is debated sporadically in social work, but, when it arises, there is a consistent position. Bowers' (1949, p 417) well-known definition of social casework, based on a review of all previous definitions, refers to it as an art and a science, seeing practice as requiring at least some artistry, while knowledge should be from science. Boehm (1961, p 150), in a contribution to an important review of social work curricula in the US, argued that it was wrong to create a dichotomy between art and science, that an artistic component was required in the practice of scientific social work and that art in practice is capable of being studied and understood scientifically and provided for in social work education and practice. He connects art with intellectual endeavour, having a high-quality response to understanding the world in a unified way, combining specialist knowledge with a general interest in forming realistic, believable ideas about it. In his view, art seeks in every situation its originality, the surprises that it offers, and it rejoices in and tolerates difference and dissent so that it welcomes conflict, tension and polarity. England (1986, pp 85–100) argued that art incorporates intuitive and subjective understanding (for example, of ambiguity) into practice in ways that rational understanding in the social sciences cannot achieve. Social work in this view involves the self of participants in situations of fluid reality, which may be understood and communicated but not finally pinned down in rational understanding.

Using art in practice involves work on understanding similarities between processes of creating art and doing social work, and using artistic materials such as literature, painting and poetry as part of social work action processes. This helps communication by providing a wider range of media. Such practices have contemporary import in the use of blogs, emojis, social media, vlogs and other information technology as forms of communication. Techniques of artistic or literary criticism can help critical thinking in social work, since they involve coherent analysis according to a consistent history of evaluation.

Assessment, reporting and recording

Social work and assessment

Assessment has been an important aspect of social work since its early beginnings, and has always been part of the social control, social order and surveillance analysis of social work actions. This is evident in the initial aims of the charity organisation societies, among the important forerunners focusing on individualised problem-solving social work in its European and US origins. The societies sought to prevent applicants for charitable relief from making unjustified claims for help from multiple almsgivers and to provide help efficiently. Loch's (1883, p 10) early guidance for people providing help states the case:

> ... whoever gives charitable aid, undertakes a responsibility; he [sic] is not, for instance, entitled to injure the person he thinks he will help. To make sure that he does not, he must learn all the circumstances, which will indicate how he can help effectually ... Inquiry then is the acquisition of such information as may make charity productive of good results. Two kinds of knowledge are required for the purpose: a knowledge of the social life of the class of which the person in distress is a member ... and a general knowledge of character – a

discernment of the value of evidence, combined with a knowledge
of the modes and possibilities of charitable assistance …

Methods of practice emphasised home visiting and effective recording and reporting of assessments of the character of applicants for help (Fido, 1977). One of social work's earliest textbooks, Richmond's *Social diagnosis* (1965 [1917]) contains extensive guidance on collecting comprehensive social information about clients of social services. It claims the English social work pioneer Octavia Hill as the first to describe '… inquiry with social reinstatement [rehabilitation] as its motive and aim' (p 29) and quotes one of Hill's letters about the importance of 'knowledge of the passions, hopes, and history of people … how to move, touch and reach them' (p 30).

During the 1920s in the US, detailed investigation, for example for social histories in psychiatric social work, was an important professional task, often so detailed that the psychiatrists refused to read them (Grinker, MacGregor, Selan et al, 1961). Early probation services provided reports on offenders' home circumstances for the courts, and this led to a system of social inquiry or pre-sentence and other reports for many different courts which developed over the twentieth century (Bochel, 1976), particularly in the UK after the Streatfeild Committee on the Business of the Criminal Courts (1961) recommended their universal adoption.

An important aspect of this assessment process is the creation of records, which are the property of the social work agency and facilitate the professional's practice and reflection.

Assessment is a process in all social work practice and is also frequently seen as a function or role of social work when it is part of wider social care services, the contemporary development of the idea of diagnosis, describing the process of understanding the nature of the issues to be dealt with in social work interventions, but 'assessment' carries more complex implications. Thus, presentations of theory in European/US individualised problem solving view assessment as an important factor in the beginning processes of practice models. For example, Perlman's (1957) 'problem-solving process' involved assessing the person, the problem, the place and the process; Reid and Epstein's (1972) task-centred practice involves exploring and prioritising problems, and extracting goals and hierarchies of tasks to work on the problems; and cognitive behavioural practice (Ronen and Freeman, 2007) involves analysing and assessing behavioural problems so that their antecedents, behaviours and consequences may be identified. Later models involve assessment of potential strengths and exceptions in difficult patterns of behaviour, so that solutions within the reach of clients may be found (Shennan, 2019). Over time, assessment has developed from a metaphorical and interpretive understanding of clients' concerns drawn from a relationship with the social worker (perhaps more artistic in its balance of the art/science duality), while more recent practice has been concerned with specifying particular behaviours and objectives (perhaps more rational technical).

Social work without assessment

Other streams of thinking give less importance to assessment. Social pedagogy is more concerned with work alongside groups and communities, allowing issues to emerge from a participative action process. Critical theory similarly seeks to build a shared view of important issues using a dialogic co-production process in which service users have an important role in defining what should be worked on and how this should be done. The social development stream is more policy-led, focusing on issues considered to be important in the communities worked with. Indigenist practice, deriving from important cultural traditions or the original populations of colonised countries (more in Chapter 5) focuses on ways of thinking within the population being worked with. In these other, less therapeutic streams of thinking the practitioner's assessment is less significant and tempered by participative structures.

Social service agencies' use of assessment

Many social work services, particularly where they are public services, use social workers to determine eligibility or need for service provision, and in case or care management in adult social care services, this is an important legal function in many care agencies. Alongside this, there may be requirements to undertake financial assessments where services are charged for. Assessment of this kind is often an initial assessment, seen as a starting point for the agency's service, undertaken before decisions to take action or provide service are authorised. They are then only periodically reviewed, whereas professional practice assessments are usually a continuous part of the process of social work action.

These agency service assessments may interfere with the practice uses of assessment because they may be used to ration services, or plan service provision in ways that are distant from clients' and carers' interests and wishes. Hence more co-productive or participative streams of thinking give less emphasis to assessment. As a result, in European/US individualised problem solving, practitioners might be acting on behalf of the managers of the service rather than in clients' interests or according to professional discretion. Social workers may deal with this, for example, by explicitly separating assessment of need from assessment as part of actions or service provision, and may be helped in this because other providers of services also carry out additional assessments as they engage with clients. The ethics of care view argues that assessment for care cannot separate formal definitions of care from the people involved in the process. This is because they must inevitably explore the interpersonal consequences of the intended caring process, and therefore must include both caregivers' and receivers' parts in that process (Tronto, 1993, pp 137–55).

Summary: theorising social work assessment

Assessment may be theorised in different ways. Consequently, the extent and specification of what is assessed varies considerably, according to the approach taken. Milner, Myers & O'Byrne (2015) use the analogy of different types of maps of the terrain of the client's life, connecting these with social work practice theories, as follows:

- Assessment of a wide range of elements and networks to place the client in relevant social contexts; for example, in systems practice, a satellite map.
- Assessment of complex interactions in life and thinking of the client and people around them; for example, in psychodynamic theory, a map of the ocean.
- Assessment of specific elements of behaviour relevant to the issues in the client's life; for example, in cognitive behavioural therapy, a detailed map of a specific area.
- Assessment of agreed issues to be worked on in the intervention; for example, in task-centred practice, a handy tourist map.
- Assessment of areas to be explored to achieve a goal; for example, in solution or strengths practice, an explorer's map covering unknown territory.
- Assessment of beliefs and issues in the client's life; for example, in community work, this might include macro and spirituality practice issues; a map of the universe in interaction with the client's feelings.

Home visiting and community presence

Social work and home visiting

Social work practice requires a presence in the community being served and often involves the intrusion of visiting clients' homes, or in indigenous practice engaging with existing community structures in, for example, tribes. It allows for the creation of social capital, links and networks among people in the community and professional human actions.

As with assessment, community presence and visiting were part of the very early formation of social work. The settlement, in which people from middle-class communities and universities lived in the area being served, is the source of the importance of being present in the community to demonstrate engagement with the daily life and experience of the people social workers were trying to help. Community workers being present in the community affirms the value of people's daily lives and struggles. An example of this during the late twentieth century is the idea of community social work in the UK, in which teams of social workers were placed alongside local domiciliary and other care services in localities, so that social workers achieved better understanding of local community concerns and built connections with local organisations (Hadley & Young, 1990; Stepney, 2018). A practice handbook (Hadley, Cooper, Dale et al, 1987) for this practice method suggests recruiting local staff and providing community facilities, for example. Other practices also developed local bases and responsive visiting. Examples are crisis intervention teams dealing with mental health emergencies, community mental health teams and co-location of social workers in local health centres.

The importance of visiting was taken up from social work's experience of the practice of Christian ministers of religion visiting the homes of their parishioners. Chalmers (1780–1847) carried out surveys of the people living in poverty in his Glasgow parish, and divided it into districts supervised by deacons who investigated families' needs (Young & Ashton, 1956, ch 4). In 1853, the municipality of Elberfeld, Germany, developed a system of visiting by volunteers (Rosenhaft, 1994, p 26). A method of 'friendly visiting' was devised by the charity organisation societies (Hancock & Pelton, 1989), based on the systematic home visiting devised by Octavia Hill for the London housing movement, and assessment and help was provided by consistent and regular home visiting. Later, debate centred on whether it was more effective in changing behaviour than interviews in clinics and offices (Timms, 1964b, p 195).

Home visits nevertheless became an important practice in many aspects of social work (Beder, 1998; Winter & Cree, 2016). They are beneficial in linking agencies such as clinics, hospitals, schools and other professions with families, improving understanding of the home setting (Allen & Tracy, 2004), and allowing social workers to experience emotional engagement with families as a useful resource in professional judgement and understanding (Cook, 2020). It is particularly essential for evaluating issues faced by clients in their everyday lives and protecting them; for example, domestic abuse, child and adult safeguarding and the realistic assessment of risk where disabled or older people are living in the community. These ideas about experiencing community, indigenous and personal experience are, again, tending towards artistic rather than rational technical forms of knowledge.

Home visiting practice

Where this may be perceived as an intrusion, good practice is to negotiate clients' acceptance of the process in the early stages of contact, even if protective visits are later performed unannounced. The most helpful approach is to try to engage clients in a cooperative, joint process of looking at and understanding difficulties in the home, for disabled or older people, or children's wellbeing in child protection processes (Scora, 2005). Developing a cooperative relationship in this way reduces the sense of intrusion or oppression when using authority or legal powers; however, it is important not to deny or sugarcoat the reality that this is what the practitioner is doing. Winter and Cree (2016) note, however, that the frequency and location of visiting are increasingly legally mandated and state regulated, forming an element of the social control and surveillance roles of social workers. This emerged in the UK child safeguarding system in the procedures about responsibility for the 'looked after child', looked after, that is, by the local authority (Parker, Ward, Jackson et al, 1991), and was increasingly focused on by an initiative to help 'troubled families' on assumptions that disruptive families created the need for intervention (MacLehose, 2011).

Recent research and professional scholarship emphasising home visiting is Ferguson's (2011, 2016, 2018; Ferguson, Warwick, Cooner et al, 2020) work on the importance of interpersonal contact during home visits between social workers and children affected by concerns about safeguarding them from abuse and neglect and their families. He argues that this is an important characteristic of practice in this social work role, which requires complex negotiations of human interactions in the private space of people's homes. Allied to this, his text (Ferguson, 2011) shows how hidden aspects of practice may occur in private spaces such as bedrooms, kitchens within the child's household and the car, which can be used for private interactions with children separate from family members. Oliver's (2017) Canadian study of strengths-based child protection work points to the difficulty of maintaining her principles of 'firm, fair and friendly' intervention in the clients' home space, balancing the exercise of authority to ensure a child's protection, while respecting the client's privacy in their home environment.

An Israeli study (Muzicant & Peled, 2018) is another example of recent research showing how home visiting changed social workers' professional relationships with clients. The journey from office to home heightened the practitioners' focus on how to conduct the visit. This arose from a combination of tentativeness and uncertainty created by social workers' intrusion into domestic settings and clients' control of their home environments. There was also the sense that the visit was 'dirty work', sometimes involving presence in an unpleasant environment. Like many social workers, I learned early in my career to take precautions to avoid picking up insect infestations and infections in clients' homes. In poorly maintained or unsafe homes of clients without income to make repairs in their homes, or disaster or war zones, it is also necessary to avoid the risk of physical injury due to accidents.

Recent research contrasts this conventional situation with practice during the COVID-19 pandemic of 2020–22 when visiting homes was often forbidden or surrounded by practical restrictions to ensure infection control. Research in the UK showed a considerable change in practice (Pink, Ferguson & Kelly, 2020; Ferguson, Kelly & Pink, 2022). While it continued to be heavily influenced by formal systems and regulatory frameworks, social workers developed considerable flexibility to 'master' the complexities of the situation that they and the children they were working with faced. This enabled them to identify contingencies, such as being unable to visit, and improvise alternatives, such as meeting in the open air near the child's home and seeking to integrate face-to-face, digital and humane interpersonal practice. The social workers sought to develop intimacy, despite practical disruptions, by emphasising 'closeness through kindness', and reflected the fact that children were often comfortable with digital communications technology. Consistent with the reality that home visits are focused on the assessment and management of risk, local authorities prioritised visits for these purposes rather than for caring or helping processes (Cook & Zschomler, 2020).

Making arrangements

Making arrangements is not routine

The case studies of Iulia and Karim in the Introduction, and the Mooney family in Chapter 3, are examples of another way of connecting human actions with developing social capital: making arrangements. Arranging for services to be provided, coordinating or organising other services, and making contacts on behalf of clients and their families are all examples of useful elements of practice, even where the focus is on behavioural or social change. This is theorised in social work as either advocacy or empowerment: speaking on behalf of clients and enabling them to have a voice in decision making or policy making (advocacy) or enabling people to take control of events in their lives (empowerment). Advocacy and empowerment are important practice methods for critical, social development and indigenous streams of thinking, but they are relevant to all social work.

Although it seems a mundane activity, making arrangements for other people has important meanings for people in human interactions. Its practicality and accepting responsiveness to people's needs and requests are important for affirming clients in their relationship with social workers and mitigating the social control and surveillance aspects of the social work process. In a study of home care services, making arrangements demonstrated the possibility of a planned, secure and shared social future, and the possibility of dividing up, negotiating and pre-planning tasks. In this way, it permits cooperation in activity and social engagement between clients, family members and practitioners (Ekberg, 2011). It demonstrates and facilitates the social basis of human actions in social work.

The practice of making arrangements

Clarity about third parties, that is, explaining which agencies and people are involved in the situation, something that might not be immediately apparent to clients, can also help them to participate in and understand the processes. It may also enable clients, for example, people with disabilities and chronic illness, to feel autonomous and secure in the sometimes complex procedures around services they receive (Wongboonsin, Merighi, Walker et al, 2021). Yates's (2018) study of decisions about family living arrangements where there is sexual abuse in the home by siblings reminds us of the importance of carefully working out practical arrangements with the cooperation of everyone involved to ensure that their interests are properly balanced. Similarly, many safeguarding situations involve careful planning of where people will be, so that potential perpetrators of abuse are not left alone in situations where potential victims of abuse may not have protection and support. Again, such practice strategies use social control and surveillance to make the safeguarding actions work in the realities of social lives as they are lived, supporting practically the security of people at risk.

Networks and relationships

Building networks and relationships

Developing networks and relationships are two different, but sometimes complementary, ways of creating and understanding the connections between people that form social capital in people's lives. Networking focuses on the links between people and groups in society, while relationship focuses on the human emotional, psychological and rational responses to connections between people. This is another example of the art/science duality: developing relationships, although it may be researched and understood empirically, tends towards an artistic practice strategy; creating networks in social life, while it may require artistry, may be pursued through empirical investigation, using mathematical and graphical analysis among other methods of understanding.

Early accounts of social work (Cannon, 1939; Richmond, 1965 [1917]) do not emphasise relationship. Robinson (1930) argued that, in the US, the period 1920–30 saw a shift from a focus on the individual to relationship in the theorisation of social work within the individualised, problem-solving stream of social work; Yelloly (1980) suggests that this occurred later in Europe and the UK. Relationship became important in this way of thinking for two main reasons. First, individuals influencing others requires an interpersonal relationship; it cannot be done at a distance (Perlman, 1957, pp 64–83). Caring, counselling and helping actions all rely on alliance and relationship. Second, social workers practising such actions often deal with people's relationship difficulties. The social work helping relationship provides models and options that help people find alternative ways of relating to others (Irvine, 1952). For example, social workers can help clients' experiences of dealing with people in authority by showing the positive side of their official and professional powers (Studt, 1959).

Biestek's (1961) important text is individualistic and focused on change in problem behaviours. Relationship created an atmosphere whereby clients could engage with practitioners' help to respond to their psychosocial needs and problems. They worked together to define the direction of change, interacting to build a conscious wish to act. Clients interacted with practitioners' sensitive responses and understanding; emotional involvement was controlled. Downie (1971, pp 134–8) points out that these relationships are both personal and impersonal. The personal element is one of openness, receptiveness and encouragement, while the impersonal element reflects the fact that the practitioner occupies a role that has duties and rights bestowed by the employing agency. The social worker is impartial, even judicial, in making decisions, and cool in their reaction to provocation. Social work's relationships reflect social work responsibilities and values, including care, control and social justice, but

Biestek sees them instrumentally, as necessary to creating a successful helping relationship. Other characteristics of the relationship include individualisation, recognising a client's uniqueness and therefore adapting interventions to clients' specific needs; enabling feelings to be expressed purposefully allowing them to be recognised and dealt with; and acceptance, dealing with clients as they are, thus enabling them to reveal themselves. The social worker is non-judgemental, avoiding evaluations of clients' attitudes, standards and actions and setting aside their responsibility for causing problems. By enabling clients to make choices in their lives and as part of their work together, they retain self-determination and autonomy. Confidentiality is important to maintaining clients' privacy.

The individualistic emphasis in Biestek's analysis is striking. Later accounts from the 1980s have varying emphases. A Marxist critique of the focus on interpersonal relationships in social work suggests that it prevents us from acknowledging that all relationships are conditioned by economic relationships, which our practice fails to tackle (Rojek, Peacock & Collins, 1988, p 50). Feminist social work accounts of relationships explore the value of women's relationships with each other in working on matters of emotional welfare (Dominelli & McCleod, 1989, pp 88–9), and a dialogic style, in which workers and women clients engage in interactions as equal participants, fostering awareness of shared interests, rather than a worker with professional status and a less influential client (1989, pp 131–54). Feminist writing identifies the importance of workers' and clients' identities, and the organisational context in which sharing is facilitated and women's identities are valued (Hooyman, 1991; Kravetz & Jones, 1991; White, 2006). Milner (2001, p 5) stresses that a narrative and solution approach is open to accepting a range of clients' – particularly women clients' – experiences, focusing on present and future (rather than past) lives and on behaviour rather than emotions.

Consumer research (for example, Glastonbury, 1976; Howe, 1993; Huxley, Evans, Beresford et al, 2009) shows that good quality, respectful relationships are valued by clients as helpful. Contemporary practice continues to see effective worker–client relationships as essential. Examples are Rapp and Goscha's (2012) empirically supported account of strengths practice and holistic models of cognitive behavioural therapy, which, even though they work with structured schemes of interventions, start from making a relationship that engages clients in working on the issues in their lives (Stepney & Davis, 2018).

Networks and relationships as community presence

Being present in the community is a resource for interpersonal practice. Networking permits practice that concentrates on comm links between communities, groups and individuals, looking at the distance between people's living and working spaces, the frequency of links, their patterns and their strengths by looking at how often people are in contact and the purposes of their contacts. Such an approach allows social workers to think about social relations without focusing on personality. Ideas of building community, group and individual social capital are crucial. Practitioners can enhance the strength of social interchange by working on the number of links, the number and quality of interactions, the range of issues dealt with and the strength of commitment to those links. All of these issues may be evaluated empirically.

Critical, indigenous and social development streams of thinking may all make greater use of networking than individualistic, problem-based thinking. Community and groupwork practices, for example, often emphasise networking to develop community connections and interpersonal links. Other examples include community mental health practice, the use of support systems for stigmatised or unconfident clients, and family networks to build resilience to stresses arising from poverty and unemployment (Walsh, 2016). Even in more interpersonal practice, indigenous groups may set aside individualised values such as confidentiality to permit community or tribal engagement in resolving individual problems. Similarly, work with socially isolated people may use networking to build support networks. Another example is how networking may be used in practice with children in adoption or foster care or who may have attachment difficulties to build mutual support or find additional attachment figures in the community or wider family.

Conclusion

This chapter argues that Chapter 3's focus on action on the human and personal cannot be individualistic because being human requires concern for the social context of the individual. Social work strategies mark out social work's distinctive way of developing the human towards the social as a unique approach among cognate professions and within the service and organisational context of its practice.

Taking action on social work practice strategies
Be aware of and open to the social requirements of social work human actions. These actions and strategies interact in tension with, and balance, challenge and enhance, each other.

In the next chapter ...
... the streams of thinking that inform how social work human actions and strategies for the social create the different social works identified in Chapter 2.

5

Social work's streams of thinking

Social work practice thinking

Chapter 2 identified four current types of social work in diverse professions. These different conceptions of social work derive from continuing cultural, historical, political, policy, social and spiritual traditions of particular regions of the world. Practice thinking is not a series of novel developments; rather, it flows from characteristic traditions, streaming from past through present to future. Chapters 3 and 4 have made it clear that social work practice actions and strategies characteristically influence and respond to the cultural traditions expressed in varying streams of thinking. In Figure 5.1, I summarise the five identifiably different streams of thinking, which have developed over the period during which social work emerged, starting in the mid to late nineteenth century in different parts of the world.

Extending the analysis of the development of international social work education set out in Askeland & Payne (2017, pp 4–7), Figures 5.1–5.3 in this chapter refer to three main periods in social work's development:

Figure 5.1: Five streams of social work thinking

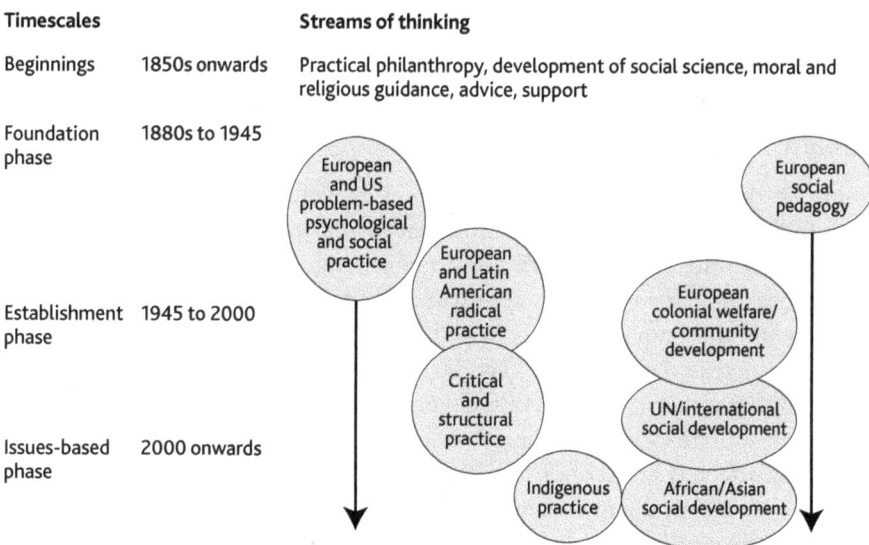

Timescales		Streams of thinking
Beginnings	1850s onwards	Practical philanthropy, development of social science, moral and religious guidance, advice, support
Foundation phase	1880s to 1945	
Establishment phase	1945 to 2000	
Issues-based phase	2000 onwards	

(Streams depicted: European and US problem-based psychological and social practice; European and Latin American radical practice; Critical and structural practice; Indigenous practice; European social pedagogy; European colonial welfare/community development; UN/international social development; African/Asian social development)

- A foundation phase, as pioneer social workers and educators began to develop professional structures. This continued from the late nineteenth century until the end of the Second World War in 1945.
- An establishment phase, as professional structures developed and institutionalised social work provision across the world. This continued through two periods of political change:
  - The post-war welfare states were economically and politically propitious for establishing and institutionalising social work professions and services. This period continued from the late 1940s until the economic and political disruption caused by the oil price shock of the 1970s. After that, economic and political thinking was more questioning of social provision.
  - The ending of the cold war between Western and Soviet political blocs, in the context of this economic and political environment in which the value of extensive social provision was more contested. This period continued from the 1980s until the early twenty-first century.
- An issues-based phase, in which, since social work education and professions were by then widely established, there was a struggle around global economic and political challenges to the nature and role of social work, which I examine in Chapters 9 and 10.

The two earliest streams of thinking both emerged during the late nineteenth century. At this time, industrialisation and urbanisation led to major social changes in many Western societies. These seemed to stretch the capacity of traditional forms of social governance through local government, itself developing, community and family support and philanthropic and religious action. Thus, new forms of social response emerged. In turn, these responses formed streams of thinking within social work, influencing the four types of social work discussed in Chapter 2. The different practice actions and strategies within each stream were reviewed in Chapters 3–4.

The European/US individualised behaviour and social practice stream

Some of the actions explored in Chapter 3 were interconnected because they focused on social problems in Western societies. Philanthropic help in European countries and the US grew, responding to social change in the late nineteenth and early twentieth centuries. Efforts to manage crime, healthcare, housing and the Poor Laws all enlarged during this period, and social security provision increased as the Poor Laws began to be displaced. Philanthropic help began to shift into social work, initially providing services for people in poverty and more welfare-oriented help for offenders, particularly younger offenders and those affected by alcohol misuse. This move also contributed to helping people with physical and mental health problems. Because the European and US experience of industrialisation and urbanisation was ahead of that of other countries, philanthropic and welfare provision often influenced thinking about social provision more widely. During the 1920s and 1930s, as social work emerged as an occupation and education for it also developed, this European and US thinking became a significant stream of thought. As an early starter, it has developed in a more complex way than the other streams, and I therefore set out various elements of it in more detail in Figure 5.2.

Figure 5.2: Developments in the European/US stream of thinking

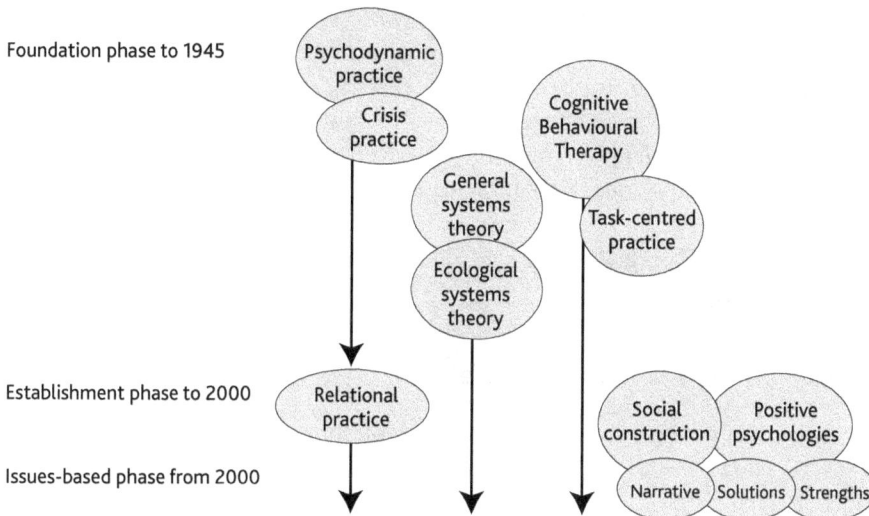

European/US stream narrative

The underlying narrative of this stream was problem based. Social change was seen as creating disruptions to the social order. Moral, religious and social constraints to disorder were thought to be breaking down. The view of change is individualistic because the problems of disorder were seen as the responsibility of individuals, families and communities in poverty. It saw social work as concerned with interventions to change individuals affected by disruption in a caring and helping way using behavioural and environmental, not social, change. Its psychological foundation was primarily psychodynamic, drawing on Freudian ideas in which the psychic drives generated behaviour and social relations. This led to a focus on caring, counselling and helping social work actions.

While the objective was social cohesion, one of the social work aims set out in the global definition of social work discussed in Chapter 2, the helping was less about empowerment and liberation, and more concerned with control and surveillance, especially where individuals were causing disruption. Social work aimed to help people manage the consequences of their poverty and other disruptions to social order by becoming the social helping aspect for crime, education, health, housing and poverty services. Sometimes, people were helped as individuals, but their families and local communities were also engaged as the most appropriate and sustainable sources of help. The thinking was holistic, aiming to link all the factors that disrupted people's lives.

Chapter 2 noted that social workers at this time focused on doing something practical, and taking action, although they maintained links with social research and social reform. The involvement with both physical and mental health services influenced the adoption of a medical model of diagnosis and treatment: people's problems should be linked to their social causes, in the way that illnesses and their causes would be diagnosed and treated.

The individualistic and social change elements of this problem-based practice aimed at social cohesion saw social change as producing pressures and problems for individuals to adapt to. Because people facing change were seen as valuing stability, this stream of thinking takes a conservative view of social cohesion. Thus, it contests possibilities for positive social change. The aim was for people to become resilient to change. Providing services and support for them was usually based on collective tax-raising powers in developed economies, and it often made progress when economic shocks or wars disrupted business, economic growth and employment.

Developments in the 'American model'

As this stream of thinking entered the establishment phase of the development of social work, it became the dominant mode of thinking about social work practice, sometimes called 'the American model', influencing social work and its education (Guzzetta, 1996). This is because of a political effort by the US to use social work to strengthen democratic regimes during the cold war with Soviet regimes during the 1950s. Adopting counselling-based psychodynamic practice, particularly with families, redirected any socialism to the more pragmatic and service-provision-oriented forms of social care in European welfare states. A good example was in the formerly legally based government services in Finland (Satka, 1995).

In the last half of the twentieth century, the US model built on its psychodynamic foundations with three developments, shown in Figure 5.2.

- First, a brief mode of practice, crisis intervention, developed, using ideas of coping; this was primarily a modification of longer-term psychodynamic helping. 'Coping' is a continuing effort to manage external demands exceeding a person's internal capacity, so conceptually it places responsibility for managing those demands on the people affected.
- Second, criticisms arose that psychodynamic ideas saw 'the social' as the source of problematic behaviour, but did not intervene in it. First, general systems and then eco or ecological systems ideas were incorporated, strengthening interventions with wider networks of clients' relationships and services.
- Finally, in the issues-based phase of the early twenty-first century, the relationship elements of pragmatic social work and psychodynamic ideas were reasserted in an explicitly 'relational' practice, which is now the primary form

of psychodynamic practice (Freedberg, 2009; Goldstein, Miehls & Ringel, 2009; Ruch, Turney & Ward, 2018).

During the 1960s, critique of the psychodynamic theoretical base of this form of social work led in two directions, again seen in Figure 5.2. The first critique was primarily about its failure to include the social as part of the explanatory base of social work. This led to the incorporation of general systems ideas into individualistic, psychological practice (Payne, 2002), allowing for indirect work with clients' networks of community and family and influencing other agencies through advocacy. Ecological systems followed up to focus on helping people adapt to their social environment, and more complex ideas about systems have also emerged (Hudson, 2010; Gitterman,Knight & Germain, 2021). Systems thinking shifted the work on clients' psychological functioning to include the social patterns affecting their lives, but still saw the people affected as bearing the primary responsibility for adaptation. This was not the only critique concerned with the inclusion of the social in psychodynamic social work, since critical and radical practice was also influential at this time, but forms a different stream of thinking, considered later.

The second critique was from a different form of psychological thought, which developed as a distinct psychological practice model: cognitive behavioural therapy. Initially, it created a rational technical theory, using social skills training and behaviour modification (Gonzalez-Prendes & Cassady, 2019). Thus, a more 'businesslike' approach sought to divert social work from the artistic, interpretive and metaphorical elements of psychodynamic theory. While this became mainly the province of specialised mental health settings and clinical psychologists, an adaptation directed to general social work, task-centred practice (Tolson, Reid & Garvin, 2003; Marsh & Doel, 2005) set a planned series of tasks to help people make progress towards an objective.

Influence from postmodern thinking

Towards the end of the twentieth century, and becoming influential during the issues-based period, social construction ideas became an important element in social work thinking, valuing a diversity of cultural, linguistic and social psychological ideas (Parton, 1996; Parton & O'Byrne, 2000). Figure 5.3 shows that two elements of this influenced social work: Seligman's (2017 [2002]) ideas about positive psychologies overlapping in social work thought with a broader social science shift towards postmodern and social construction thinking (for example, Sands & Nuccio, 1992; Pease & Fook, 1999). The positive psychologies challenged the emphasis on problems in the European/US stream of thinking and cognitive behavioural and task-centred practices. Looking instead at 'solutions', what people wanted to achieve, and the strengths they had to make progress towards them, shifted the emphasis from problem-based ideas in this stream of thinking. And social construction ideas challenged the rationalistic basis of many psychological interventions by encouraging social workers to look at how cultural and linguistic factors in society directed people's thinking about what was happening to them.

Streams of thinking and poverty

All these developments draw attention to a feature of *streams* of thinking. While there are important changes in theoretical and practice understanding, streams maintain an underlying model, which is sometimes hidden by new interpretations of practice. In this case, the continuity comes from broad social preferences for focusing on claimed social problems and helping people manage resilience to poverty within their communities, families and individual capacities. Shifting away from the focus on poverty, the same problem-based approach moved to work on resilience to behavioural, identity and social issues. But the practice emphasis remains on individual, family and social resilience rather than the issues faced, whether it be poverty or social issues of later concern. This may be compared with the approaches in social development, discussed later, which focus on *poverty alleviation* not resilience to poverty, and in the critical practice stream to transforming the sources of the issue and their impact on people, not resilience to a socially identified problem.

The European social pedagogy stream

Social pedagogy, the European conceptualisation that emerged from the same period of social change, but responded to it differently, offers a further example of how a stream of thinking maintains its consistency of approach, even though the social issues changed. While Western in origin, it emerged in central Europe and the Nordic countries and did not influence the problem-based approach in other European and US social work, since the original writings in German, Nordic languages and Polish were not translated (Kornbeck & Jensen, 2009).

Social pedagogy does not see social change as problematic, but as natural and continuing in everyone's life and every society. People join a process of shared learning within community and group endeavour, action based on improving their grasp of the issue, not just acquiring knowledge and understanding and being left to adapt. They need to appreciate how understanding the world better goes alongside learning and practising social engagement.

Social pedagogy achieves this through shared activities with other people, engaging people's communities. Examples include after-school care for young people residential care and community organisations such as the folk high schools of some Nordic countries. This educational approach sees helping as 'coming alongside' people to overcome the difficulty of intruding in private relationships. The social and community location of social pedagogy and its focus on group, personal and social cultural and educational development facilitates engagement without the individualistic assumptions of the problem-based approach of the European/US stream of thinking.

This stream continues, developing different aspects of its theorisation, and being adopted experimentally in the UK in residential care (Cameron & Moss, 2011; Charfe & Gardner, 2019), and as part of social work education. Some of its ideas also influenced care for refugee children, through the influence of Pestalozzi's educational work during the post-Second World War period (Charfe, 2019).

The radical, critical and structural social work stream

Radical and critical thinking in social work

Critical social work is the current iteration of a stream of thinking, which has gathered various elements of thinking over time, as set out in Figure 5.3. This stream emphasises how social structures in society generate and sustain conflicts of interest between different social groups. Such conflicts are an important source of social difficulties, rather than the claimed problematic behavioural disruption of the European/US individualistic problem-based stream of thinking. This broadly socialist formulation of social work is present in Western social work, but it has often been sidelined by problem-based thinking adopting social-cohesion conceptions of social work that emphasise psychological change theory and service delivery. There are historical and political reasons for the scepticism about these alternative ideas. They are disregarded partly because of the US minimisation of explicitly socialist social critiques characteristic of the cold war period, and because of their critique of dominating liberal/neoliberal economic and political ideas in Western political debate (see Chapters 9 and 10). These

Figure 5.3: Radical and critical streams of thinking

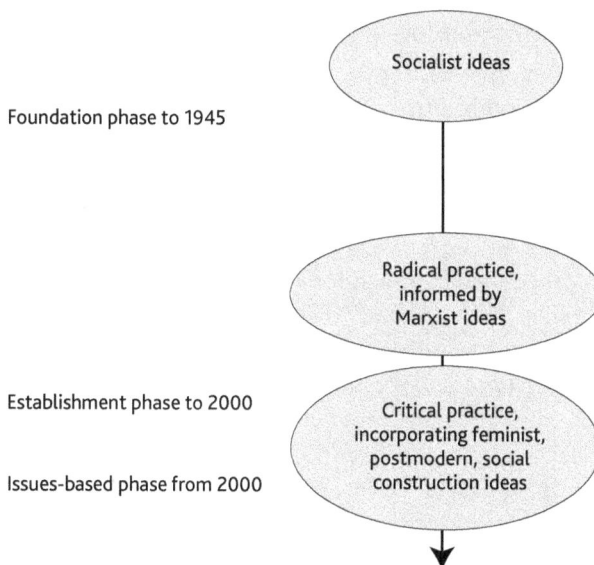

Socialist ideas

Foundation phase to 1945

Radical practice, informed by Marxist ideas

Establishment phase to 2000

Critical practice, incorporating feminist, postmodern, social construction ideas

Issues-based phase from 2000

ideas are, nevertheless, significant in all societies because they underlie the same change and social justice discourses about social work actions.

Figure 5.3 shows this stream of thought's influence on social work during the 1930s economic depression, in a left-wing analysis of the approach of liberal economics to welfare provision, in social provision services for Black populations, particularly in the impoverished southern states of the US and in the work of social work writers such as Lurie cited in Schriver (1987). The Second World War, the development of European welfare states and US cold war policies in the post-war period obscured this analysis.

The 1960s radical resurgence

There was a resurgence in radical social work during the 1960s, incorporating an explicitly Marxist analysis of the role of social work as an aspect of social control in capitalist societies and their economic systems (Bailey & Brake, 1975; Corrigan & Leonard, 1978; Langan & Lee, 1989). Marxist theory problematises socialisation, the process by which children are knitted into the networks of social expectations that rule their lives and behaviour. It regards the family as an important site of social reproduction preparing children mainly for industrialised work roles, or latterly precarious unskilled employment. This process also leads, in feminist thinking, to women being oppressed by fulfilling family domestic roles, caring for children and disabled and older people rather than being able to pursue more financially and intellectually rewarding roles in the wider economy.

Radical practice encouraged collective community action and mutual help, particularly in working-class communities where socialisation for industrial and precarious working patterns takes place. By engaging people in the struggle against oppressive conditions, they are empowered to understand and engage in tackling the barriers and limitations in their lives. Practitioners should look at conflicts generated by these structural conflicts, and build alliances with representative organisations in people's communities, such as activist and advocacy groups, community organisations and trades unions, rather than working on people's problems within social structures which focus on adaptation.

To achieve this, a significant influence on radical practice is Freire's (1972, 1974 [1967]) conscientisation, a collective process of working with people who share similar experiences or concerns; in feminist practice, consciousness-raising in dialogues with other women. Practitioners help people explore their experiences of difficulties in their lives to identify collectively how others' power and privilege affect them. Exploring and sharing experiences in this way enables people to see that their experience is not individualised, but has been privatised instead, blamed on individual and family problems. Unlike informal education in social pedagogy, radical processes of this kind aim to enable people to see their troubles not as individualised, private affairs, affecting them only, but created through broad economic, political and social processes. Doing this allows people to gain the capacity to be critical of and to understand the processes by which they are oppressed. Because the experience is shared, moreover, the effects become a matter of wider concern, so that policy and political action may be taken. This creates a praxis, actions directly derived from their experiences and shared dialogue, that can be taken forward both individually and jointly. Research in social work has shown that groupwork of this kind leads to useful shared action Gutiérrez, 1995; Gutiérrez, DeLois and GlenMaye, 1995).

Critical practice emerges

Critical practice emerged during the issues-based phase of social work's developments in thinking. It built on radical practice's class-based analysis, but in tune with the times shifted towards identity politics and global social movements for change. Postmodern critiques contest the deterministic aspect of radical practice and positivist social work education, research and practice. Contemporary critical practice incorporates feminist gender-based critiques and movements for anti-oppressive practice, decolonisation and social justice (Kleibl, Lutz, Noyoo et al, 2020; Webb, 2020, 2022). It also takes up identity concerns relevant to social work client groups around the political economy of ageing, sexuality and social models of disability. When they are used to pursue critical practice objectives, elements of advocacy, empowerment and macro practice are valued. Critical sociology, such as the work of Bourdieu (1980, 1991), questions how ideas in society become authorised ways of thinking in people's habitus, the cultural patterns by which they live, and fields, the networks of relationships in their social environment. Foucault's sociology, discussed in Chapter 3 referring to social work's role in governance and management, shows how this becomes part of creating that social order. Ideas from feminism and social construction have built a critical social work (Fook, 2016) that encourages people to learn how to overcome the limitations in community and family life, how pension systems frustrate a good quality of life as people age, and how discriminatory attitudes to disability, LGBTQIA+ sexuality and mental illness are replicated in society.

Critical practice theory uses both structural and social construction analyses of how oppressive cultural, economic, political and social ideologies are implemented in social relations. This take place within important social structures informing or providing for cultural life, education, employment, family, healthcare, housing, leisure and social provision (Mullaly & Dupré, 2019). Such an analysis contrasts with the radical theory emphasis on class- and economy-based explanations.

Critical practitioners respond in three main ways to these issues:

- Look for opportunities to meet people's human rights, combat social justice and reduce inequalities.
- Focus on social models of disability, health and relationships and promote participative and citizenship approaches to benefit clients and the people around them.

- Practice in dialogic, equal relationships with clients and colleagues and build cooperation to achieve social improvements.

An important critical practice strategy is disruption, to disconnect oppression and inappropriate use of power from clients' lives. Three disruptive practices involve:

- Changing adverse impacts of organisations and policy on people's capacity to develop and survive by advocacy, dialogical practice, family support, self-help and peer support.
- Challenging adverse impacts on people's social identities, for example by enabling gay and lesbian parenting to be acceptable to local agencies such as schools.
- Helping people become aware of and combat political and social policies that lead to barriers or demands upon them, such as inappropriately restrictive safety concerns affecting the lives of disabled and older people.

Structural and eco practice

An important strand is structural social work practice, and concerns about inequalities and social injustice baked into many important social structures affecting education, health and social assistance for people in poverty. Structures might include matters such as attitudes to parenting or offending, or gendered discourses in childcare issues (Robb, Montgomery & Thomson, 2019). Critical analysis of social work in childcare and child protection services, for example, starts from listening to the voice and experience of the child to guide its direction (Rogowski, 2013; Esquao & Strega, 2015).

An important new development is eco or green practice, concerned with combating the effects of climate change and helping people and communities cope with its consequences (Dominelli, 2012; Gray, Coates & Hetherington, 2013; McKinnon & Alston, 2016). This also is concerned with general social change. While this requires behavioural and interpersonal change, the focus on long-term broad social adaptation to a changing natural environment suggests that caring, counselling, helping and support actions are less relevant to the change objective than social justice and human rights actions.

The initial critique of radical practice was that an activist stance and broad political and social aims meant that social work ignored the immediate needs of clients in favour of broad social objectives and structural change. Also, it might create hostility towards clients and within client groups who are already stigmatised by social attitudes. This is contested with the more practical bent of contemporary critical practice, and the recognition given to clients' voice and participation. Many practice strategies with a critical emphasis are possible, and activism compatible with social workers being officials is also increasingly theorised, for example by Fenton (2019).

The social development stream

Social development is a stream of thought originally derived from the fairly minimal welfare development practice in British, French and Spanish colonial administrations, influenced also by the thinking of Christian churches. It was taken up by the United Nations, influenced by US political objectives during the cold war. In that context, it was seen as contributing social welfare objectives to economic and industrial development in globalising economies (Midgley, 1995; Midgley and Conley, 2010). More recently, however, this perspective has been taken on by African and Asian writers (Desai, 2014; Patel, 2015; Tan, Chan, Mehta et al, 2017).

As with other streams, an approach has been maintained as the issue has shifted. In this case, the shift is away from adding a social focus to economic development, towards an emphasis on participation in alleviating and eradicating poverty, building environmental sustainability and food security, gender equality and women's economic liberation, and responding to health and education inequalities and needs. The aim is to generate social entrepreneurship and political and economic capabilities as community resources, rather than as contributions to global economic objectives. As with the critical practice stream, interpersonal actions such as caring, counselling, helping and support actions may not be relevant to the development aims, but may contribute to helping people participate in resolving their community and individual responses to the issues that the development aims are trying to achieve.

The indigenist practice stream

Indigenous practice reflects an indigenist ideology (Gray, Coates & Yellow Bird, 2008; Hart, 2019). It connects with social development and has emerged in the issues-based period in the early twenty-first century. It is also connected with a critical emphasis on responding to the issues of colonialism and sometimes a history of slavery, rather than seeking adjustments to alien and colonial cultures and lifestyles. It has become important where colonisation displaced pre-settler and pre-colonial populations. The United Nations (United Nations Permanent Forum on Indigenous Issues, n.d.) identifies indigenous peoples by the characteristics set out in Table 5.1. Providing an analysis of the cultural and linguistic oppression of communities of such populations, it has proved influential in Aotearoa/New Zealand, Australia, Canada, Arctic regions in Nordic countries and parts of the US where there are minorities from pre-colonisation countries. More recently, it has become influential in formerly colonised African and Asian countries where cultural or religious groups, sometimes majority populations, have experienced the suppression of important traditions by Western thinking.

Early discussion of indigenisation (for example, Walton & El Nasr, 1988) discussed adapting Western social work models to local traditions, making them more authentic for use with other cultural and ethnic traditions. More recently,

Table 5.1: UN statement on characteristics of indigenous peoples

---

- Self-identification as indigenous peoples at the individual level and accepted by the community as their member.
- Historical continuity with pre-colonial and/or pre-settler societies.
- Strong link to territories and surrounding natural resources.
- Distinct social, economic or political systems.
- Distinct language, culture and beliefs.
- Form non-dominant groups of society.
- Resolve to maintain and reproduce their ancestral environments and systems as distinctive peoples and communities.

Source: United Nations Permanent Forum on Indigenous Issues (n.d.)

Kreitzer (2012) argued that colonial academic influences have inhibited the development of distinctively African cultural traditions relevant to social work practice. Graham's (2002, p 69) proposal to build an African-centred practice includes many factors common to other indigenous practices:

- The interconnections of both natural and human environments.
- The spiritual nature of human beings.
- Families and people possess both collective and individual identities and are part of collective structures.
- There is a unity of both mind and spirit, contrary to some Western philosophies.
- Relationships between people should be valued.

Asian research proposes a blended approach in which local people should explore aspects of non-indigenous practice that might be included in a culturally relevant practice (Pulla, Das & Nikku, 2020), similar to more globally relevant proposals (Payne & Askeland, 2008, pp 51–3; Payne, 2014a) for 'cultural translation' from a dominant to a minority culture. These contributions acknowledge the issue of decolonisation from colonial power not clearly established in the earlier work. Another formulation, 'Indian' social work, is proposed by a group of social workers (Dash, Kumar, Singh et al, 2021) claiming an ancient cultural history of social welfare provision, for example from the *Arthashastra* (Kautilya, 1992), an accumulation of traditional wisdom on public administration for a monarch. The emphasis in much of this work on restoring cultural traditions and practices, however, fails to focus on the important structural issues of colonialism and racism in the social work practice prescriptions, and detailed analysis of how local traditions should be included in social work is not available. Accounts of practice in previously oppressed cultures and ethnicities are becoming available which explain indigenous concepts and show how they are applied. Examples are Mafile'o (2004) and Mafile'o & Vakalahi (2018) on Tongan ideas; Spitzer, Twikirize & Wairire (2014) and Twikirize & Spitzer (2019) on African ideas. Indigenous practice proposes that social workers must 'struggle gladly' (Payne, 2014a, p 13) to open themselves to receive the culture of people from another culture and ethnicity.

Indigenous practice, therefore, seeks to formalise the position of practitioners who see their profession as allied to culturally and ethnically distinct, local social norms and structures in communities of such populations. More broadly, the aim is to draw into current social work practice the cultural, environmental, political and social identity knowledges and understandings of pre-colonial populations or peoples with suppressed identities. For example, family group conferencing, a process in Māori culture of engaging all family members in decision making about a child in difficulties (Crow & Marsh, 1998; Burford, 2017) has been taken up internationally and extended to youth restorative justice and policing (Wachtel, 2017 [2000]; McCold & Wachtel, 2012). It is similar to involving tribal mechanisms when collectively resolving community issues in African cultures. This innovation contests the Western preference for advocacy practice to achieve participation by children and parents in decision-making processes. Contestation between streams of practice draws attention to where the stickiness of loyalty hides inflexibilities in dominant streams of thinking. This stream of thinking emphasises people's cultural and social identity as an important factor in social work practice and an important opportunity for increasing social work's diversity. Thus, while not every national social work has a pre-colonial traditional culture to respond to, this stream of thought draws attention to the availability of traditional cultures, which means people may resist social work actions following other streams of thought, or provides opportunities to incorporate innovative social thinking from other practices.

Conclusion

This chapter uncovered the different ways of thinking that underlie the four social works described in Chapter 2.

Each formulates a dominant way of practising that is culturally typical of particular countries or regions of the world. Other streams of thinking might also be present as part of the social work services in any particular country or region, as contributions to helping people respond to different aspects of the issues and because of cross-border influences. The critical stream of thinking is present in most countries, challenging the dominant streams of thinking in European countries, for example, or influencing particular social work agencies. Or the interpersonal, problem-based or social pedagogy thinking of European countries can be incorporated to help communities, families and individuals respond to climate change or poverty in many African and Asian countries, which can only be fully tackled through social development thinking.

Within these streams of thinking, there are often formulations of practice that are in themselves specialisations. The long-standing problem-based social-cohesion stream, for example, contains ideas such as systems-, cognitive behavioural- or task-centred practice. These form particular theoretical approaches, seeking to tackle problems in that stream's mode of thinking. There is something of a shift from practice theories that emphasise work on analysing and tackling problems that people are worried about towards looking at people's goals and finding solutions or strengths within their present lives that move towards those goals. While many of these can be used as part of most forms of social work, some people take up particular forms of therapy, or they are used within particular services, and we can see these as specialisations. For example, crisis intervention theory emerged from mental health work and continues to be used in emergency services for mental health problems, but can be applied more widely.

Action on social work streams of thinking

Explore with colleagues and team members how you are affected by streams of thinking typical of your location, and identify learning from other cultures and streams of thinking that could offer wider forms of practice action and strategy.

In the next chapter ...

... exploring the context of agencies and professions builds an understanding of how social work's aims and practice contribute to social provision. It questions whether social work agencies facilitate or hinder practice actions, strategies and thinking. It focuses on the impact of agency and managerial policies and responsibilities on social work's unique practice focus on social capital.

6

Social work's agency contexts

Social work's practice in agencies

Social work is always practised in an agency. Even private practitioners have to develop policies about their specialism and a system for managing their work. Often, they form a group practice that becomes an agency. Previous chapters have concentrated on the ideas and influences from within social work that created professional identity and practice. Throughout, they identified influences and pressures on social work from the wider societies in which it exists. This chapter, and those following, concentrate on those influences.

The focus of this chapter is the impact of agencies that provide organisational contexts for practice. The space for social work to be practised is created through formal decisions by organisations and informal negotiations among the people working in the agencies, including professions working with social work. What agency arrangements are good, or not, for social work practice? Conversely, what do agencies and other professions want from social work?

Social work agencies are the intermediary between the cultures and expectations of the society they operate in and the ideas that developed social work practice. Chapter 2 showed that social work education and agency settings strongly influenced social workers' identities. Agencies have an impact in the opposite direction, because providing social work services carries social work into society, influencing economic, political and social views about social work practices. As social work became widespread, even universal, during the twentieth century, the state has become an important organisational structure for social work agencies. There are, however, alternative structures; I discuss five of these structures in this chapter, deriving from sectors of the economy:

- The community, family and social context.
- Public or state social services.
- For-profit or private sector social services.
- Charitable or 'third sector' social services.
- Social enterprises.

I set out relationships between these structures in Figure 6.1.

None of these structures is limited to social work provision; wider social services and wider economic and social actions are present in each structure. Social work services therefore mesh with the other aspects of these structures and interact with other professions, and with social care workers who are

Figure 6.1: Five social work practice agency contexts

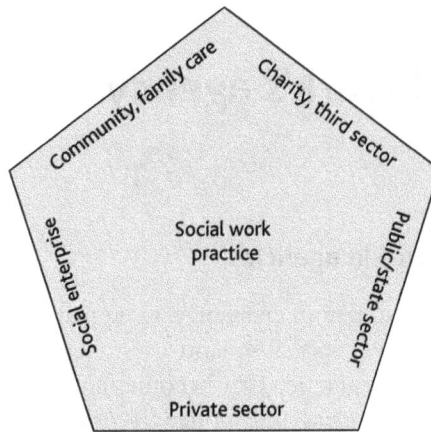

not social workers. Chapter 5 showed how social work practitioners develop practice strategies about how to take forward their responsibilities on behalf of their agency. In this way, social work creates and expresses strategic knowledge about 'how to go on' (Kearney, 2004, pp 163–80) when social work is practised.

Each structure and way of working together brings both advantages and problems as a base for social work services, often reflecting issues of finance and power, and modes of working together within these structures.

The following three case examples, based on real cases with details changed to protect confidentiality, suggest some of the debates agencies and practitioners have with contexts for social work practice. In all of them, maintaining the agency's policy aims is set against people having the freedom to take control of their lives and having human rights and social justice through their voices being heard. All these examples arose in the context of the UK's main emphasis on social work as part of broad social provision in a democratic Western society. I look at alternatives to that social context in a later part of the chapter.

Case examples: individual need and voice and the agency context

Christina, her advocate and her social worker

In Christina's case, two different kinds of social work responsibilities come up against each other: the caring, controlling work of child protection processes and advocacy that expresses a child's voice within the agency's processes. The agency's procedures expected both aspects of social work to be present, but did not facilitate holistic work between them.

At a child protection case conference, the residential school, following the local authority's policy, asked its child advocacy service to provide an advocate to represent 15-year-old Christina in the decision-making process about her care and education arrangements as her time at the school came to an end. The local authority's social worker, after some reflection with her team leader, prepared a report with recommendations from the social work team. The advocacy service contracted an independent social worker to act as Christina's advocate. After reviewing the social worker's report with Christina and her lone-parent mother, the advocate argued at the conference for what Christina wanted, a return home to her mother's care. After the conference, the social worker complained about the advocate, saying it was unprofessional to argue against the local authority's considered opinion of what was in the best interests of the child. The advocate pointed out to her that the advocate's responsibility was to act as the voice of the child. The local authority's responsibility, and that of their social workers, was to decide on and act in the best interests of the child, which might be different.

Here both practitioners are using their social work skills in different ways and through different agency structures to contribute to a service that as a whole makes official parenting decisions in the best interests of the child, but the local authority agency had not sorted out a way forward if these practices came into conflict.

Appealing against Mrs Chartin's funding assessment

In Mrs Chartin's case, the local authority's adult social care department, while making formal provision for social justice by designing appeal procedures in its decision-making processes, sought to mitigate the financial consequences of an adverse appeal decision by limiting the range of social work practice interventions from Nirmal's agency. The social worker is faced with institutional and organisational pressures to move her practice away from enabling clients' and their families' human rights and to avoid facilitating social justice in the administration of resources.

Nirmal was a social worker with a local association for older people, which was substantially financed by the local authority. Her client, Mrs Chartin, an older woman with severe disabilities, was receiving local authority funding for care assistance. A reassessment of the financing led to a substantial cut in the funding for Mrs Chartin's care and Nirmal, after discussion with her team leader, advised Mrs Chartin's daughter to appeal against the funding decision. This was successful. Later, the director of Nirmal's association asked Nirmal's team leader to stop the team from advising people to appeal, since the local authority's director of adult social care had told him this was causing a big increase in costs.

Here, economic priorities are being asserted against appropriate social work practice by the naked use of organisational and political power.

Chidike's child protection plan

In Chidike's case, social work decisions deriving from child protection procedures, respecting the human rights aim of not subjecting the family to unnecessary control and surveillance, were subverted by the education priorities represented by behaviour management in the school, a tension between potentially different professional priorities.

At the child protection case conference, Chidike's social worker and her team leader argued that there was no need to continue with a child protection plan, an organised response to the risk of child abuse or neglect, for Chidike, since he was not at risk from the difficulties in his family. They could be worked through with the staff from the local children's hub. The school's headteacher argued that Chidike's relationships with other children at school reflected poor emotional control and this was disruptive in the classroom. Because the child and adolescent mental health service was under pressure and unable to offer treatment for Chidike, no work had been done on this issue. The conference chair pointed out that the director of education took the view that it was important for children's social care services to support the school where behavioural difficulties were inhibiting the child's educational opportunities. Social workers argued that this was important but did not justify the imposition of a child protection plan where there was no risk to the child in the family setting.

Here, different social priorities were represented by the perspective of different professions supported by different services.

Agency in agencies and co-production

These examples represent a common experience for social workers; agencies represent economic, political and social pressures that torpedo good practice. The pressures sometimes operate covertly, there is a surface commitment to values that social work practice espouses, but the power seems to be coming from elsewhere.

A starting point to reflect on this is to understand that the word 'agency' has two different meanings. One, the one I have so far been using, is the organisation in which social work is practised; I call this the 'organisation agency' to distinguish it from the other kind. The second is the capacity of human beings or organisations to use rational thinking to have an impact on the social structures of the world around them; I call this 'impact agency'. The two ideas are connected: social service 'agencies' are called this to denote that they enable social policies to have impact agency on the quality of life and structures in society. Part of that impact comes through sponsoring social work practice. Chapters 1 and 2 noted that social work emerged pursuing idealist and progressivist ideologies. These are beliefs that it is possible for human beings, working collaboratively, to influence and improve social relationships. Social work cannot exist without believing those two things, and society sanctions them through its agencies. Social work organisation agencies are the instruments of having that positive impact on social relations, while social work is an impact agency for agencies to get the outcomes they want to achieve.

Co-production is the current model for social work practice to have impact agency. It does this by engaging clients with practitioners as participants in the work of the organisation agency. It aims to produce good social work practice together with service users, with agency colleagues and with other professions. Co-production requires structures to work together to originate the best work: structures around the client and other service users, and structures between agencies and between professions. To have impact agency in social work, social workers in their organisation agencies need to pay attention to and work for co-productive structures. Because social work starts from promoting human cooperation and solidarity and contesting competitive behaviour, co-production is integral to social work practice values.

Summing up the messages of this book so far, to facilitate co-production as part of getting results, agencies have to offer contexts that work for social work. Here, I draw together, in brief, what social work needs social service agencies to do:

- Promote human cooperation and solidarity; contest competitive human behaviour (Chapters 1 and 2).
- Offer at least one of the main types of social work: interpersonal intervention, services for social wellbeing, social education and social development (Chapter 2).
- Balance social cohesion, solidarity and cooperation with social change and collective and individual freedom for communities, families and individual people to take control of their lives (Chapter 2).
- Facilitate social workers taking on an appropriate balance and integration of all social work's actions: care, behavioural and social change, counselling, help, social control and surveillance, social justice and human rights work and, finally, support (Chapter 3).
- Facilitate social workers adopting a range of social work strategies: art and science, assessment, community presence and home visiting, making arrangements, networking and relationship (Chapter 4).
- Facilitate social workers adopting at least one of the five streams of thought, balanced with understanding of and sometimes incorporating other streams: individualised behavioural and social practice, informal social education, critical and structural practice, social development and indigenous practice (Chapter 5).

The organisation agency asks the opposite question: does the social work practice that results from these requirements meet its social aims?

Social service agency contexts of practice

Social work practice takes place in one of the five agency contexts set out in Figure 6.1. People first and foremost engage with and are helped by their community, family or social network, the first context. All professional work, social work too, interweaves with this context.

Social work agencies reflect constantly changing ideas in society about the social objectives of their professional work. An authoritative Scottish literature review (Asquith, Clark & Waterhouse, 2005) identified a succession of underlying philosophies influencing the management of social work agencies in Western countries in the latter half of the twentieth century:

- Welfarism: a paternalistic helping and caring approach based on social democratic ideas.
- Professionalism: underlining the authority and expertise of practitioners.
- Consumerism: focusing on the needs and rights of service users.
- Managerialism: privileging economic and managerial requirements.

- Participationism: stressing equal partnership between service providers and users.

I would add a point because history has moved on:

- Neoliberalism: using public services to promote individuals' freedom of action in economic markets in some countries during the twenty-first century, and the current importance of economic and managerial policies arising from it, which contest the philosophies outlined here and further discussed in Chapters 9 and 10.

This historical analysis reflects tensions between action for the individual and for the social within social work. There are also tensions between requirements expressed in conflicts between the agency and the organisational context of other agencies, professionals and service users. Social service provision seeks a social work that is more impactful because it is acceptable to and valued by the community, family and individuals. It must, however, also respond to economic, managerial and political policy, expressed in the agency's social role and powers. These tensions were present in the three case examples.

The struggle between social work's practice needs and values and economic and political policy control of the agency context is always present in social service agencies, an important theme of the discussion in the next section. This particularly arises around the significant role of the state that emerged during the twentieth century.

Community, family and informal organisations: the continuing context

Before organised social work in agencies, social care was provided through family and informal organisations in the community. Many, like the churches, were not primarily focused on social service provision. Links between community, family and informal providers provide the social capital in the places people turn to as significant sources of social care in any society. The first social work was not provided by a formal agency, let alone the state with its economic and political objectives; it was a restructuring of relationships in everyday life. Agency structures and policies in the early twentieth century expressed people's existing social relationships. Existing class relationships, social assumptions and status hierarchies influenced early social work, as they still do. Helping responses in most European countries and the US, therefore, were led by local elites, officers in the armed forces and their wives and the churches. Solidarity was strongest among leading and skilled workpeople, such as craft guilds, or where there was a high enough income for saving and mutual insurance schemes. People in poverty, struggling to live and work, were neglected by these structures but sometimes found support in local communities, trade unions and other social groups with mutual interests and concerns. Social actions also reflected commonplace social relations of caring and helping, so that helping was women's work and organising was often done by their menfolk. These historic conventions continued in the early social work profession and persist, sometimes hidden, in the formal structures of the present organisation of social services.

Because natural community and family engagement and helping is the starting point of all social work, early social work organisation came out of those human settings in the foundation phase of social work (see Figure 5.2). Chapter 3 noted social work actions around caring, community change, social control and surveillance all emerged from local and traditional organisations. In doing so, it often represented specific interests such as cultural and ethnic roots and existing power relations. Streams of thinking such as social pedagogy, critical, social development and indigenous practice equally emerged from concerns about the needs of local and ethnic communities and indigenous minorities.

Social work strategies such as assessment, community presence, home visiting and networking came, on the other hand, from the need of agencies to engage with, understand and, crucially, govern, local communities and social groups that were economically, ethnically and socially different from their helpers. Examples were churches, folk high schools in some European societies, settlements and local community organisations. Social workers also took up positions in public institutions which both governed and had helping responsibilities in these communities. Examples include general and psychiatric clinics and hospitals, temperance organisations leading to probation services and general welfare organisations such as Poor Law workhouses. In the UK local guilds of help, associated with developing municipal institutions, were important as well as the charity organisation societies discussed as one of the sources of practice in Chapter 3 (Burnham, 2012). In Germany, the Elberfeld system of local welfare visiting with its influence in Japan is a well-known example (Rosenhaft, 1994). In Europe and North America, many local child welfare organisations, often with connections to Christian churches, or motivated by Christian charity, created a diverse picture.

Public or state sector social work agencies

Public sector structures

Public or state sector social service organisations may be national, regional or local. The arrangements depend on the size and administrative structure of the country and the impact of national standards or local responsiveness on the national system. How they are managed and regulated therefore depends on the interaction of local, regional and national political systems. They are financed by national and sometimes local taxes and charges for services. Social work is consequently influenced by economic decisions about the extent to which (and how) government finance should provide for social work and political decisions about what should be financed in this way. Often social work is managed by the public authority that finances it, but decisions may be passed up to higher levels of the state, or national and regional policies passed down to local government to manage the service. Some services may be outsourced to be provided by other sectors of the economy. The extent to which this happens depends on the economic and political philosophy underlying the outsourcing decision; I look at this further in Chapters 9 and 10.

Four arguments for public sector social work

There are four main arguments for public sector social work services: solidarity, rights and powers; all leading to security. The first argument is that public or state provision provides for mutuality and solidarity in providing services. A state accepts collective responsibility on behalf of the population for social provision, using its tax-raising powers. This accepts the humanistic position that social helping is a natural characteristic of human societies. The extent to which social work is included depends on the political interpretation of public views about its legitimacy and usefulness in providing social services; I consider this issue in Chapter 9.

The second argument for state social work services is the other side of the coin: the rights of citizenship. Citizenship is a status that goes with a connection with a territory, a state or a local area, and it is also the process of building that connection, or losing it or aspects of it. The rights of citizenship include legal, political and social rights to receive benefits from the local or national collective and participate in the social relations of the nation, to have a voice. Citizens also have duties towards the state, to fight for it, to participate in other ways by accepting duties to other citizens, paying taxes to support the nation and its collective responsibilities and taking part in politics and voting.

The third argument for state provision of social work services is the need for political authority to provide legal powers of compulsion, where this is required for public protection. It can also provide legal entitlements to particular elements of the service, rights to ensure public confidence that a service will be made available if required, and the security among potential service users that their needs will be met. Such rights also permit compliance with standards and responsibilities under international law. For example, service provision can be made to comply with international agreements such as the United Nations Convention on the Rights of the Child (UNICEF, 1989).

The fourth argument, leading from the three previous points, is that the state is the best hope of providing consistency and security of provision across a community or territory, with steady financing from lawful taxation. By legislating or giving other public authority for a service, and by using tax-raising powers to provide a similar service across the area that it covers, state provision allows people to have the security that there is no postcode lottery. They all get the same extent and standard of provision wherever they are. But this security is only a hope: it depends on the stability of the state. A weak state cannot provide its citizens with the security that social work will be there; a state that does not value this offer of wellbeing to its citizens will direct its policies elsewhere.

From a successful state concerned with wellbeing for all, a welfare state, citizens get the secure advantages of participating in and receiving services that include social work. A state with other objectives, perhaps the economic security of elites or the hegemony of other ideals, may only provide a limited social work.

Critiques of public sector social work

Critiques of these arguments for public or state provision of social services make three points: that they depend on the effectiveness and management of the services, on resources and on access to rights.

On effectiveness and management, although legislating for provision, governments can decide not to provide the services themselves. Both third sector and private sector provision are commonplace across the world. In the UK, for example, the National Society for the Prevention of Cruelty to Children has historically had legal powers to prosecute parents for cruelty or neglect, and private and third sector services both in the community and in residential care are widespread. Even if services are directly managed by public sector organisations, conflicts over how services are provided may arise, as in the example of Christina, her advocate and her local authority social worker, or the conflict of interest between education and social work in Chidike's case, all mandated by organisations working with state responsibilities. Public services may be inadequately managed, and even if they are provided according to legislation, different interpretations and approaches to services may arise in different areas. On resources, taxation depends on political decisions and public support (see Chapter 9), and may not meet legal requirements, as in financial support for Nirmal's agency. On access to rights, oppressed or poorer people may not have the emotional strength and financial resources to take legal action to have their rights implemented, or understand and use the mechanisms to get help.

One important area of concern about public organisations is that they derive from and are accountable for government and legal responsibilities that are diffused within them and because they implement legal powers. This often leads them to be cautious, constrained and reactive in their responses to social issues; bureaucratic behaviour, when social work requires creative, innovative and responsive behaviour. The freedom to practise creatively may be balanced by the duty to be accountable for public constraints because belief or support in social work is lacking. The advantages of state welfare may be vitiated by managerial and political foot-dragging.

The legal and organisational aspects of public and state sector social work provision also raise questions of oppression and inflexibility. On oppression, because they represent public attitudes, can politically directed and taxpayer-funded organisations reflect the need for openness to diversity and meeting the needs of stigmatised groups? Historically, state organisations have been slow to take up the needs of minority groups, have been discriminatory towards minority groups of all kinds but perhaps particularly minority ethnic groups, and have been unsympathetic with conscientious objectors to participation in war. A longstanding example is the fear of parents that social work involvement in their families will lead to their children being taken away from them; research suggests (see Chapter 11) that this power is the main thing that many people know about social work roles and responsibilities. State organisations, partly because they are large and hard to understand, but also because of political accountability and legal requirements to stick to legislated mandates, have sometimes been inflexible in dealing with new challenges (Chapter 1's case example of Iulia and Karim is relevant to both of these points). Welfare states have therefore sometimes been seen as bureaucratic and inflexible in their decision making and capacity to act, as in the three case examples. Also, their management approaches may be too rigid to balance the different aspects of social work in all their complexity. A recent example of these concerns in the UK is conflict reflecting public disquiet over gender identity services, including social work, trying to respond to rising demand from young people to transition to a different gender identity.

Summary: for and against public sector social work

In summary, the theoretical right to secure public sector provision might be the best organisational basis for social work, offering service users rights and consistent service provision. Characteristics of public sector organisations, however, may get in the way of practitioners being able to balance complex social work actions, methods, objectives and streams of thinking examined in previous chapters. Co-production may be the answer because it offers mutuality to drive the appropriate reaction, but there is a risk that, led by a public organisation, it too becomes over-complicated and oppressive.

Because of these doubts about whether the state can provide a flexible basis for social work, many people argue for a market, or a quasi-market, that includes both some of the benefits of state security and also alternative pathways to social work. Are such alternatives the answer to the inflexibilities of the state?

For-profit, private sector agencies

Profit and occupational social work

Profit-making, private sector organisations may provide occupational social services, that is, social services for employees or services for the public.

Occupational social services are present in many economies, including Nordic countries and the US, providing welfare services for employees of large companies. In Japan and some other countries, large companies sometimes provide extensive health and social care services for their workforce, including retirement facilities. In India, training for private sector personnel and human resources roles is provided in many schools of social work; it is a career option for social work professionals.

There are question marks about whether all practice within companies is consistent with social work values. Bakalinsky (1980) argued that difficulties included achieving neutrality in the context of economic pressures from employers, rather like the conflict over Mrs Chartin's funding and Nirmal's position as an employee. Intrinsic conflicts between corporate and humanitarian aims and values and a professional focus outside resolving work conflicts, might better be tackled by trades unions which can take the side of employees or other mechanisms that provide for mediation. The workplace is an important aspect of many people's lives, however, and may thus be an important location for help (Kurzman, 2000). This may particularly be so for men who are not well served by social services aimed at domestic caring. Working with an employers' coordinating body, providing services to a range of employers, may avoid some of those difficulties. Also, access to some groups may be better through welfare provision in employment settings than in conventional social services: for example, people with long-term physical disabilities or recurring mental illness (Akabas & Gates, 2000). It has often been difficult for people with mental illness to maintain employment. A variety of community mental health projects support recovering patients in work, for example in sheltered employment schemes, but a higher proportion of mentally ill people in open employment have better wages (Rüesch, Graf, Meyer et al, 2004).

There is a case, therefore, for occupational social services, but their existence depends on the history and traditions of particular cultural and national contexts.

Private sector service provision

Residential and home care are often provided by private agencies, charging fees for their services, although these may be completely or partly financed by government. Some for-profit organisations are small- or medium-size enterprises, and like third sector organisations may be part of local, regional or national coordinating groups or federations. Others may be part of national or international companies. Profits are distributed to the people who financed the setting up of the organisation. In small organisations, this may be the people who provide the services, so the profit in effect pays their wages. In large organisations, some of the profits are distributed to people who invest in private companies to make money.

The arguments for developing for-profit agencies are economic, ideological and structural. Economically, they provide additional capital investment into a sector of the economy which otherwise mainly receives public funding, which at times is in short supply. Ideologically, they provide an alternative management structure outside the public sector, allowing for private sector engagement in what is otherwise a wholly public sector provision. Structurally, they allow a choice of provider both for public agencies that commission and plan services and for service users. This may be particularly where, for example in providing care homes, a large proportion of clients finance their own provision and the provision has similarities to other commercially provided services, such as housing or hotels. Some political views are critical of making profits from helping people in difficulties or in poverty, as many clients of service providers are, but this is not inherently different from providing other kinds of services. Also, profits are part of an economy which provides other benefits. For example, many pensions are financed by profitable investments, and third sector provision is also provided by indirect payments from profits, where companies or rich entrepreneurs make donations. Another concern with for-profit social work is that private sector activity is inherently competitive, and so may make it more difficult for practitioners to develop co-production through collective practice and solidarity with both colleagues and service users. Against this view, self-funding might allow greater control of co-production decision making for clients.

Summary: for and against private sector social work

In summary, for-profit agencies can generate their capital and income free of political pressures and thus be a good base for independent social work and other social care provision. Also, fee-paying may develop co-productive control for clients. But the competitive ethos of the private sector and making profits from people in poverty raises question marks.

Third sector agencies

Third sector structure and advantages

Charitable and voluntary organisations are collectively sometimes called non-profit-making organisations or 'non-profits' and are the 'third sector' of the social services economy. Business (for-profit) enterprises are the first sector, and the state is the second sector, but in history the third sector came first, emerging from community, family and local activism. As with state organisations, third sector agencies may be local, regional or national. If local, they may connect with national or regional federations of local organisations, or be a national organisation with a branch structure. Church and religious organisations are sometimes important providers of social services and considered part of this sector, often by setting up charitable organisations connected to but separate from the church. Third sector agencies are financed by charitable donations by individuals or companies or the income from charitable trusts, or by grant aid from national or local government. Charitable donations are made for the benefit of others, community benefit, but the donors are often people with surplus capital or income. They express their political and social views in how they choose to donate.

Third sector representation

While third sector organisations are free of the potentially oppressive political and tax-funded pressures of public sector agencies, therefore, they present their own decision-making and funding pressures for social work agencies. This is because decisions, funding and management may be influenced more covertly by individual donors and supporters without the requirements of political accountability of state organisations and public transparency of for-profit organisations.

Case example: dealing with the government minister – negotiation or pressure?

I worked with the coordinators of a group of local social services third sector organisations. After a funding dispute, they secured a meeting with a government minister. In a pre-meeting, they resolved to express their experiences and views to him and then walk out of the meeting. Some of the larger and better-funded organisations did not agree with this, because they felt that, to protect their funding, it was better to negotiate about the issues. The coordinating team that organised the meeting felt it appropriate to join the walk-out. After I arrived home, I received phone calls from very influential local donors and members of management boards about walking out rather than negotiating. Later, there were fraught meetings representing the two clashing strategies and pressure on the coordinators to dissociate themselves from the more conflictual strategy. Eventually, the reality was that the negotiations went ahead anyway, and the robustness of the initial response did not seem to disconcert the minister or obstruct the negotiations. As with the earlier case examples on practice with individuals, clashing perspectives on how to achieve social change were raised partly because of donor influence, that is, influence from the economically powerful, who may have political and social power also.

Concern about external pressures also affects international philanthropic or charitable organisations. Often called 'non-governmental organisations' (NGOs), they provide services on an international scale, often in countries that are less developed economically or resource-poor. These are financed by international agencies, for example the United Nations, or by charitable and philanthropic donations from richer countries. Much of this provision is emergency relief or poverty alleviation. Crucially, international NGOs are usually financed from outside the countries where they work, and management and policy-making may also be outside the area or country in which they operate. The policies of third sector organisations about what social work services they should provide and how to do it are influenced by the donors of the finance in ways that may be less transparent than the political decisions made about state social work. On the other hand, social work in third sector organisations may experience less direct political constraint and direction from government.

Summary: for and against third sector social work

In summary, the arguments for providing social work through third sector agencies are that they are independent of political considerations and provide an alternative to state services, which in a local area may be a monopoly provider.

Also, if they emerge from local concerns, they are an important route for people's voices, especially for social groups who are excluded from mainstream and in particular public services. Examples might include serious drug users and gambling addicts, where lifestyle choices may disconnect people from everyday helping provision, but whose children and families may need support and protection. The problem is that funding may reflect inappropriate external pressures, and is less secure than tax-funded public sector or profitable private sector provision.

Social enterprise agencies

What is social enterprise?

Social enterprises are, usually, small private sector companies established and distributing their profits for social purposes and not to the owners of the business. There are two main characteristics. The first is that they aim to be entrepreneurial, that is, energetic in a forward-looking way, using business techniques to promote innovative ways of meeting social objectives. The second is that because they are profit making, if successful, they avoid dependence on government or private sector charitable financing. Social enterprises may therefore be able to set their social objectives separately from political processes, although they also may be subject to economic pressures on businesses.

Social enterprise in resource-poor countries has used a microfinance approach to alleviate poverty. Microfinance provides loans to enable small businesses to take off. Other important areas are healthcare, education and training, particularly to improve the participation of people with intellectual (learning) disabilities and their relatives in society; environmental projects; community and housing regeneration; welfare projects to combat unemployment; alcoholism and drug abuse projects; and advocacy and campaigning, for example through Fairtrade and Traidcraft, which provide a good economic return for businesses in resource-poor countries that export to richer countries (Nicholls, 2006, p 14). Kummitha (2016) describes a variety of social entrepreneurship activity in India, focused on social inclusion, including the participation of people with disabilities, revitalising rural living and rights to appropriate clothing. A UK experiment to set up 'social work practices' like family doctors' general practices to provide elements of local government social care provision, including child safeguarding, involved some successful social entrepreneurship agencies (Le Grand, 2007).

Four arguments for social enterprise social work

There are four reasons for the interest in social enterprise as an organisational form of social work. First, its focus on social responsibility and mutuality potentially connects with social work's objectives for the social, promoting social cohesion and solidarity (Oham & Macdonald, 2016). Second, many social enterprises are small scale and emerge from and remain connected with local roots in contrast to public sector agencies that dominate the local scene in many cases (Frank & Muranda, 2016). Third, their independence from state policy making insulates them from political pressures on social services policy (Ashton, 2010). Fourth, the possibility of financing themselves from commercial activities might relieve funding pressures in the social services sector (Hulgård, 2011). All these factors suggest a more community-near presence and the freedom to act in service users' interests, rather than according to the agency's concerns and interests. Moreover, the variety of possible organisational forms offers flexibility in management and structure (Weerakoon & McMurray, 2021).

The value of social enterprise in social services is, however, challenged. A Scottish study (Henderson, Hall, Mutongi et al, 2019), in the context of the introduction of service users' self-directed care using personal budgets in adult services, found that where social service provision was the main focus of the work, there were tensions with official agencies. Some were supportive, but there were concerns about social enterprises 'creaming off' less complex or less expensive cases. A Bangladesh study (Hackett, 2010) identified a range of issues arising in developing social enterprises, including complex market failures, problems with the boundaries of social enterprise and other sectors and conflicts around contending political objectives and donor and creditor expectations. East Asian studies (Defourny & Kim, 2011) suggest that government, rather than civil society or community endeavour, is often the driving force, and a Chinese study (Wang, 2022) proposes a top-down model in which government decides on objectives and organises the setting up of the enterprise, perhaps the antithesis of the Western conception of social enterprise, but consistent with a political system in which participation in constructing provision locally displaces Western national democratic participation in constructing policy nationally.

Social enterprises are, however, for-profit organisations, and their entrepreneurial style often relies on charismatic, perhaps individualistic, power among the leadership, missionary zeal (Gray, Healy & Crofts, 2003) rather than a participative engagement with service users or other organisations in co-producing services. For example, Kenny, Haugh and Fotaki's (2020) study of 28 UK social enterprises found that participants often believed that they would be pro-social, even pro-social-work, in values and approach. These values, however, were in tension with commercial and economic needs, and difficulties arose when founders departed from the agency or when risks arose to the organisation's survival. Participants sometimes had to abandon pro-social goals as a result.

Summary: for and against social enterprise social work

The precise form and role of social enterprise as part of the whole system of agency social provision is, therefore, unclear, although there have been some successful innovations. Froggett and Chamberlayne's (2004) study of social enterprise and active citizenship models of achieving engagement and leadership in disadvantaged communities found that careful exploration, in their case using biographical narratives, of the intersection of organisational experiences was needed to understand the complex interactions of the organisations involved.

Conclusion

This chapter explored different types of 'organisation agency'. It examined how they emerged from the informal community and family care to form structures within which social work is practised. In the quest to gain 'impact agency' through social work, each structure for organisation provokes complexities in social work practice, which in turn raises issues for managing social work in agencies.

Action on agency contexts
Use understanding of both social and organisational contexts to develop impact agency for economic, political and social policies and structures to implement practice actions and strategies.

The next chapter ...
... explores how the complexities in relationships between agencies and social work practice present issues for the role of the social work profession.

7

Social work, profession and agency

Agency issues for the social work profession

Chapter 6 identified 'impact agency' and 'organisation agency'. A reminder: impact agency refers to having an influence on the world, and organisation agency is the social structure in which social work practice is based. Chapter 6 looked at the pluses and minuses of the range of organisation agency settings where social work is practised. This chapter moves on to explore first, how those agency settings connect with and have their impact on wider society, and second, the impact of social work as a profession on how organisation agencies use it to have impact agency on social issues.

Case example: palliative care services in a hospice

I worked for some years in a large hospice providing palliative care services. Palliative care provides health and social care services for people who are dying and their families and communities. In the UK, hospices provide in-patient care and care in people's homes; in some other countries, the term 'hospice' refers mainly to provision in the community and people's homes.

The hospice movement emerged in the 1960s. Its initial aim was to provide comfort and palliative healthcare where curative healthcare ran out of options. Thus, it extended healthcare services to provide good care to ensure the comfort of people where curative medical treatment was unable to achieve recovery from an illness. It had a strong association with cancer care and pain control; people were fearful of serious discomfort because of physical pain in terminal cancer. Later, palliative care became important during the 1980s when younger people were dying with the newly emerged disease HIV/AIDS. All medical conditions came to be included where younger people died, such as degenerative diseases like motor neurone disease and multiple sclerosis, and the final or 'end' stage of diseases affecting major organs such as the heart and kidneys. Later still, palliative care became an important provision for older people who became frail later in life. This history means that palliative care shifted from giving priority to oncology (cancer care) towards a wider relevance in all kinds of healthcare. It also changed direction from being concerned with deaths in a small population of younger patients with identifiable medical conditions, towards being a service for everyone at the end of life, most of whom were older adults. This meant that it shifted from a connection with the end stage of acute medical care to gain responsibility in matters of ageing, of geriatric medicine and of health and social care for older people.

An important element of palliative care social work is bereavement care; research in this field also emerged during the 1960s. This became a social work responsibility in palliative care because it was concerned with the family and relatives of the focal medical and nursing patient. The fact that this is so implies the other professions' and service managers' attitudes to the main focus of palliative care (that it is medical service to identified patients) and to social work (that is it not central to the main healthcare focus on a particular patient with an identifiable condition and is concerned with 'the social', a set of relationships outside health provision).

The agency was multiprofessional: the biggest staff group was nurses, doctors were influential because of their social status, and there were also priests, various allied health professionals and administrative and care staff. The social work team provided social work both within the hospice, as part of the daycare and ward teams, and outside it, as part of the community teams. Most patients were in the community; only a few were admitted to the hospice wards. Social workers were, therefore, attached to community teams, not ward teams; if patients cared for by their community teams were admitted, like the doctors and other professionals, they joined the ward team caring for their patients. That agency decision reflected the priority given to continuity of care. The social work team organised bereavement care, maintaining continuity with clients of their community teams, but organising groupwork and memorial events separately, and financial and welfare benefits advice, which was treated as specialised and provided by separate staff. The team leader managed safeguarding for the whole hospice, provided training, responded to referrals, and supported other social workers where safeguarding issues arose through the everyday work of the hospice.

This case example shows how the agency's aims changed as different patient groups emerged as the focus of the service. It also shows how the agency's requirements for social work derive from social perceptions about the service's aims, and may be organised in different ways. Those different ways are established through decisions made by the social work team itself and by negotiation with other colleagues in the hospice, which in turn are affected by the social expectations of healthcare and of social work.

To explore how organisation agencies mediate impact agency for economic, political and social policy and thinking, this chapter picks up on the social contexts of provision within which social work and agencies employing social workers have an impact in their areas of responsibility. It covers:

- welfare states as a location for social provision and social work;
- agency power and social work empowerment;
- mixed economies of social service;
- manualisation, proceduralisation and deprofessionalisation;
- managerialism;
- community, generic, holistic and specialised practice.

Welfare states and social work practice

Welfare state regimes

Welfare states are nations that accept broad responsibility for social provision for their populations. Social interventions emerged in Western societies during the nineteenth century and through the first half of the twentieth century developed towards welfare states; social work was part of every stage. Welfare states emerged from the experience of liberal economic policies in the late nineteenth century in a range of European countries, developing strongly after the Second World War ended in 1945 (Corneo, 2012). Initially, there were three main components, reflecting global social protection policy, discussed in Chapter 2:

- Social insurance against the risks of old age, sickness and unemployment.
- Comprehensive and usually state provision of education and healthcare.
- Taxation giving priority to progressive taxation, that is, where richer people paid more tax than poorer people.

Early on, such developments sought to mitigate the risks of structural economic change, but proved insufficient to cope with serious poverty arising from the economic depression of the 1930s. Some developments sought to substitute for the loss of moral and social controls deriving from small communities, family life and religious observance as European countries became increasingly industrialised and urbanised. This included support for social work, making it part of governmentality and surveillance of people in poverty. There were also explicit efforts towards achieving greater social equality through social mobility, economic and social redistribution, and greater dissemination among European nations of the benefits of scientific and technical gains, such as computerisation and more efficient work practices.

There are many shades of 'welfare state regimes', reflecting, according to Esping-Andersen (1990), economic and political choices which seek to balance the pressures of social class with the national economic system. He identified three main models:

- Liberal regimes, typical of countries such as the US and the UK, means-test social assistance, limiting it to low-income, mainly working-class people who become dependent on the state, but with incentives to participate in the market economy.
- Corporatist-statist regimes, like many countries on the European mainland, grant social rights within state support of traditional allegiance to social class and status, preserving family values.
- Social democratic regimes, like Nordic countries, provide universalised social assistance promoting social equality.

During the 1990s, there was some convergence between countries' regimes, because neoliberal ideas and concerns about financing high social costs became prominent and contested regimes that offered broad or universal social rights (Kautto, 2001). Globally, however, various arrangements reflect the interaction of social factors in different countries at various points in history. For example, the social democratic character of Nordic welfare states, particularly Sweden's (Sipilä et al, 1997), initially responded to the separation of church and state in rural economies, which meant acceptance of local government as provider. Reserving family interventions to the church is more typical in Catholic countries. In various historical stages, Sweden needed to provide comprehensive care for older people and daycare for children, allowing women to work and contribute to family budgets and the national economy.

Social work emerged around the beginning of the twentieth century as part of the shift to idealist thinking that social intervention was possible and useful (see Chapter 2). Was developing the welfare state a prerequisite to social work development? Alternatively, would social work have been amplified by growing industrialisation, urbanisation and populations and the powers of nation states anyway? Sipilä's (1997) analysis of Nordic welfare states suggested that women-friendly social care for children and older people was key to its development. But there are alternatives: social work has been strong in some liberal regimes and corporatist-statist regimes. Another point is that Esping-Andersen's (1990) widely quoted analysis focused on the commodification of regimes and the extent to which they incorporate market mechanisms for individual choice rather than developing social interventions through official policy. It is also concerned with social protection, broad policies for income redistribution, employment and social security rather than with social work services. Even though Sipilä's (1997) research saw social care as key to Nordic welfare state development, it focused on daycare for children and residential care for older people rather than the full range of social work. In British terms, this represents a social care, rather than social work, focus. Social work's development may benefit from incorporation in wider social provision, therefore, but like welfare states, it emerges from many different factors.

Origins of the UK's welfare state

The UK was typical of industrialised European states in developing its social provision towards its particular kind of welfare state. Probation regulated provision for offenders outside prisons. Poor Law organisations, relieving poverty, developed from the fifteenth century and strongly in the nineteenth century as industrialisation and urbanisation required organised services for poverty relief. Institutions housed orphaned children and disabled, older and sick people; asylums and colonies for mentally disordered people developed (Parker, 1988). More enlightened provision shifted early in the twentieth century towards less controlling, less punitive provision in smaller institutions. Services concerned with care rather than the governance of working-class people in poverty led to community provision to avoid institutionalisation through foster care and adoption for children and less restrictive provision for adults. Child guidance emerged to improve 'mental hygiene' for children, and services for 'problem families' began to emerge (Timms, 1964a; Starkey, 2000a, 2000b).

After the experience of a serious economic depression in the 1930s, political support grew for more state social work provision. This began to develop in Europe, particularly in the provision for orphaned and neglected children. Salomon (1937) argued, in her international survey of social work education, that some countries had established social work education more strongly than, for example, the UK and US, because of stronger government regulation and control of service provision and training programmes, the beginnings of corporatist-statist welfare state regimes.

US, European and global welfare states

In the US, political thinking called on the individualism of the frontier, popularised as 'rugged individualism' in the 1920s by Republican President Herbert Hoover. This was contrasted with European 'socialism' creating dependence on the state (Bazzi, Fiszbein & Gebresilasse, 2020). Roosevelt's subsequent Democrat administration, alongside financing work programmes for unemployed people, also supported states to provide help to families with children affected by poverty, through the Aid to Families with Dependent Children (AFDC) programme. This became an important basis for social work actions to help families in local government social provision (DuBois & Miley, 1999, pp 39–40). Despite this provision, valuing individualism persisted as a philosophy in the US, for example, in Republican presidential candidate Barry Goldwater's arguments in the 1970s (Hammerback, 1972). In European states, collectivist ideals influenced further development of the helping services that emerged to provide for children, disabled and older people during the world wars when women carers took up the jobs traditionally done by men. Increasingly, in the post-Second World War period, experience of social work during the 1930s depression and the Second World War (for example, in the UK, evacuating children from the cities) led to the increasing incorporation of social work into state services in Europe. Even though social work continued developing in the US and influenced global conceptions of social work, a stronger individualist ideal continued there. As a result, there was less commitment to the idea of a welfare state.

By the 1970s, most Western countries had substantial social work services as part of official provision for child protection, including adoption and foster care, services for adults with long-term disabling conditions (both mental and physical), for older people and those recovering from mental illness. In Europe, during the 1970s there were moves to make these services more comprehensive and integrated. In the UK, for example, local government 'personal social services' and social work (Scotland) were brought together in local government agencies creating an integrated and generalist social work provision.

This was not the picture in less developed or 'Third World' economies in Africa, Asia and Latin and South America, where colonial and post-colonial administrations had rarely concerned themselves with social provision until the 1960s. Nevertheless, it was thought that economic development would lead to similar social progress. Neither was it the picture in the 'Second World' communist countries, where state welfare provision excluded a role for social work as a profession and there was 'a period of silence' (Bagdonas, 2001, p 37) for social work. Social services were provided through other structures such as employing organisations, housing and local community welfare organisations and trades unions.

Looking back at the post-war period, idealist and progressivist assumptions seemed to be borne out in many Western countries: reasonable quality social service provision was diverse and secure in comprehensive state provision. Ideas of service born experimentally from perceived social ills led from piecemeal charitable and voluntary innovation to acceptance and adoption by the state. The role of the remaining charitable provision was to provide for stigmatised groups such as offenders and drug addicts that voters would not finance through the state and to experiment and lobby for adoption for further innovation. But there were also social service systems that did not use social work or did not have the economy or social structures to develop it extensively. The overall assessment must be that, always, it is important to understand the economic and political choices being made or avoided. Since the 1970s, welfare states in many countries have generally become less comprehensive.

Agency power and social work empowerment

Authority and power in social work

Social work experiences a tension between the power expressed by its institutional position as a profession and the political and social power expressed through the agencies that use it. The German sociologist, Weber (Gerth & Mills, 1948) influenced social work thinking on authority, the power that comes from the right to dominate others bestowed by legal or political processes, and by economic resources such as the way agencies are funded (Weber, 1978, pp 941–8). Weber analysed charisma, leadership where personality allows a leader to dominate others, and bureaucratic authority, which distributes power from political sources according to legal rules in an organisation. Where social workers are government employees, political authority is diffused to them as officials in this way. Sometimes, social work uses legal powers to enforce public policy or for the benefit of clients, such as children in care or mentally ill people who could not, at least temporarily, accept intervention for their own benefit. The philosopher Russell (1938) examined power achieved by physical force, through education and establishing routines, by social practices in local government such as social pedagogy and social work, and by economic incentives, such as supporting employment.

During the 1950s, as it became more generally available in many Western societies, social work sought to distance itself from the implications of using power in this way by focusing on authority given by legal and procedural rules, and by developing a professional model of practice whereby social workers sought to ensure that clients had self-determination in deciding the direction and approach of the help they received (Foren & Bailey, 1968; Yelaja, 1971; Biestek & Gehrig, 1978). This avoided the direct and obvious use of compulsion and power by a non-directive approach to practice, pursuing clients' interests through forming interpersonal relationships to influence them by consent (Biestek, 1961). Social workers tried to avoid ritualised, inauthentic relationships, acting humanely in their work. This value system continues in much social work practice, but may nevertheless conceal oppressive actions disguised as beneficent practice.

Broader analyses of power challenged this professionalised position. Lukes (2005) identified three dimensions of power:

- Weber's one-dimensional analysis that power was someone in control imposing their will on a respondent, who in a conflict resisted the use of the resources or violence that enforced the controller's will. This is not typical of social work uses of power.
- A pluralist view that suggests that in decision making, many interests may be represented and what happens depends not only on resources and violence, but on excluding some people from the decision-making process. For social work, this analysis provides for actions such as advocacy on behalf of people who are excluded and participation in decision making.
- A three-dimensional view, which argues that one- and two-dimensional views are too behavioural and rational. That's because they assume that power only operates where those involved are aware of conflicts or differences and can exercise their minds to understand the situation. But power may also involve controlling the agenda or the rituals of the social situation, which participants may not be fully aware of. People may take for granted the privileges of people who are accustomed to having power and influence. These uses of power are frequently experienced by people working with social workers, and social workers may, knowingly or not, be part of such uses of power.

Power is widely distributed among people and organisations. The weight of their influence varies; depending on how they exercise it, they may be powerful in some situations and not in others and may not control everything they are involved in (Dahl, 1968). Power is often exercised through behavioural means, such as agenda setting, influence and persuasion, and therefore is not absolute or everywhere. There may be opportunities for finding other ways to construct relationships and social work actions may enable people to respond to misuses of power by collective engagement with and resistance to it. Habermas (1977) argued that power is necessary for political conflict because it is what politics is about, as the idea of *realpolitik* proposes. This refers to the nineteenth-century political view that a natural aim of relationships between nations and among people is to gain power over other nations and people. Bew (2016) argues that *realpolitik* re-established itself in international, religious and social identity conflicts in the twenty-first century.

Empowerment and social work

Social work practice seeks to be empowering, suggesting that using power in social relations is often inappropriate and ineffective. The potential exists, therefore, for acting to counter inappropriate power relations. Confronting and engaging with difficult issues in social life is usually better than using power for dominance to influence people. In particular, it does not work well for private matters that are emotionally important to people. These views about power in social relations underlie empowerment ideas, which address the use of power in community practice and in individual helping by facilitating people to find and use power that is available to them.

Empowerment became a significant analysis in the 1960s as the civil rights movement brought racial discrimination and oppression to the forefront of social concerns in the US. Arising initially from oppression against Black people in the US (Solomon, 1976), it is applied to wider practice situations in Lee's (2001) analysis of empowerment, which includes domestic violence, women's empowerment and refuges. European countries such as Britain and France similarly grappled with maintaining links and post-colonial influence with countries in former empires and also the immigration of significant minority ethnic groups from those countries.

Social work practice therefore placed significant emphasis on anti-racism (Dominelli, 2017), anti-discrimination (Thompson, 2016) and anti-oppression (Dominelli, 2002). Such approaches start from avoiding racist thinking and actions in practice. They move on to combating them in the organisation and structure of social work agencies. Then, it follows logically to help clients, their families and communities overcome barriers in their lives arising from racism. Anti-discrimination goes beyond racism to deal with a range of discrimination affecting clients, including on grounds of age, disability, gender and sexuality. The analysis is that discrimination on these grounds leads to barriers and disadvantages limiting the life chances and wellbeing of people in social groups affected.

Anti-oppression sees discrimination as part of class and other power relations leading social groups with power to dominate other groups and the individuals within them. The idea of anti-oppression thus proposes that practitioners' increased political and social awareness of how such structural factors create barriers and discrimination enables them to understand and respond to the inequalities in many societies. A practice concerned with violence towards children examines how adults claim inappropriate domination of young people. Violence towards women by men, towards people of diverse sexualities, towards older people and people with disabilities by able and younger people is also generated by structural factors in the way societies are organised to permit the misuse of power. The structural analysis is taken further to consider how privilege for some groups leads to uncomprehending oppression of others (Mullaly & West, 2018; Mullaly & Dupré, 2019)

The main approaches to empowerment are:

- Clarity about how people in oppressed groups are affected by exclusion from opportunities and social structures in society.
- Using the sociological understanding of power to help people identify and understand the mechanisms by which they are oppressed, ways to combat those mechanisms and ways of using alternative sources of power.
- Giving people positive experiences of using their power and resisting oppression.

Empowerment analyses have been criticised because they assume individuals can gain power in an oppressed situation. This puts pressure on already oppressed people to resolve problems created by oppressive structures in society, rather than changing those structures. In family and gendered violence, the least powerful people in a family or relationship may be given responsibility for protecting themselves and blamed for not doing so. This critique led to a stronger emphasis on advocacy alongside or on behalf of oppressed people, and organised community and group support to enable oppressed people to build skills in achieving change for themselves (Dalrymple & Boylan, 2013; Hoefer, 2019).

Mixed economies of social service

Chapter 6 noted that social service organisations interact with each other and in the community and family context. They therefore form a mixed economy of social provision, sometimes called a 'mixed economy of welfare' or 'mixed economy of social service provision'. How services participate in the economy is an important factor in professional and service policy making, and how social work practice develops. For example, although not-for-profit and for-profit organisations can, independently of government policies, set objectives and service provision policies, they must also operate in the context of the political policies of state social provision.

Part of the reason for this is that economies are interacting cycles of exchange. Finance flows to third sector organisations via government grants and finance for service provision, donations from companies' profits and surplus income from people who may work in the private sector. Also, fees for day, home and residential care provision are paid to state, not-for-profit and for-profit providers of services, such as domiciliary or home care and residential care homes. In the cases of Christina's advocacy agency and Mrs Chartin's funding assessment, described in Chapter 6, there was an interaction between the state and a non-state organisation that affected how social work was practised.

The community and family context of the services in most countries is largely a local one; only a few social services, usually specialised ones, are national in scale; even fewer are international. The local community and family contexts also affect the balance of provision between the sectors and the nature of the provision required. For example, in the financial year 2021–22 across England, 34.5 per cent of people in residential care homes paid their own fees, but in the south-east of the country, 44.1 per cent did so, statistically significantly higher than the proportion paying for themselves in the north-east (21.5 per cent) (ONS, 2023). The scope for private sector development, therefore, is stronger in the south-east than the north-east, and the demand for state provision greater in the north-east. The relative wealth of the area affects the mode of service, because self-funding is much less common in more-deprived areas. Care homes with the highest quality ratings had the highest proportion of self-funders, and vice versa. This may suggest that self-funders, or their supporters, were more able to demand higher standards, or that they were able to pay for better or more services than residents funded by the state.

Another example is the way in which the attitudes and opinions of companies and individuals who make donations to third sector organisations affect their choices for what they will support, and therefore potentially influence how independent their decision making may be. This is a continuation of the class and social factors that affected third sector services throughout the history of social work. All providers of social services are also part of a wider economic context, which influences both economic and political policies for agencies, considered in Chapters 9 and 10. This is a 'context of a context': the economic and political context of the community, family and local state context of social work.

Manualisation, proceduralisation and deprofessionalisation

One of the consequences of the power elements of state social service provision is concern about bureaucratic power disrupting practice. Three processes involved are manualisation, proceduralisation and deprofessionalisation.

Manualisation

Manualisation involves establishing processes to be followed, rather than allowing for the discretion and flexibility of professional practice. Both agencies and professional sources have manuals of procedures for practitioners to follow. This suits clients or workers who like to be involved with an ordered, explicit approach to problems that can be clearly explained and justified. While manualisation gives useful guidance and support to less experienced practitioners, universal use of it may become dehumanising and inflexible. Psychological therapies, such as cognitive behaviour therapy (CBT) and motivational interviewing (MI) often use manualisation to guide practitioners in appropriate processes. With effective training, support and experience in CBT, practitioners can use such methods flexibly; however, less experienced practitioners without qualifications and supervision may use manuals in a more limited way, only helping with specific life issues, for example. Research on MI shows that it is most effective when practitioners are guided by a detailed practice manual and closely supervised, thereby ensuring careful application of the model (Miller & Rollnick, 2013, p 381), but this reduces flexibility required by broad-ranging services.

Proceduralisation

Two important areas of practice, child protection or safeguarding and care management in adult services, are examples of proceduralisation of social work practice; the development, by policy makers and managers of social workers, of increasingly detailed procedures for social workers to follow in their practice. It is part of the bureaucratisation and politicisation of social provision and may develop from the increasing distrust of professional discretion (Banks, 2004, pp 149–94). It contests and devalues discretion and professional judgement and, consequently, professionalisation as a way of regulating practice. It is often a product of 'new public management', in its turn an element of neoliberal thinking; see Chapter 9.

Proceduralisation in child protection arose from the shifts in thinking about the care of children. Ferguson's (2004) historical account of responses to child abuse found that during the period 1914 to 1970 child death became an unusual event in people's lives, compared with the nineteenth century when it was commonplace. A focus on child death was, consequently, repressed in professional discourse and thinking, until the resurgence of public concern about child abuse during the last third of the twentieth century. In an analysis of management education, Weick (2007) discussed the process of practitioners in a wide range of professions 'dropping their tools'; he means developing agility in switching focus when traditional methods don't work for new approaches to practice. One example he gives is research in the US on the pioneer medical and paediatric teams developing ideas about child abuse (Westrum, 1993, cited in Weick, 2007, pp 8–10). Doctors found it hard to accept that parents were injuring their children, but part of the problem was that medical practice did not offer the skills to deal with such parents. Social workers introduced to the team were accustomed to child protective work and had the knowledge and skills to separate the interests of parents and children and support the families involved. This made it psychologically easier for doctors to diagnose child abuse.

Parton (2014) puts the subsequent history of public concern and government involvement into the context of political shifts during the late twentieth and early twenty-first centuries, connecting these with professional orientations. Comparative studies of child protection systems (Gilbert, 1997; Gilbert, Parton & Skivenes, 2011) suggest that there were two political and professional orientations to child safeguarding, with a third later emerging:

- Child protection: putting an individualist, moralistic frame of thinking on the issue, intervening initially in a legalistic and investigatory approach, becoming adversarial in the relationship of the state to the parent and eventually using involuntary out-of-home placements to protect children.

- Family service: putting a social and psychological frame of thinking on the issue, starting with a therapeutic and needs assessment, seeing the relationship between the state and parents as a partnership with mandatory reporting of child abuse or neglect signifying trust and making out-of-home placements on a voluntary basis.
- Child-focused: framing the issue as the needs and wishes of the child, with a psychological and social emphasis on their development and wellbeing, avoiding mandatory reporting of incidents of child abuse or neglect, and risk-based actions validating the child's participation and voice.

Hetherington (2006, p 43) suggested that cultural factors were important in deciding which perspective was adopted nationally. Parton (2014, p 8) links this to the form of welfare state regime present in a society, relying on Esping-Andersen's (1990) analysis, discussed earlier in this chapter. Child protection approaches were typical of liberal welfare state regimes, family service approaches of social democratic regimes and child-focused approaches of corporatist regimes. Hearn, Pösö, Smith et al (2004) similarly show how legalistic, child protection with limited child daycare provision in England and preventive family approaches with good daycare in Finland led to different styles of social work practice.

The political changes in UK provision that Parton (2014) identifies include a phase of developing central government guidance following the identification of child abuse as an important concern, with an investigatory and controlling approach. Because of concern about poor outcomes for children who were looked after by local authorities, this was refocused on assessment of risk, rather than the needs of children and parenting. Later, a political shift to the left led to a focus on tackling child poverty as a preventive factor and policies supporting social inclusion. This was driven by a generalised top-down, policy-driven approach.

Subsequently, serious child protection scandals suggested that this broad population approach had not led to improvements in child protection provision, so there was a shift back to emphasising safeguarding processes. Then, a rightward political shift led to criticism from a liberal and neoliberal perspective of centralised management and social breakdown. A greater emphasis on competition, consumer influence and private sector innovation would contribute to opening up public services enabling a more flexible system. Part of this led, through the Munro Review (2010) of child protection, to a policy focus on early intervention, trusting better-developed professional practice, thus allowing greater accountability and transparency.

The later final report (Munro, 2011) proposed a more child-centred system. At much the same time, a more general report on social work proposed a system for all social work that relied on improved qualifying education, and professional development of 'a confident, high-quality adaptable' workforce (Social Work Task Force, 2009, p 6) with better professional leadership nationally and in each local government area. Many of these professional developments occurred, but a review of children's social care more than a decade later (MacAlister, 2022) found that inadequate resources had been applied to provide the necessary services, and there was a 'broken care market' (p 5) and little voice for children themselves.

Proceduralisation in UK adult care services also took place around the turn of the twenty-first century. Whittington (2016a, 2016b) studied government guidance for England on the implementation of the Care Act 2014, claimed by social work professional interests as congruent with social work aims and values. This was argued to be so because of the person-centred, holistic model of practice of the individualistic, problem-solving kind, open to creativity rather than the narrow 'care-management' models of practice previously used. He argues, however, that the economic and political context of austerity and resource constraint threatened this position.

This may be compared with my analysis of government guidance during the previous practice revolution in adult care services (Payne, 1997b). Care management is an adaptation and renaming of US case management (Payne, 1997a, 2000). Through research, political judgements, professional guidance and how it was implemented by agency managers, proceduralisation and managerialisation of practice occurred, leading to the later shift towards person-centred self-direction in the practice approaches that Whittington's work refers to. And yet, the same thing happened with the professional reforms that Whittington discusses.

Why does this process repeat itself? Lymbery and Postle (2015, p 4) argue in a retrospective assessment of both these policy reforms that there were three factors:

- The appeal of the reforms both to ideals of personal responsibility in neoliberal thinking, as well as collectivity in left-leaning ideologies.
- Widespread support for a historic shift towards deinstitutionalisation from long-stay hospitals.
- A period of retrenchment in public expenditure.

First, the development of case management ideas showed the potential for flexibility and responsiveness to clients' needs in the initial research (Davies & Challis, 1986). The aim of this research by social policy scholars, however, was to make professional decision making about priorities for clients' services more rational, not a practice focus. Legislative implementation of the idea focused on the political objective of reducing costs (Lewis & Glennerster, 1996).

Second, the changes achieved a shift of social care from public to private provision accidentally, by responding to escalating social security costs in the previous system. Rising property values made it lucrative for entrepreneurs to invest in large properties to use as care homes. At the same time, the availability on the job market of a cohort of people with nursing experience in long-stay hospitals which were being closed provided a workforce for private operators of care homes.

Political decision making paid little attention to how case management would be implemented. Government guidance issued by professional advisers in the Social Services Inspectorate and research left open many ways of implementing care management, but cost and management imperatives led to a highly proceduralised approach (Payne, 1995b, pp 51–82). As this developed, care managers found that the social work elements of the practice were disappearing in favour of rationing decisions and completing documentation for meetings-based managerial decisions about priorities, rather than offering the creativity and flexibility in working with clients and their families in the community envisaged in the original research and the reform that developed from it (Postle, 2001, 2002; Gorman & Postle, 2003).

Deprofessionalisation

Processes of manualisation and proceduralisation may in this way lead to deprofessionalisation. This arises when social service agencies establish less-skilled social care roles to displace more complex and holistic social work roles. In the 1990s this process, called 'flexibilisation', began to happen in social work, paralleling the changes a century earlier in industry. Twentieth-century Fordism (named after Henry Ford the US motor car manufacturer) led to complex tasks being divided into actions carried out sequentially on a production line. The resulting routine repetitive tasks cut costs and increased the speed of production of complex products like motor cars, by using less-skilled workers rather than traditional craftspeople. Less-skilled workers' tasks can be readily changed to fit the requirements of production. And employees are more easily replaced, so that representatives of workers' interests, such as trade unions, lose influence. Flexibilisation gives employers greater socioeconomic control of labour resources. An industrialised economy results, with low-paid workers having little influence over their work and life opportunities. This is how social workers experienced changes in many welfare states.

In post-Fordist and post-industrial societies, even these workers are displaced by robots, as low-skilled, low-paid industrial work becomes less available, unemployment more commonplace and employment less secure. This leads to 'massification', where individual workers are seen as part of an undifferentiated herd that can be treated as a mass.

During the late twentieth century, flexibilisation began to be applied in service economies as well as industrial settings. Ritzer's (1996) sociological research refers to 'McDonaldisation', proposing that neoliberal economics applies rigid Fordist organisational principles to services to break them up into small elements of unskilled work. Producing a beefburger for the fast food restaurant chain McDonald's becomes not a skilled chef's operation, but a process of assembling standardised elements, with both ingredients and work processes defined and applied internationally. Service costs are reduced, and the organisation's management is simplified. Applied to social services, surveillance of the operations and personnel maintains quality through information technology, target setting, control of production and close supervision of outcomes. As in industry, so in social work; massification led to social workers and other care workers feeling like low-grade operatives rather than independent professionals.

James (2004) argues that McDonaldisation leads to a degeneration of focus on clients' needs and inflexible responses from practitioners. Dustin's (2007) consumer research saw this process occurring in care management in the UK adult social care services, where social workers and other professionals construct 'packages of care' from standardised elements. Services become commodified, that is, made capable of being turned into paid-for commodities, endlessly substitutable by other services. Consequently, in self-directed care, clients either receive elements of service selected mostly from private sector suppliers or receive funding to buy services through 'direct payments' in a cash-for-care system. Although this process may be financially efficient, in social care, as opposed to commercial services, clients dislike the dehumanisation of the processes of assessment and prefer help to use services in a flexible way. McDonaldisation leads to reduced choice and reduced personal help, for example with emotional and psychological difficulties. It may also lead to public agencies withdrawing from responsibility for working towards the overall benefit of the community, avoiding responsibility for failures of coordination and changing needs. This happens because continuing service is replaced by episodic engagement with clients, the contrary process to social work's original conception of 'the case'. In this way, social work is deprofessionalised, devaluing a service committed to human social cohesion and solidarity. Opportunities for clients and their families and communities to benefit from creativity, discretion and flexibility in the construction of services to fit their needs is lost. Dressel (1987) argued that one of the factors in social work deprofessionalisation is the high proportion of women social workers. As the demands of neoliberal policies deprofessionalised the labour process of social work, the subordinated position of women facilitated these moves.

While in North America, professionalisation continued with an increase in counselling-style and psychotherapeutic professional practice, in much of Europe, the position is more ambiguous. In welfare states, the primary roles of social work lie in government provision, and regulation of professional activity also derives from government policies. The professional status of social work is, therefore, affected by global economic trends towards post-industrial deprofessionalisation. In the UK, however, there have been moves to reprofessionalisation in response to criticism of proceduralisation in child safeguarding and the public sector generally. Experiments in social entrepreneurship (Le Grand, 2007) and changing organisational culture to support professionalised practice are examples (Cross, Hubbard & Munro, 2010).

Managerialism

Managerialism is an important factor in thinking about the management of social service agencies. The Scottish study (Asquith, Clark & Waterhouse, 2005) of their underlying philosophies identified four sources:

- The increasing size and generic roles of social service agencies in the late twentieth century. Their consequent political significance meant more interference on economic and political grounds. Also, management became more separated from practice. Previously, in smaller agencies, managers were more concerned about and in touch with daily practice. For example, before the reorganisations of the 1970s, as a basic grade social worker, I saw the director of my agency most days both in meetings and informally; there was only one hierarchical step between him and me. Afterwards, I saw the director no more than once a month, probably less, usually only in meetings and there were four steps in management between him and me.

- Management processes, particularly in the public sector or state agencies, became less concerned with the supervision of professional tasks. Instead, there was more rational and technical measuring of success in defined objectives set in compliance with political policies. This change was part of a shift towards 'new public management' in public sector organisations generally (Clarke & Newman, 1997; Cheung, 2002; Newman, 2002). It may have been one of the reasons why child protection seemed out of control during the 1980s, discussed earlier in this chapter, as professional discretion became displaced by rational technical target setting.
- Claims that, in a 'fiscal crisis of the state' (Pollitt, 1993, 2002; Hildeng, 1995), tax income was insufficient to pay for the extent of public services in the European welfare states. This argument was associated with neoliberal economic and political thinking (see Chapters 9 and 10).
- Since management became increasingly concerned with meeting economic and policy objectives, there was also a move towards generalist management. From a time in the mid-century when service administration was considered part of professional social work and its education (Kidneigh, 1950; Warham, 1975), management thinking meant it became no longer necessary for social services to be managed by social work professionals (Ryan, 1963). In the US, the education and engagement of social workers in the administration and management of services declined (Wuenschel, 2006), and generalist managers without social work connections became acceptable, or even preferred, managers (Perlmutter, 2006). In the UK and other Western countries, managers sought business-oriented management training, rather than public administration or specifically social work management training (Frahm & Martin, 2009). Harris (1998) argues that this was also associated with a rational technical 'scientific management'. Previously, as 'bureau-professionals', they exercised professional discretion and judgement within the powers of a public authority or the policies of private and third sector managements; now they complied with number-crunched rules. Such trends used business terminology rather than professional or public policy language (Harris, 2003a, 2003b), and transferred management ideology that treats social work like a business, using private sector management techniques and performance management by measuring outcomes (Harris & Unwin, 2009; Harris, 2014).

The neoliberal business model of social care management was only part of this direction of travel, however. Lawler & Bilson (2010) argue that social work's complexity requires a reflective and pluralist approach to social work management, building on human relations techniques of management. Such methods aim to challenge and explore what social workers are doing, rather than solely evaluating objectives with outcome measures in a rational technical management style. Both are needed: facilitating a reflective approach to complex social work tasks and the management process, rather than directively requiring compliance with inflexible organisational objectives. This validates the traditional social work supervision approach to management analysed in Pithouse's (2019 [1984]) study of childcare supervision. Supervisors extracted holistic, increasingly complex accounts of interactions with clients from practitioners. Evans's (2011) study of managers and practitioners found that the professional skills and status of social workers allowed them to undertake child protection using flexibility and discretion. Professional actions and judgements were almost invisible from managers. He compares this with Lipsky's (1980) sociological analysis of 'street-level workers'. In that study of bureaucratic decision making in public services, professional actions and judgements were invisible from managers. Interactions with service users were often treated almost as delinquent or deviant because they did not fit with organisational requirements. Kitchener, Kirkpatrick & Whipp (2000) found that, despite pressures for bureaucratic conformity in social work, autonomy and discretion nevertheless existed, unlimited by management control systems, probably because social work cannot be done without it.

Community, generic, holistic and specialised practices

Another longstanding issue for social work of agency organisation is how it responds to social work's holistic philosophy. Should the agency remain generalist, or should social work be organised into specialisms? This issue arose in discussion earlier in the chapter about the development of welfare state regimes and the emergence of managerialism.

Starting in the nineteenth century from the idea of working with the 'case' rather than dealing with separate applications for, or episodes of, service, social work has concerned itself with the whole person, adding connections from within the family and community. This is expressed in concepts in European/ US individualistic psychological practice such as the 'person-in-situation' or 'person-in-environment' (Karls & O'Keefe, 1994), later using systems theory to analyse and express how social work interacts with other agencies and with people in clients' networks (Trevillion, 1999).

Holism as a social work practice ideal is, however, relevant to all the streams of thinking discussed in Chapter 6. In social pedagogy, holism is demonstrated in bringing together hand (action), head (cognition or thinking) and heart (emotion and feeling), in seeing action in the community as the focus of practice and in the objective of aiding the personal development of people as part of their community (Charfe, 2019; Stephens, 2013). Community and social development connect individuals with the environment and social world in which they live and with policy and social change (Patel, 2015). Indigenous practice seeks to connect people with community, cultural and traditional social structures, environment, family and emotional, psychological, social and spiritual issues in the community and in people's lives (Hart, 2019).

Early social workers were employed by agencies for their specific purposes, for example in child guidance, family social work, hospitals, mental health or probation. But much of this was underpinned by working with families in poverty. This focus continued in the US and European countries during the 1930s depression and with European wartime services during the 1940s. As welfare states developed, family social work therefore began to be the most generalised form of practice, relevant with young offenders and in physical and mental healthcare also.

Colonialism transferred the social work of Western cultures to resource-poor countries in Africa and Asia, continuing with this family and individualistic style; however, greater urbanisation meant a need for services for managing adoption, young offenders or street children. US social work education in major urban centres developed master's degree-level education on casework practice in major family charities. Smaller towns and rural areas often centred on more collective and public service approaches to social work, especially in the major economic depression of the 1930s, and in areas with substantial Black populations. In the early 1950s, American social work education coalesced around a generic master's degree-level education (Kendall, 2002, p 81). This became the global gold standard when the US developed international social work to support Western democratising policies during the cold war (Askeland & Payne, 2017, ch 1).

Genericism therefore influenced the perception of social work globally in the 1950s and the subsequent reorganisation of public social services in the UK during the 1970s based on the Seebohm report (1968) to provide a broad official social work service. Generic practice theory emphasised understanding agency objectives, social concepts such as the family or power, and building good interpersonal skills and knowledge of practice theory. The aim was to create a system similar to 'general practice' in primary healthcare. Social workers would assess new clients, provide basic care and services, and refer complex problems or be supported by specialist advisers. Not every generic social worker was well suited to serve all client groups, leading to a loss of confidence by clients, families and professionals in education and healthcare, in social workers' expertise and understanding (Timmins, 1996).

Increasingly, however, a detailed understanding of the issues facing particular client groups came to be more valued. Issues concerned with child protection and assessment for adult care were also policy priorities in agencies. In the period of the Blair and Brown Labour governments of 1997–2010, implementing policy priorities led to an emphasis on specialised jobs being created to meet specific policy objectives, even though their practice largely implemented generic skills (Jordan with Jordan, 2000).

Specialised social work and specialised agencies imply a decision that selects one issue requiring social work as more important than another (Wilson &

Wilson, 1982, pp 72–101). An agency that throws open its doors to anyone who might choose to come to it is allowing the service user to decide how to define the services they want. To say 'we only do this', or 'the policy priority is that' forces people to define their request for service in a particular way. They cannot then present more general issues, such as the consequences of poverty, and those who do, for example, rough sleepers, come to be excluded from services.

The shift to generic practice in UK services during the 1970s led to focusing on closeness to the community in 'community social work' (CSW). A general social work service was located in neighbourhoods within a local government area, including domiciliary social care, newly incorporated into social services provision by the Seebohm reform, and local links to other social care provision. The aim was for social workers to develop fuller involvement in and understanding of the class interests, culture and interests of local communities. Social workers also built networks among local organisations that could provide information about individuals and resources in the community that could support social care and social work provision. Reports began to emerge of different modes of practice and structures (Hadley & McGrath, 1980). Evaluation research (Hadley & McGrath, 1984) demonstrated its effectiveness in keeping the social work community-near (Bayley, Parker, Seyd et al, 1987). The main focus was to develop social work practice at a neighbourhood level, which would encourage reductions in state bureaucracy and improving local responsiveness in service provision (Hadley & Hatch, 1981).

A government committee of inquiry into the roles and tasks of social workers (Barclay Report, 1982) recommended adopting CSW; however, a dissenting view in a minority report (Pinker, 1982) saw it as a distraction from the main care responsibilities of social work. Some agencies adopted CSW as the main mode of organising their area teams, with some positive outcomes (Hadley & Young, 1990). An independent consumer-oriented study, however, found that CSW did not engage with service users effectively (Beresford & Croft, 1986). The model died out as social services departments were reorganised in the 1990s according to client-group specialisations.

Conclusion

In concluding this chapter, I want to reflect on the issues raised for social work by its practice being placed within social service agencies. Its agencies bring social work into relationship with the power structures and cultural and social changes affecting the society in which it operates. Because, as in the case example in Chapter 6 about the government minister, social work sometimes helps people at odds with those structures, it cannot sit outside the power structures, because their agency is within them. This produces tensions in practice, and it also brings social tensions that have to be faced in practice. These may be tensions in societies like the UK where I was practising in the case example, in which although there was conflict, this was accepted as a natural part of the democratic power structures, and the minister accepted a robust conflict approach.

But in societies where economic, political or religious power does not permit transgression, social work may face more restrictive consequences for or limitations on their practice or leave practitioners only with influence where there is space for practice development in planning and managing services rather than in changing policy or political directions. For example, in some countries, political and religious movements challenge abortion and social workers may face difficulties in responding to some needs that women want their help with. More politically, social workers in Russia during the present war with Ukraine may be involved in the 're-education' of children transferred from Ukraine and placing them for adoption with Russian families (Khoshnood, Raymond & Howarth, 2023), which is raising human rights concerns at the time of writing; they would not necessarily be informed enough to refuse, neither would it be possible for them to do so. In such societies, forming social policies for political reasons runs alongside and is integral to implementing those policies. Thus, in China, agenda setting, decision making, the diffusion of policy ideas, experimentation around new initiatives and policy implementation may develop in different locations locally, regionally and nationally and lead to interacting mutual influence, rather than separate processes of policy development, legislating and policy implementation dominated by a national political process (Yang & Yi, 2023). Elsewhere, similar interactions may easily involve activists, interested professionals and service users in policy making and implementation processes.

Social work internationally needs to think, therefore, about how to respond to the requirements of its professionals in authoritarian regimes, and not assume that policy advocacy and resistance is the most practicable strategy. In countries where social work practice is part of policy formation, social work practice, thinking and tactics must be part of social reactions to issues at the policy and practice level simultaneously, but this cannot always be so.

Citizenship and its legal, political and social rights, even in democratic welfare states, may sometimes facilitate or hinder, through agency pressures, the range that social work can offer and the possibilities for action. The same is true of the economic and political power represented in the aims and organisation of agencies. Social work struggles with clashing interests and objectives in their work, with using authority and power engaged by their responsibilities that may be oppressive. This has stimulated the development of an empowerment practice as part of social work, but it has also demonstrated how difficult it is to use social work methods to overcome the barriers in people's lives.

The structures of economic and political power over working-class people in poverty are expressed in the economies and social policies of social service agencies, and systems of compliance that tend to deprofessionalise social work practice, to limit its discretion and flexibility and to seek governance and surveillance over working-class people through managerialism in agencies. Similarly, social work has struggled with the demands for a specialised practice focused on political and social priorities against a community-near generic practice responsive to the range of issues that are highlighted by service users' needs.

There are signs of opportunities in the struggles between agency and social work explored in the section. First, although there are barriers and ideologies hostile to social provision and social work, a range of factors have influenced the creation of a wide variety of regimes in welfare states, and generally there has been movement towards more widely spread social work expressed in service and policy initiatives globally. Second, although social work sometimes struggles with policy, political and other limitations, policy trends are to pick up and use social work. There have been periods of both community-near practice and specialist practice, worldwide typically social care services and social work are provided and variety of political and welfare regimes are taking them up.

Taking action on professional and agency interactions

Watch for developing trends in agency organisation and their impact on how professionals can practise, and create space within the political and economic structures for influence in the interests of social work and the people it works with.

In the next chapter ...

... the twenty-first-century development of co-production is explored as a practice strategy. It is relevant to all streams of thinking and practice actions, and addresses the interaction of agency and professional interests in the economic and political context discussed in Chapters 9 and 10.

8

Social work and co-production

Co-production: a partnership model

This chapter argues for co-production as a helpful model of partnership among people who use care and social work services, practitioners in care agencies, social workers and other professions. Examining agency and professional contexts for social work in Chapters 6 and 7 made clear that such a cooperation model is required. The social nature of human flourishing requires that the human and the social together, in all their complexity, are the focus of social work practice actions and strategies. The complexity, the human and the social must therefore be part of agency and professional models of cooperating and co-production is currently seen as a good way to do it. This is because it enhances cooperation, mutuality, partnership and solidarity in carrying out its actions across organisational and professional boundaries.

But doing this raises difficulties for agencies, other professionals and practitioners that sometimes challenge the position and status of social work, reflected in the following case example.

Case example: the status of social work

In 2021, a social worker from a European country wrote to me, expressing her worries about the future of social work in her country. This is an anonymised and edited version (that she has approved) of what she said:

I am a social worker who has been working in mental health for many years. I am currently very concerned about the social work profession. The supply of social workers graduating from university is nowhere near the demand. Compensating for this, the main social work agency is employing recruits as social welfare workers who are not qualified in social work. They are often doing the same work as social workers.

In mental health, nurses are taking over our profession, with us supervising and guiding them in how to do social work. The numbers of doctors, paid at three times the social work salary, are increasing, but their workload is decreasing, and they are progressively relying on social work reports and interventions to do their work. It boils down to government policies and direction and investment in the profession. Everyone knows how important we are to the organisation, but no one is ready to invest in social work.

These concerns arise in many countries. The email introduces two separate issues: social work's standing in relation to other professions and to care workers. To respond to these issues, this chapter considers:

- The role of social care services and social work in relation to other professions.
- The perception that social work is not more than 'basic psychosocial skills'.
- The history of service partnership structures.
- Co-production as a partnership structure.

Social care, social work and other social provision

All professions are part of an organisational and social territory which other professions also inhabit, each with different roles and contributions. This territory is the sphere of biopsychosocial spiritual practice (Payne, 2006, pp 153–9), drawing on biological, psychological, social, legal and theological knowledges. Most social workers in the territory find themselves working with the following fields of practice and occupational groups:

- Education, in particular with psychologists and teachers; using social science pedagogical and psychological knowledge, particularly of children.
- Employment and unemployment, in particular with administrators, civil servants and employment advisers; using social science administration and management knowledge.
- Physical and mental health, in particular with doctors, nurses and other health professionals; using biological and healthcare knowledge.
- Income transfers, social security and poverty, in particular with administrators, civil servants and financial advisers; social science administration and management knowledge.
- Housing and homelessness, in particular with housing managers and housing welfare workers; using social science administration and management knowledge.
- Justice, civil and criminal, in particular with lawyers, legal paraprofessionals, police and security workers, using legal knowledge.
- Spiritual care, with chaplains, ministers of religion of various denominations and faiths; using theological and pastoral care knowledge.

Knowledge territories in each area overlap; each service and occupational group knows something of and often uses knowledge and skills from other groups. Roles and identities between professions are continually renegotiated (see Chapter 2). More numerous occupational groups and professions are often more familiar to and better understood than social work by the public; examples are nurses and teachers. Their professional needs and views have the power of numbers to influence the organisations they are involved with. Other occupations and professions that social workers work with have 'manifest disaster criteria' (Nokes, 2013 [1976]). Prison officers prevent escapes and riots; doctors prevent death and suffering, both potential disasters easier to understand than what might go wrong in social work practice. In some countries, such as Asian countries in the former Soviet bloc, or Eastern Europe 'transitional economies' shifting from a Soviet regime to connect more with Western European nations, social work had a period of being 'new' or being renewed and needed time to establish a position in cultural understanding. But positions in cultural understanding change all the time everywhere, so this process is universal. Chapter 1 outlined an ideological and political position taking up social Darwinism that de-emphasises social issues and solidarity and emphasises competitive, individualistic relations, devaluing social intervention and professions engaged in it; see Chapters 9 and 10 for further discussion about economic and political ideologies affecting social work.

Because of these factors, I have argued in earlier chapters that it is important to think through how to explain and express what social work is and what it does. There is also evidence, see Chapter 11, that other professions and the public are not as negative as social workers sometimes think. Demonstrating social work contributions and skills needs to go alongside reinforcing positive perceptions and combating negative ones; see the Mooney family case example in Chapter 3. The important issue in all these situations is to establish a position in cross-boundary engagement.

Social work and 'basic psychosocial skills'

Another issue for social workers, raised in this case example, is the issue of what the World Health Organization (2022) describes as 'basic psychosocial skills', developed for use by people dealing with emergencies and in particular during the COVID-19 pandemic of 2020–22. This identifies the following skills required by many different occupational groups dealing with difficult or emergency situations:

- taking care of and maintaining one's health and wellbeing;
- supportive communication in everyday interactions;
- helping people to help themselves regain control of the situation, access practical support and manage their problems better;
- supporting people who are experiencing stress to identify when to call specialised service providers;
- helping in specific situations such as working in care homes, law enforcement and displacement or refugee situations;
- supporting those who are grieving.

These would be relevant for people in many different occupational groups working in the biopsychosocial spiritual territory. They are closely related to social work skills and responsibilities, and, as in the case example, social workers may be using their skills to supervise and support other workers, both paid and voluntary, to use such skills well. The human element of social work's unique contribution is here being used to improve the human quality of the more practical elements of the agency's provision using other less skilled staff.

Research in social work settings during the 1960s tackled this issue through the functional analysis of social work roles or tasks (see Chapter 3) that influenced conceptions of social work specialisation (Briggs, 1973). Getting lower-qualified, and cheaper, employees to do social work tasks has been an ambition across the years in many countries. It connects with a perception that many care tasks are not particularly skilled, like making a meal for a child, or bathing an older person, but require the 'basic psychosocial skills' to do them well in many social situations. Doing the job of making a child's lunch well, for example, involves helping the child make choices, involving the child in some of the preparation and chatting about life and their preoccupations.

Case example: making a child's meal

I made Ezra's breakfast last week. We discussed which of the various options he knew were available that he wanted that day. He supervised the toaster (he likes his toast only lightly brown) and he checked that I was frying the other elements the way he likes them. We have a world map on the wall; we discussed the Roman empire and the Punic wars and he pointed out on the map where the historic state Carthage was in relation to the city of Rome. This came about because I was acting in a Christian play, and he was studying these wars at school at the time. We connected how territorial security was important to nation states, using the examples of the wars and the persecution of dissidents by the Roman empire. Making this child's meal was not just the task as it might appear in a list of tasks to be done by a care worker or cook, but involved him in the process, used the resources in the room to broaden out some of his education, and also led to some relationship-building between us.

Agency organisation and political policy often tries to separate the human element of such contributions organisationally, to be able to employ cheaper and differently qualified staff. Being connected to the cultural traditions in the local community may often be more important than professional qualifications in some kinds of care work. But, a good care worker making Ezra's breakfast would do more than cooking. And, as in the case example about Leilani's human rights work and peer support for a mentally ill man in Chapter 3, the human element of social work includes supervising practice to support effective practical actions by social care practitioners. Doing this helps to link social work-qualified and social care-qualified people, when agency and political boundaries want unwisely to separate more available, more community-near and cheaper staff groups from social work.

Discussing genericism, Chapter 7 explored how the early-1950s US standard for social work qualification gained global influence (Kendall, 2002, p 81). While this enhanced the professional recognition of social work, it shifted social work's focus away from service delivery in rural and urban areas with substantial minority ethnic group populations. By the 1960s and 1970s, services needed to expand to deal with an urban mental health crisis in areas experiencing great poverty and disturbances concerned with civil rights, particularly of minority ethnic groups, but social work education was not producing enough qualified social workers. This was a similar situation to the case example's 2021 European country; new thinking about social work roles and tasks developed as a result.

Another similar situation arose in the UK in the 1960s at much the same time as the American developments. The Younghusband Report (1959) led to new courses to provide a qualified workforce for expanding welfare departments delivering adult services. The graduates were considered less skilled than the medical and psychiatric social workers, many qualified on post-graduate courses, employed mainly in hospitals (Timms, 1964a). All these courses became equal social work qualifications with the reform of social work education in the 1970s (Payne, 2005, pp 236–7). Generic agencies established then employed an increasing number of non-qualified 'social work assistants' and other care staff needing 'basic psychosocial skills'. This led to the development of a certificate in social service qualification, involving agencies and further education colleges, rather than universities. With a reorganisation of social work in the 1990s, this was again treated as equivalent to the social work education of the time (Payne, 1995a).

These continual attempts to distinguish 'basic psychosocial skills' from social work suggests the difficulty of distinguishing social work from these skills. Just as UK social work responded to agency expansion to provide more comprehensive general social services, US social services expansion also needed to provide broader services for a larger troubled urban population. But limited numbers of master's degree-level social workers mainly doing interpersonal social work needed supplementing with people from minority ethnic communities and other local people (Barker & Briggs, 1968, pp 23–31). Widely cited US studies (Barker & Briggs, 1968; Teare & McPheeters, 1970) analysed social work roles or tasks in 'intra-professional' teams in social work services that could be undertaken by non- or para-professionals, what would now be called 'social care workers' in the UK. Teams, including qualified social workers and paraprofessionals, were allocated tasks according to how complex they were and the kinds of tasks to be undertaken (Barker & Briggs, 1969; Brieland, Briggs & Leuenberger, 1973). The analysis identified three aspects of social work tasks:

- Domains of living (like the contemporary concept of 'activities of daily living'), where clients experienced difficulties.
- Status of clients' functioning (assessing the seriousness of their difficulties, from wellbeing, through stress, problems, crisis to disability).
- Obstacles to clients' functioning (personal or environmental deficiencies, rigid law or regulation, disasters).

Lists of roles and tasks were produced by different studies, both in the US and the UK (Baker, 1976; Jeans, 1978) and the British Association of Social Workers (1977, pp 38–41) picked up this work to differentiate what it considered professional social work tasks. These included assessment and diagnosis, attitude and behaviour change, consultancy, counselling, directing social work service provision and planning care. In this analysis, such skills distinguished the professional task from 'basic psychosocial skills'.

Social work and service partnership structures

Social work and agency priorities

Social work coordinates, cooperates and interacts with a variety of agencies and professional practices in doing so, building on practice actions and strategies discussed in Chapter 3. Its approach in doing so, however, is often at odds with how organisation agencies deal with this issue. What makes the difference is that social work, with its professional commitment to participation and solidarity, seeks to incorporate links with carers, the community, families and other social services within its agency services.

Agencies, on the other hand, develop cooperative and partnership structures to take forward services, pursuing their objectives and policies. This is a primarily managerial approach deriving from policy and political concerns that distinct agencies should operate together effectively, avoiding 'silos'. Management thinking takes the analogy of silos, grain stores containing different cereals, to describe organisations that separate activities into service divisions.

I illustrate this in Figure 8.1. All services, social services as well, start from a concern to respond to the needs of their consumers in the context of service priorities identified by their management and policy making. Education, healthcare, social housing, social security and social service agencies all pursue links with other service providers in their sector. Social work services, for example, do so with care homes, domiciliary care services and between public, private and voluntary sector social work organisations. But social work has different priorities: to link across boundaries and to make links with community, family and other services. Social work partnership, using co-production, needs to balance these priorities with the organisation's approach to partnership.

Among the organisational strategies are the co-location of practitioners from different professions and the coterminosity of geographical areas covered. In the UK, for example, the National Health Service [NHS] Act 1973 required health and local authorities to set up joint consultative committees, and joint care

Figure 8.1: Social work and organisation service provider partnership approaches

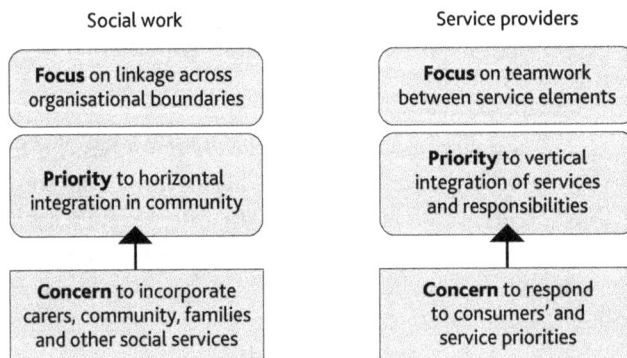

Source: Adapted from Payne (2017, p 64)

planning encouraged cooperation on health, housing, transport and education, mainly using joint finance to transfer funds from healthcare to social service agencies. In 1973, an integrated structure of health and social services boards in Northern Ireland was established, similar to the system in the Republic of Ireland. The NHS and Community Care Act 1990 introduced a marketised system for both health and social care to set up a commissioning process for health and social care services in all sectors of the economy.

Social workers have always been important players in making links between agencies, for example in healthcare (Browne, 2019). Skills in cooperation and coordination include:

- Liaison, making and sustaining contacts with other agencies, both in general and around particular service users.
- Coordination, ensuring through liaison that organisations work together when required.
- Representation, acting on behalf of your agency or service user to influence another agency or person; this includes advocacy.
- Presentation, promoting and demonstrating the value of the role of your agency, practice and service users' needs. (Payne, 1993)

Partnership working

Partnership working developed in the early twenty-first century. To continue the UK example, the New Labour government elected in 1997 introduced the concept of 'partnership', to refer to coordination that combined organisational and professional actions (DH, 1998), and provided for formal involvement in strategic planning, service commissioning and service provision. The follow-up Health Act 1999 permitted health trusts and local government social services to delegate functions to each other and pool funds. This sought to deal with the funding and structural issues. Similar arrangements under the Children Act 2004 mostly did not come to fruition. Consumer research suggested that service users could identify improvements arising from health and social care partnership development, including continuity of staff, sufficient staff and a range of resources, including the availability of long-term and preventive services (Petch, Cook & Miller, 2013). Research concentrated, however, mainly on management processes rather than service user outcomes (Dowling, Powell & Glendinning, 2004).

Professionalisation and division

It is often argued that professionalisation leads to divided functions in organisations because professionals are educated and practise in different academic and intellectual traditions, and Chapter 2, examining the development of professional identity, referred to the process of socialisation into a profession, building on choices arising from life experience. Professionalised services such as education and healthcare, with high levels of education and specialised training, often devised structures that respected the separate professional skills of different staff groups. Examples include doctors concerned with diagnosis, medication and other treatment regimes, which were implemented by nurses undertaking physical care and physiotherapists concerned with physical rehabilitation. Loxley's (1997) analysis of the reasons for these professional divisions included power relations by different professions to maintain control of expertise and knowledge and control of their work, the role of the state in challenging claimed professional autonomy, the development of occupational cultures, increasing differentiation of specialisation and division of labour among different groups of staff and organisational and policy failures in bridging divides.

Interprofessional/multiprofessional practice

Extensive commentary, particularly in healthcare-related activities, develops interprofessional or multiprofessional practice as a practice strategy, particularly seeking connections between interagency, interpersonal and interprofessional practice (Hornby & Atkins, 2000). Similar commentary and development activities arise in connections between education, youthwork careers guidance and work with young offenders. The problem with the education or healthcare focus is that, although social workers are sometimes included, the emphasis is on teams of education or healthcare professionals and their interests. The British literature often follows the government policy of referring to 'children's services' or 'health and social care', although often without substantial inclusion of social work issues. An example is Day's (2013) text, which includes Nursing and Midwifery Council materials and does not index social care or social work despite its title, which refers to 'health and social care'. Consistent with the research, interprofessional practice developments focus on developing shared values, clarifying different professional roles and improving communication in interprofessional settings, especially in regular meetings such as ward rounds or patient reviews. Another focus is encouraging the development of group relationships among people who regularly work together, for example the team around a particular service user or in a community team covering a specific area, a day or residential care home or ward (Slusser, Garcia, Reed et al, 2019).

A weakness of the focus on interprofessional practice is that such practice needs to be within service structures that resolve finance and management discontinuities that often make joined-up professional practice more difficult (Glasby & Dickinson, 2014).

Approaches to developing interprofessional work included interprofessional training either at the initial qualifying pre-registration stages or in agencies (Freeth, Hammick, Reeves et al, 2005). Carpenter and Dickinson (2016) summarise research showing that pre-qualification interprofessional education may be less effective than post-qualification work. Also, work settings may benefit from a chain of responses in which encouraging collaboration improves cooperation and support and reduces demands on any one profession, thus reducing stress. Service user participation in interprofessional education has also been shown to strengthen its impact.

Social work in multiprofessional healthcare

Within healthcare, social workers claim specialised understanding of emotional and psychological reactions to disability and illness and supportive family and social links that facilitate more effective management of illness in community settings. Early examples were Cockerill's (1953) paper arguing for social workers to develop skills in promoting interdependence with other healthcare professionals, and Kane's (1975) work in interprofessional practice in several US healthcare settings.

Social work in mental health

Community healthcare settings in primary care and mental health services are important locations for shared practice. See Collins (1965), Corney (1982, 1993) and Corney & Clare (1983) for studies of social work in primary healthcare in the UK; for projects on the work of support teams for people with intellectual disabilities (a condition once referred to as 'mental handicap'), see Webb, Vincent, Wistow et al (1991) (Nottingham), Grant, Humphreys & McGrath (1986) and Humphreys, McGrath & Grant (1986) (Wales). These generally found that local cooperation among teams working with particular patients or groups of patients worked well but financing and organisational boundaries got in the way. Recent systematic reviews of social work in primary healthcare (Fraser, Lombardi, Wu et al, 2018; McGregor, Mercer & Harris, 2018; Zuchowski & McLennan, 2023) found that there were positive outcomes for patients when social workers were included in primary healthcare medical teams. Among the advantages were improved patient care, good value for money and good interdisciplinary practice. But as with the earlier research, funding constraints, organisational barriers and poor understanding of the potential social work role obstructed progress. Fraser et al's (2018) study identified three main roles undertaken by social workers in interprofessional community healthcare teams: providing behavioural treatment, managing care and engaging community services.

There is evidence that social workers are important players in professional services in mental illness. A recent example (WHO, 2018, p 47) identified the main types of government social support available to people with mental disorders as follows, all of which connect with social work roles:

- social care support: 67 per cent
- income support: 59 per cent
- family support: 46 per cent
- other support: 46 per cent
- education support: 35 per cent

- housing support: 34 per cent
- legal support: 33 per cent
- employment support: 32 per cent

High-income countries, particularly in Europe, generally have markedly larger mental health workforces than low- and middle-income countries. In most countries, social workers (qualified personnel) were part of the workforce, globally about 0.3 per 100,000 of the population, as compared with psychologists (0.9), nurses (3.5) and psychiatrists (1.3). They were a more significant part of the mental health workforce in Eastern Mediterranean (0.3 compared with 0.7 psychologists) and Southeast Asian regions (0.2 compared with 0.1 psychologists, 0.4 psychiatrists and 0.8 nurses) but there were more of them in the Americas (0.6) (WHO, 2018, pp 31–3). In the US, clinical social workers are the 'most abundant' type of mental health professional. Reasons for this include their salaries often being lower than those of equivalent nurses and psychologists, and the requirements for licensure are generally less demanding than those for psychologists and doctors (Heisler, 2018).

Co-production

This brief historical account shows that there have been attempts in different countries to overcome the disadvantages of service divisions in organisational territory that social work is part of. Co-production is the current iteration of this. An important element of practice in this territory is emphasis on professional assessment of clients, patients and service users as the basis for service provision. In turn, this means that professional collaborations and perceptions dominate the context for social work practice, despite the historical emphasis on self-determination in social work thinking and self-direction in current policy management thinking.

Including clients and service users in social service management emerged from mental health and disabled service users' movements (Bartnik & Chalmers, 2007; Beresford, Branfield, Maslen et al, 2007; Norton, 2023) and from the attempts to make social work education more practically relevant at the turn of the twenty-first century. One strategy included agency management and service user representation in qualifying and post-qualification courses (DH, 2002). It is not clear, however, whether there is substantial change as a result in outcomes for students (Robinson & Webber, 2013). Recent international studies suggest that joint participation by educators and students and in social action projects in the community may be an effective approach (Ramon, Moshe Grodofsky, Allegri et al, 2019) but requires preparation, including appropriate resourcing, training and facilitative skills (Driessens, McLaughlin & van Doorn, 2016; Tanner, Littlechild, Duffy et al, 2017).

Co-production has diverse meanings in different settings. An important source in social development practice described it as '… a process through which inputs from individuals who are not "in" the same organisation are transformed into goods and services' (Ostrom, 1996, p 1073). This draws attention to the fact that it involves:

- people ...
- ... working in different organisations or social systems ...
- ... a process of transformation from a previous state to a new form ...
- ... of production ...
- ... of goods and services.

Ostrom emphasises that the systems are polycentric, that is, they involve two or more centres of influence on the process; while one person from one organisation might take a lead, others also have an impact on the process and the outcome. Both process and outcome are important. Hunter & Ritchie (2007) exemplify four main strategies for changing the orientation of service philosophies: re-engineering how services are delivered, a standard-setting and monitoring approach, diversity and equality strategies for representing excluded communities and individuals and consumer empowerment. Realpe & Wallace (2010), in a healthcare context, suggest it might include co-governance and co-management as well as co-production.

In a more recent review of the concept, Filipe, Renedo & Marston (2017) suggest that it involves the creation of new knowledge, values and social relations between different groups of people. It does not, therefore, privilege one sort of knowledge (for example as evidence-based practice privileges particular measurements of success or methods of investigation), set of values (for example, behavioural expectations) or relationships (for example, between professionals rather than community activists, family members, students, non-professional workers, volunteers). Clark (2015), with a mental health service perspective, emphasises seeing the people involved as bringing personal assets and skills to the process and building reciprocity and social capital, the range of social networks that people have links with. Because it requires transformation, it requires social change to occur, rather than being concerned with managing decline or maintaining rather than improving services. Also, it moves on from consultation or participation, seeing carers, clients, family members, non-professionals and service users as experts by experience. The Social Care Institute for Excellence (2022) emphasises both the engagement of service users as a necessity, and cultural and organisational change, requiring collective examination of culture, structure, practice and review through monitoring processes and outcome evaluation.

This is another reason why problem-based analysis of social issues is often unsatisfactory as a basis for service design. If policy making just looks at a 'problem' and organises to deliver undifferentiated services, it undermines the service by not providing for the social complexity that leads to the issue being problematic to those involved. Social service agencies and legislation for social provision do not provide adequately for more complex issues that professions such as social work deal with holistically; they are not services to be 'delivered'. The human and social quality of Ezra's breakfast preparation is not catered for by the 'delivery' of breakfast, and this can only be understood through qualitative judgements.

Policy-based political and social analysis of issues leading to legislation and service provision, together with economic issues in providing financing, often fail to identify more complex needs that social work must meet. Critique of social work practice by its clients makes this clear. Hallett's (2016) qualitative study of young people's experiences of interventions in child sexual exploitation, for example, shows that services saw only a surface 'problem' of exploitation but failed to respond to the reasons why young people were vulnerable to exploitation in the first place: the instabilities in care and support in their lives and living arrangements. Removing perpetrators from contact did not deal with those issues in their lives that might lead them to return to being exploited. In a completely different field, Stajduhar, Giesbrecht, Mollison et al (2020) found that 'structural vulnerabilities' meant that the capacity of people to help family members in dealing with end-of-life care was variable and required flexible actions to deal with three major vulnerabilities: poverty and substance abuse, housing instability and challenging relationships. A service designed merely to deliver supportive services failed because it did not tackle how these vulnerabilities got in the way.

Thinking carefully about what participants want to achieve is important. For example, Jaspers and Steen's (2019) Belgian case study identified tensions about pursuing efficiency and effectiveness, facilitating individual freedom of co-producers, reciprocity and inclusion in their project.

Conclusion

Co-production is more than using basic psychosocial skills to deliver services. As a community-near solidarity practice, it engages holistically with those being served, their surrounding social connections, and other agencies and professions. Unlike self-determination and direct payments of cash for care, it takes up the basic social work requirement to act with others in doing something purposeful and strategic in people's lives. Co-production does not just accept management and policy aims but articulates them in worthwhile shared actions to enhance human flourishing and social capital.

Action on agency and professional contexts
Value the opportunities that your agency and professional contexts offer for worthwhile co-productive practice with people who need social work, demanding that the contexts adapt to enable the human and practical contributions of social work.

The next chapters ...
... take a step away from the direct context of social work practice and look at the 'context of the context'; first the political (Chapter 9) and then (Chapter 10) the economic contexts of social service agencies and social work practice, and some of their implications.

PART III

Social work under pressure

This part of the book starts by exploring the influences on social work, both external (policy and politics, and economics) and internal (clients' and service users' views). Finally, I look at trends for the next quarter century. Care, and social work within it, are going to be more important, but economic, human, political and social resources to provide it will be increasingly difficult to find.

9

Social work, policy and politics

Social work and politics

Social work is affected by social policies that are created through politics. Policy and politics are but one of the contexts of the contexts: they influence the agency and professional contexts considered in Chapters 6–8.

Policy is a consistent course of action carried out by a decision maker. It may arise pragmatically, by a decision maker following a consistent pattern of behaviour. Alternatively, policy may come from debated and planned programmes and strategies determined by decision-making structures. Most people think of policy as coming from political authorities, governments or parliaments, and the management boards of private or third sector organisations.

But thinking more broadly, all activities have a politics. This is because in human society any important activity develops a social life, in which different groups of people with varying views about the activity interact to decide among or combine some of these views about how they will act. Political ideas, political philosophy or political thought, often connected with social and spiritual beliefs, influence the political process. Political economy includes economic power in the power dynamics that politics engages in; political debate often calls on economic assumptions to support political influence.

Politics operates at every level in society. There is a broad political system in which all social groups participate, and this engages in national and international relations, but there are also political relations among social groups at local and regional levels and between social structures in informal relationships. Each level and each social structure influences the others. For example, international agreements such as treaties or declarations by bodies such as the United Nations of the European Union may direct, encourage or inspire national political ideas and actions, which in turn might influence regional, local or personal actions.

The main issues considered in this chapter are:

- Debate about whether and how social work is a political activity and what this means for practice and the profession.
- Influential political philosophies and their implications for social work practice and the profession.
- How social work's practice in state organisations engages with political ideas.

Because all activities have a politics, therefore, social work does too. Since social work is part of the agency and professional structures discussed in Chapters 6–8, it is also clearly part of a politics in how it relates to government structures and with other professions in its interagency and interprofessional practice. Decisions are made within these structures which lead to policies, consistent courses of action. Both the decisions and the policies may be written down and published, or they may simply be reflected in consistent courses of action that social workers take or that are reflected in agencies' decisions. You can sometimes see policies and political views expressed in what groups or individuals do, even if they are not talked about.

Is social work a political activity?

The reasons for the sometimes hidden influence of political tensions are that in bureau-professional roles (see Chapter 6 on managerialism) professional discretion is constrained by bureaucratic authority often used to implement political policies. Social workers carry out their work roles within a system of what Garrett (2018a, pp 79–81) describes as 'embedded liberalism'. The bureau-professional in social service organisations is part of a social system where ideas are in tension. Social democratic ideas supporting empowerment in social work through broad social provision in a welfare state come up against underlying liberal capitalist structures. These give priority to economic growth and epitomise attitudes of social Darwinism. Important ideas in politics therefore run contrary to social work values, rather than humanistic concerns which are integral to social work.

Case example: Carrie's local authority job interview

A social worker, Carrie, who had been active in a well-known third-sector organisation went for a job interview for a promoted post in a local authority. One of the questions was: 'Do you think that your membership of the Child Poverty Action Group is consistent with being a team leader in our children's social care team?' She answered that poverty was an important factor in the families her team was working with, and the membership gave the social worker lots of up-to-date information and access to specialised training. Already, colleagues often called on her to talk to their clients and families to see if their incomes could be improved or to help with appeals against welfare benefits decisions. Her confidence in using information sometimes enabled improvements in uptake for the local authority's financial aid to families and supported the accepted social work role of advocacy for clients with other agencies.

What's not to like? The evidence of activism, it seems. Social workers for a public authority should be quiet, many people think, about pursuing rights and the social aspects of social work action for change (see Chapter 3). My commentary on the case examples in Chapter 6 suggested that the pressures were often ambiguous and covert. In this case, there was a challenge about the political in a private process, the job interview.

The kinds of political activity that social workers take part in include the following kinds of action:

- Acting in an environment that reflects (and therefore implicitly accepts) the political system of the nation or political influences on an international organisation.
- Implementing government decisions and policies, whether they work in a government agency, which inevitably reflects political decisions, or another agency, which may represent indirectly political decisions through its finance or management or in response to the social environment containing its work (see Chapters 6 and 7).
- Influencing decisions about individuals in their agency, through making reports, social histories or participating in allocation or prioritising systems.
- Influencing decisions about individuals in other agencies through advocacy, reports and participating in decisions about priorities or services.
- Influencing the policy of their agency through internal representations or making decisions within the bounds of their discretion; if this is a public agency, they may be influencing political decisions, or how political decisions are carried out or enforced.
- Influencing the policy of other agencies through advocacy or representations to that agency.
- Influencing public policy or political debate through representations through their agency.
- Influencing public policy or political debate through representations via representative bodies such as interest groups, professional associations and trades unions; that's possibly what Carrie in the case example was doing.
- Participating in policy and political debate through presenting professional experience or research, for example to official inquiries or working groups.
- Participating personally in policy and political debate through collective or individual activism.
- Seeking election to a political party or representative organisation.

Many people might consider that only the last two of these are clearly political activity because they are activity in relation to a political party. But all are political because they engage with political systems and with informal political processes between groups. They are all part of the distribution of power and of powers across society, but Garrett's 'embedded liberalism' constrains their expression in the local authority in the same way as, in the government minister case example in Chapter 4, it constrained their expression in relations among third sector organisations.

Baldwin (2011, pp 197–8), referring to these sorts of examples, argues that the political nature of social work should be made explicit. Since social workers work in an arena in which the scarcity of resources is frequently being contested, they assess needs and advocate for clients in resource allocation processes. Social service agencies are using social workers to ration scarce resources, sometimes exercising powers covertly as in the case example of Mrs Chartin's funding assessment in Chapter 5 and demanding that social workers avoid even beneficial and restrained social activism, as implied in Carrie's job interview. Baldwin argues that where uses of power produce a gap between how decisions ought to be made and what happens, they should be exposed.

But the question is how and who exposes it, to whom and what will the effect of exposure be? The bureau-professional role, at least, is constrained by Garrett's 'embedded liberalism', which censures the overt expression of ideas. Ferguson and Woodward (2009, ch 4) described a study of new and experienced social workers who found that bureau-professional roles in public sector social work prioritised manualised and proceduralised aspects of organisation, and controlling rather than more positive social work actions. This fails to reflect any of the streams of social work thinking outlined in Chapter 5. Garrett (2018a, pp 81–4) suggests that state social provision is being remade from a system in which embedded liberalism, constrained by social democratic thinking, was a consistent underlying political core in welfare states, towards unconstrained neoliberal thinking. To understand this shift, the next section explores some of the main political ideas implicit in social work thinking and practice explored in Chapters 1–8, and how neoliberalism has remade that influence, and the extent to which it has done so.

Political philosophies and social work

The three aims of social work from the global definition (see Figure 2.1) are connected with groupings of contending political ideas, liberal, socialist and social democratic philosophies. These three philosophies are present in interpretations of social work's aims, in accounts of social work and in how practitioners interpret their actions as they practice. In balancing their aims within their field of practice towards empowerment, social change or social cohesion, social workers inevitably express something of the relevant political philosophy. If they express a preference assertively, publicly or transparently, their practice may come to be seen as political action – in other words, activism. Even when they are less assertive or transparent about their aims, their practice can nevertheless be interpreted as political, particularly where it is evaluated against opposing political concepts. Understanding social work therefore requires a sensitivity to the political expression of its practice.

Liberal ideas

Historically, liberalism in Western politics was about freeing people from the medieval system of control within the all-embracing powers of the monarchy and the church. The English revolutions of the seventeenth century and the French and American revolutions of the late eighteenth century were an important part of that process; this European/US history underlies the European/US stream of social work thinking discussed in Chapter 5. Liberal political philosophy sees people as individuals, free to make their own decisions, with legal rights to protect them from the arbitrary power of social institutions such as church and monarchy, protected and nourished by more personal social institutions such as the family and local community. This influenced the ideology of individualism in Western social work values: for example, advocacy, co-production, giving clients voice, participation and self-determination (McDermott, 1975) and individualised services such as UK care management, described in the US as case management or managed care, or person-centred, self-directed care (Duffy, 2007; Alakeson, 2010; Beadle-Brown, Murphy & Bradshaw, 2017; SCIE, 2020). People's rational minds are liberated by education and greater understanding through the development of scientific research.

Liberalism was about people's liberty to pursue their own lives, interests and individual rights to enjoy their property, with the state operating by their consent. The state's role in people's lives, therefore, according to liberal ideas, should be minimal, allowing people to pursue their interests as individuals. Democratic structures enabled people to hold governments accountable. They balanced individual needs against citizens' collective interests. Political views in the nineteenth century distinguished between people who knew how to use their freedom in the economic system to accumulate wealth, and the poor, who had demonstrated that they were unable to use their economic freedom successfully to manage their lives and households, employ labour and contribute to the growth of wealth. The influential self-help movement wanted to enable poor people to develop educationally and socially but excluded them from political participation. These ideas underpinned early social work practice with how poor people managed their household affairs.

The oppressive impact of liberal ideas was limited by the extensive development of charitable work. In Britain, more than four times as many people received relief from charity as from the Poor Law (O'Brien & Penna, 1998, p 25), partly because of the restrictions of the Poor Law. The primary restriction, lesser eligibility, intended to make it less acceptable than any other form of help to potential users. Reacting against such policies, humanitarian movements sought legislation against extreme forms of exploitation. Industrialists and merchants displaced the aristocracy, and collective action by working-class people, such as trade unions and friendly societies, began to protect and defend them against exploitation. But it became apparent that people did not have equal chances to succeed, and so their fate could not be left to the market (Carr, 1960).

Socialist ideas

Socialist ideas, crystallised in the nineteenth century by Marx, picked up many of the same issues but countered liberal ideas. Rather than the liberal value given to self-interested individuals, it emphasised social cooperation to displace conflict between a capitalist class who were rich enough to control the means of producing goods and services and a working class whose poverty meant they had only labour to sell to the capitalists, who used this dependence to oppress them. Entrepreneurs in industrialising countries captured the state to organise society to their advantage. The state, as it became more democratic, became a site for struggles between capitalist advantage and workers' attempts to create institutions and services that enabled them to resist control and pursue their own interests. Working-class organisations, such as trade unions, brought people together to oppose capitalists' interests. Organisations such as co-operatives and friendly societies sit uneasily between working-class movements and self-help. As the German state formed amid rapid industrialisation, at the same time that social work was emerging in the late nineteenth century, it incorporated social provision in response to the fear of social disorder and resistance. Institutions providing for social security and social care would secure the state by responding to working-class demands for participation and service provision. Such ideas also contributed to the influence of the problem-solving, psychological stream of thinking in social work as it emerged in the early twentieth century. However, because of the anxiety in European countries after the Russian Revolution in 1917 about the possible influence of socialist ideas leading to revolution, Marxist sociology had little impact on social work as it emerged in the 1920s until the 1960s (Younghusband, 1981, p 11).

Liberalism and Marxism are materialist since both look for an explanation of human social structures in the external, material world and see economic imperatives as the drivers of social systems. Later developments incorporated broader ideas. For example, the Frankfurt School of critical theorists, including important writers such as Habermas (1986 [1971]; Houston, 2013) focused on how ideas and cultural values created hegemony for powerful elites in societies. This idea means domination through assumptions about how the world is. Spirituality and religion have also, during the late twentieth century, reasserted the concern within social work for many people who take a less materialist view (Canda, Furman & Canda, 2019; Crisp, 2017).

Social democracy

Social democratic or democratic socialist ideas emerged as Marxist social science lost its influence in the early twentieth century, with the state becoming an important site of social and economic management. More democratic processes allowed for social change benefiting working-class people. This was achieved by giving people, through the state, social rights both to services and participation. The experience of the 1930s depression led increasingly in Europe to a social democratic consensus about state social provision, contesting the liberal preference for charity and philanthropy.

The separation of social democratic from socialist ideas in British thinking and their impact on the Labour Party as it developed during the 1920s and 1930s meant that Marxism was distinguished from social democratic ideas about reform. In the US, on the other hand, there was a greater association between ideas of promoting radical social change and socialism, and consequent opposition to both. Thus, in the 1930s the radical rank-and-file movement of social workers in federal services concerned particularly with New Deal provision for the poor associated social work with communism (Reisch, 1998). British social workers continued in a relatively liberal mode of thinking, in which social work was concerned with individualised extensions of charity and philanthropy and those committed to social change were concerned more with social protection and general social change through legislative and institutional reform. The British separation between social work and 'the dole', the Liberal (political party) unemployment insurance scheme that displaced the stigmatised Poor Law for working men in the economic depression of the 1930s, meant that social work was, in the same way, not radicalised until the 1960s.

Citizenship and welfare state politics

Chapter 6 explored the importance of the idea of the welfare state, where governments accepted a broad responsibility for making social provision for their citizens. Citizenship exists to provide a structure of social order and social cohesion: it connects a population with a territory and with each other. Marshall and Bottomore's (1992) analysis, developed from Marshall's (1949) earlier work, linked citizenship with three sets of rights:

- Civil rights to legal protection of their freedoms and equality.
- Political rights to vote, stand for election and participate in political processes.
- Social rights to welfare and participation in social relations with others.

Among those social rights, according to this analysis, are access to social service provision and social work. Recognising such rights inevitably implies values that may be contested in political debate (Faulks, 2000). The social relationships of citizenship are not just individual matters: they involve the creation of collectives, social groups in which civil and political rights are invested, forming part of social capital and its connections. In any nation's society, an important collective is the state, the political system established to maintain the nation in the interests of its citizens. Different social groups in a nation and its society may have different and perhaps conflicting interests; participation by citizens in a society, therefore, involves both social collaboration and also social conflict. The state, therefore, is not monolithic, not one collective, but many. There is a national state, but there are many and perhaps conflicting aspects of it, with many different roles, and there are local and regional states, too, of varying influence.

By making social provision for all their citizens, therefore, welfare states inevitably position service users and providers in political relationships. It means that the agency context discussed in Chapter 6 interacts with social work and its practice, with the needs and wishes of people who use social work services (see Chapter 11) and with the wider population who finance and have interests in what the services and social work are. But citizenship is not just a status, it is also a process, in which people may gain or lose citizenship.

▨ *Case example: Daniela's citizenship process*

Daniela was a Ukrainian woman who moved with her three children to England as a refugee during the war between Russia and Ukraine in 2022, leaving her husband behind to join the army. She lived with a retired couple, occupying an apartment on the top floor of their large house. She saw herself as temporarily in the UK and very much a Ukrainian citizen. She received the UK universal credit and a number of other benefits, including education for her children and healthcare services for the whole family. Soon, she found a job as an adviser working with other Ukrainian people as they arrived in the country. After the initial settlement period, she found a separate apartment and began to establish a home. Shortly after this, her husband was killed in fighting in Ukraine and their house there was bombed. While her parents were still in Ukraine and she could ring them regularly, they advised not coming to visit because the situation was so insecure. She began to settle into a local authority job which offered training and particularly benefited from good education for her youngest child who had intellectual disabilities. She began to see that rather than return immediately, she would perhaps stay during her children's childhood, but she felt a great many personal losses and began to receive help from a retired qualified social worker from Cruse, the bereavement service. In her mind, she began to see her bereavement as not only her husband's death, but the loss of a way of life and her country. Meanwhile, political debate suggested that perhaps the war would continue for some years. But she retained her Ukrainian citizenship and the long-term intention of returning. She wondered: what would her position be like in five years?

Looking at Daniela's story, she was clearly a Ukrainian citizen throughout. But she received welfare and other benefits from the UK social capital in its civil society and through its welfare state. This was a bit of citizenship participation. She also contributed to this new nation through her work and paying taxes. Connections with Ukraine began to fall away with her husband's death, the loss of her house and her parents' anxieties. This was a bit of citizenship loss. She is getting security and stability, the beginnings of social cohesion and social order, through involvement in her children's lives, a new home and roots and her work. In this way, she experienced some more UK citizenship gain. At the time of writing, it is too soon to say, but perhaps by the end of five years, a continuing war (more citizenship loss), a better job and flat, a new partner and settled children (all citizenship gain) will change things. Perhaps she will think of regularising her position, marrying and gaining UK (official) citizenship.

Looking at the kind of carers, clients and service users that social workers often deal with, it is also possible to see gains and losses of citizenship. Children looked after in care will move towards adulthood and therefore increase their citizenship as all children do. Mentally ill people may be excluded from social relationships by a possibly disabling illness. But building up social capital again in a day centre through peer support is gaining citizenship back. An older person is losing digital citizenship because they are not keeping up with new technology. That is why in Chapter 3, I discussed citizenship as part of human rights actions and thinking. Citizenship participation in welfare states is expressed in all the ways that Daniela gained elements of citizenship through being part of life in the UK, eventually also benefiting from a volunteer social worker.

Neoliberalism and social work

Social democratic ideas are the source of welfare state provision, and influence one of the global definition aims of social work. But this is increasingly challenged not only by liberalism and socialism but also by neoliberal trends in the late twentieth and early twenty-first centuries. The result is that social work and social work practice lives in a less secure relationship with the state than in the welfare state era from the 1940s to the 1970s. Clarke (2004) suggested that social provision changed from a secure system that people could rely on, to one which was unstable. This came about because the global economic system was less stable in a new phase of globalisation. That social instability, generated by economic and political change, affects social services and social work and also their service users and clients. Their lives are made more precarious by economic change and the political reaction to them. Social work therefore has an increasingly insecure role in a less comprehensive and more unstable welfare state. Social work's insecurity comes from rejection of its commitment to the social, by the reassertion of social Darwinism through neoliberal thinking.

Neoliberalism describes a broad turn in social thinking that emerged in the 1980s and gathered pace thereafter. It is a new formulation of liberal ideas, starting from an international shift in policy away from the post-Second World War consensus in favour of welfare states. The main argument was about a 'fiscal crisis of the state' (O'Connor, 2017 [1973]). In this view, taxation to support state expenditure on social provision (fiscal policy is about taxation) was damaging the capacity of the economy to continue to develop. As welfare states declined, they were replaced by retrenchment in public expenditure (Mishra, 1990), marketisation and privatisation of public services including social provision. A consequential struggle by activists and others such as social workers sought to sustain the gains that had been achieved in the welfare state period on behalf of people in poverty (O'Connor, 2017, p xvi). States that did not have extensive welfare provision shifted away from policies to build it up, or developed regimes relevant to the particular issues they faced and the politics of the nations, particularly in relation to family life and poverty (Mishra, 1990; Cochrane, Clarke & Gewirtz, 2001).

What does neoliberalism mean? The term has been used across different economic, political and social science fields to mean a variety of things; it would be hard to get agreement about it even in a specific field of study (Venugopal, 2015). A number of points clarify the sort of concept it is:

- It is an idea within political economy, so it is concerned with how political systems interact with, and are influenced by, economics; thus, I consider its economic position in Chapter 10. There are implications for social policy, but social policy is not a priority for neoliberal thinking.

- As a political philosophy, neoliberalism is about broad, high-level ideas that make up the economic and political context of social action and policy. It is not a highly specified theoretical idea whose detailed practical implications for social work have been carefully researched and thought through.
- Mostly, people do not claim to be neoliberals, and policies are not labelled 'neoliberal' by their proponents. It is a term used by critics, usually hostile to these policies.

'Neoliberal' ideas and policies are, therefore, defined critically. How, then, have concerns about the context of social work come to be seen as deriving from a neoliberal political economy? Mostly, this is because it is a convenient conceptual hook to express a number of issues about the economic and political contexts in which social work operates.

The concerns about neoliberal policies affecting social work include the following points.

- Neoliberal thinking is against the state but uses it. This is a crucial distinction between liberal and neoliberal thinking. While liberalism opposes state action, neoliberalism's concern with freedom in the market (Friedman, 1962) leads it to use the state to enforce marketisation and privatisation. It does this to increase markets' freedom of operation by controlling state action and expenditure. Neoliberal policy, therefore, recruits state services such as social work as a way to enhance and regulate markets and to privatise provision. As neoliberal ideas became more important in the later twentieth century, therefore, public services in welfare states, such as social work, became an object of economic and political policies which devalued and undermined their humanity and social objectives.
- Social work is particularly affected by the neoliberal preference for marketisation because it is primarily a state-provided service. It serves people, often in poverty, who cannot usually afford the cost of social care and social work services in a market. It therefore complicates the social work task by using social work to diminish state action which is essential to social work with people in poverty.
- In this, social work is unlike healthcare. In some countries, healthcare is mainly a private, market-based provision. Even where, as in the UK and many European countries, it remains mostly a state service, a significant number of private providers operate in a market system, which inspires neoliberal thinking to extend private markets in healthcare to social provision inappropriately. This is because it increases their business opportunities in a related field and reinforces neoliberal disregard for the social.
- Social care is also unlike housing. A significant economic market in housing is widely accepted, and private house ownership and renting is a common feature of life worldwide. State provision is less widespread in housing than in social care because housing is nearly universal, while social work mainly focuses on a smaller proportion of populations with specific issues to

face, mainly people in poverty who cannot use the market to sustain their communities and lives.

Not all current right-wing policy positions are, however, drawn from neoliberal political thinking. Chueri (2022) and Moffitt (2020, ch. 3) both identify three further political positions: authoritarianism, nativism and populism. These are commonplace in the 2020s because they help radical right-wing political thinking to achieve votes in a democratic system. This works because they are attractive to a wide range of interests, some of which are relevant to social work. Such radical right-wing ideas have become important because right-wing political parties have influenced more centrist right-leaning politics in coalition political systems in European countries and elsewhere or where they make it possible to take political support away from centrist parties, making them less electable.

Authoritarianism

Authoritarianism raises questions about practice because of government or professional powers and responsibilities. Authority in professional practice has been an important aspect of social work value debates around self-determination and self-directed practice (see Chapters 3–5). Glasius (2018) argues that authoritarianism arises from a deficit in democratic accountability of people with powers within a society, such as social workers. It is revealed in practices, sets of rules and ways of working, that lead to controlling systems of behaviours in a society without accountability for the exercise of power. In authoritarian regimes, systems for accountability are present, but people with power can avoid them, while maintaining the semblance of accountability. This is revealed in, for example, focusing social provision on 'hard-working people', or 'people who have made a contribution to society'. These are vague categories that defy practical definition and allow unspoken values to be used to define eligibility for help. When politics does this, in matters that affect social work services, it often counters the professional values of social workers who are working in state services. It also wants to make social work a form of authoritarian control, rather than being focused on caring and helping actions.

Nativism

Nativism has a long history, particularly in North America where historically it referred to anti-immigration views. Now, it often describes a view within radical right-wing politics that expresses concern for social cohesion in the face of inward migration to a country. Betz (2019) identifies three elements:

- Economic nativism: preserving jobs for a native population.
- Welfare chauvinism: that native populations should have priority in receiving social benefits, such as social housing, social welfare payments or social work, as in Iulia and Kasim's case in Chapter 1.

- Symbolic nativism: concerned with preserving a claimed but sometimes unclear or debated historical culture. Newth (2021) connects the idea to regionalism and it could also relate to localism.

For social work, nativism in politics has implications for the global definition objective of social cohesion (see Figure 2.1). Working for social cohesion may be misdirected from its social work intentions towards protecting local populations against outsiders. Nativism might also provide a political justification for directing social work actions and priorities towards local rather than wider populations and potentially raise questions about strategies to achieve community-near social services and indigenous practice (see Chapters 3 and 5, respectively).

Nativism also refers to the debate about where people get their understandings of the world from. Do we know about the world from observation and rational analysis or from emotional reaction to innate understanding and early experiences and relationships in childhood? A nativist might say: 'I don't need to analyse people's rights, I learned what is important at my mother's knee' (Samuels, 2002; Margolis & Laurence, 2013).

Populism

Populism refers to diverse political movements that claim to speak on behalf of 'the people' against various alleged elites. These may be cultural, economic or political elites. Cultural elites are pilloried for supporting 'healthy' food, minority forms of the arts or 'politically correct' or 'woke' attitudes. Cultural leaders are criticised for liking opera and gourmet food rather than appreciating burgers and pop music. Professionals like teachers and social workers are criticised for being open to supporting freedoms to live gay or lesbian lifestyles and encouraging new movements such as gender transition for young people, rather than emphasising 'practical' political objectives benefiting 'ordinary people'. The diversity of political projects that are called populist, rather like neoliberalism, has been criticised: does this category of movement really reflect any identifiable political position? Or is it a politically and morally charged term stigmatising appealing to the mass as in the massification of workers as an undifferentiated herd in 'McDonaldisation' (see Chapter 4)?

Brubaker's (2017) analysis proposes that populism is a repertoire of public debate that can pick up political objectives from both right and left. It thus increases the range of attraction of politics of the far right, although it often represents the economic interests of the rich and seeks to denigrate the political views of educated middle-class professionals. It opposes, on behalf of 'ordinary folk' both elites and also, pursuing nativism, outsiders. Outsiders are both elites: for example, people who value worldwide classical music, or migrants who have an alien religion or way of life. An example might be Hindu nationalist ideas affecting Islam in India. Four elements of populist claims are apparent:

- Antagonistic re-politicisation rejects rational, scientific and evidence-based thinking that underlies the role of professionals, in the way Margaret Thatcher, the UK prime minister in the 1980s, argued that 'there is no alternative' to neoliberal economic reform. The only acceptable politics rejects the value of experts or legal and professional advice about human rights and social needs in favour of some kind of unspecified 'common sense'.
- Majoritarianism claims the opinions and rights of the many, the 'silent majority' or 'decent, hard-working ordinary people' are to be followed against the views of what a British Home Secretary called in Parliament 'Guardian-reading, tofu-eating wokerati' (Hansard, 18 October 2022, col. 628), which might include, stereotypically, social workers. Another familiar trope, sourced from the popular television cartoon series *The Simpsons*, is 'cheese-eating surrender monkeys' as a US pejorative reference to French people and indirectly all non-authoritarian, left-wing opinion (Younge & Henley, 2003).
- Institutionalism rejects the mediating value of institutions, such as social work and other professions, against immediate responses to the claimed popular will, such as long prison sentences for unspecified but unpopular criminals.
- Protectionism protects 'ordinary people' against economic threats from cheap foreign goods, migrant labour and global creditors, against insecurities from crime and terrorism and from cultural pollution by migrants and other outsiders. The valued cultural style of populism is Faragist or Trumpist (to refer to politicians popular at the time of writing in the UK and the US): this means plain unrestrained speaking, avoiding rules of politeness or respectful language.

Social work and the state

Social work's relationship with the state is made complex in the context of neoliberal and similar tropes in thinking by the moral, political and social choices involved in providing social services. Twentieth-century development in social services and social work leading up to the welfare state period sought to make its provision more secure and accessible to more people by state provision, provided to citizens as a right. The retrenchment from the welfare state outlined in Chapters 6–8 has broadened the range of providers. In the case example of Iulia and Karim in Chapter 1, however, this meant that policy, derived from political decision, led to needs of asylum seekers not being met by the state. Chapter 6 identified a range of organisational locations that offer social services, with the public sector being only one of them. Political policy after the 'fiscal crisis of the state' meant that only selective help, often requiring engagement with the private sector, was available. But social work is mainly for people in poverty and therefore requires taxation or other financial resources to support it. The alternatives may be no better, since private, social enterprise or third sector provision depend on the suppliers' decisions rather than the public sector responsibility to provide for the social wellbeing of the nation's citizens. The nature of the different sectors means that personal decisions by donors or operators of services may prevent social work being available. Or private sector provision may be affected by profitability, as in the following case example.

Case example: profitability affects decisions to provide residential care for children

A newspaper report suggested that a chain of private sector care homes for children, contracted to provide places for several local authorities, decided to close smaller homes because they were less profitable than larger homes. Children would lose otherwise successful placements altogether or would be transferred to less homelike larger units (Wall, 2023).

The policy and services of the state, including social services and social work, reflect the range of political ideas present in discourse with the nation, but also global trends in political thinking. Chapter 1 noted that the aims of social work, which set its field of practice, incorporate and represent, in a balance which influences practice, the three important historical political philosophies present in Western countries: liberal, social democratic and socialist philosophies.

Two issues arise from this. First, the discourse in social work in many countries still largely represents the discourse in political philosophy in the European/ US problem-based stream of thought identified in Chapters 2 and 5. With the present global reach of social work, alternative discourses are not fully represented. This means that social work in authoritarian regimes deriving from political and spiritual discourses outside Western democratic assumptions is ill thought through. In turn, this points to weaknesses in thinking through authoritarian pressures in Western countries. It is often unreal to assume that citizenship accords rights to public provision. Similarly, it is not clear that social workers and their clients are entitled to pursue resistance to those pressures, and can achieve that resistance. Second, connected with that, because alternative political philosophies are not adequately thought through within social work value debate, it often assumes that a neoliberal discourse is unsatisfactory for social work and a socialist social change discourse reliant on human rights is to be preferred. Such a view does not explain how to implement professionally appropriate and politically acceptable change in a hostile political context.

Social work in authoritarian regimes

Considering the first issue, in countries with an authoritarian system that constrains political accountability, it is not clear that the balance struck in the Western interpretation of social work practice values between alternative aims of social cohesion, liberation and empowerment and social change is politically acceptable or possible. Looking at Staub-Bernasconi's (2011) commentary on different human rights traditions in social work discussed in Chapters 3–5, it becomes clear that responding to authoritarian regimes is one of the intersections that require global professional debate to develop and understand the position of social work in a range of political regimes. Simply asserting the need for European/US forms of democratic system seems not to recognise the reality of alternatives. What does this mean to practitioners? Do they practise as best they can within the parameters of the political system in their country? But many European and American practitioners accept such compromises with the political leanings of their countries. When they do that, they often pursue a subterranean resistance to injustices and grasp opportunities for their clients. Is that what is ethical or realistic for social workers in authoritarian regimes? How might that be evaluated internationally? As an ethical requirement, or as a practice choice that they might make or ...? After all, children and women experiencing domestic abuse still need safeguarding and that requires social work skills, both the human contribution to practice and the practice strategies discussed in Chapter 3–4. And disabled, mentally ill or older people also need social work services and skills whatever the regime of their country. What does a social worker do if pursuing the practice ideal of co-production pulls them into trying to do something that clients want but that the state's administration doesn't accept?

Such issues are present in all social work practice. Looking back at the case examples in Chapters 1–6 drawn mainly from the European experience, many of them present the question of how far the social worker or their manager can or should challenge a political or resource decision on behalf of their clients or initiate a complaint procedure. Not all political decisions in Western countries are open to challenge, and a social worker who is an employee of the state may not have the right to raise questions in a particular matter.

For example, Gardiner, Morrison and Robinson (2022) review the idea of a 'duty of candour' which has been proposed in healthcare and police services in the UK and might become an extension of social work regulation. In healthcare and policing, inquiries into failings in service provision have found that past reports revealing similar failings have not been acted on. The Francis Report on a healthcare scandal in the UK (2013, p 41) suggests: '... it is far more effective to learn rather than to punish. To place too much emphasis on individual blame will perpetuate the cycle of defensiveness, concealment, lessons not being identified and further harm.' A statutory duty of candour was subsequently imposed on organisations by the Health and Social Care Act 2008 (Regulated Activities) Regulation 2014, s.3, extended to all Care Quality Commission-regulated providers (therefore including social care and social work) where any event causing death, severe harm, moderate harm or prolonged psychological harm must be notified to the CQC by the organisation and investigated. The General Medical Council and Nursing and Midwifery Council subsequently issued ethical requirements for a 'duty of candour' on regulated professionals, with detailed guidance. I set out the duty in Table 9.1. The regulatory body for social workers in England publishes weaker and less detailed requirements for social workers that cannot really be described as a 'duty of candour'; this is also reprinted in Table 9.1. There are, therefore, in the UK, some provisions in organisations that employ social workers or that they have connections with, for openness and transparency. But Gardiner, Morrison & Robinson (2022) recount

Table 9.1: Examples of duties of candour

Healthcare professionals in the UK: the professional duty of candour

Every health and care professional must be open and honest with patients and people in their care when something that goes wrong with their treatment or care causes, or has the potential to cause, harm or distress. This means that health and care professionals must:

- tell the person (or, where appropriate, their advocate, carer or family) when something has gone wrong;
- apologise to the person (or, where appropriate, their advocate, carer or family);
- offer an appropriate remedy or support to put matters right (if possible);
- explain fully to the person (or, where appropriate, their advocate, carer or family) the short- and long-term effects of what has happened.

Health and care professionals must also be open and honest with their colleagues, employers and relevant organisations, and take part in reviews and investigations when requested. They must also be open and honest with their regulators, raising concerns where appropriate. They must support and encourage each other to be open and honest, and not stop someone from raising concerns.

Source: General Medical Council/Nursing and Midwifery Council (2022)

Social workers in England. Professional Standard 6: Promote ethical practice and report concerns

As a social worker, I will:

6.1 Report allegations of harm and challenge and report exploitation and any dangerous, abusive or discriminatory behaviour or practice.
6.2 Reflect on my working environment and where necessary challenge practices, systems and processes to uphold Social Work England's professional standards.
6.3 Inform people of the right to complain and provide them with the support to do it, and record and act on concerns raised to me.
6.4 Take appropriate action when a professional's practice may be impaired.
6.5 Raise concerns about organisational wrongdoing and cultures of inappropriate and unsafe practice.
6.6 Declare to the appropriate authority and Social Work England anything that might affect my ability to do my job competently or may affect my fitness to practise, or if I am subject to criminal proceedings or a regulatory finding is made against me, anywhere in the world.
6.7 Cooperate with any investigations by my employer, Social Work England, or another agency, into my fitness to practise or the fitness to practise of others.

Source: Social Work England (2019)

---

a long history of organisations and public servants fudging or neglecting their responsibilities. They note that to take on their responsibilities, practitioners need considerable competence, self-awareness, skill and persistence against organisational constraints to openness.

Complexities to openness include:

- Organisational or professional objectives and responsibilities are unclear.
- Plural accountability to carers, clients, the public, the agency and to managers and colleagues makes it hard to understand the best course of action.

- Making an agency work needs complex negotiations around areas of conflict and difficulty. (Gardiner, Morrison & Robinson, 2022, p 223)

Social work's social humanity

Turning to the second issue, I said in Chapter 1 that all social work, public sector social work particularly, seeks to incorporate elements of a range of political philosophies because its concern is the social humanity of any society. It is, therefore, authoritarianism, nativism and populism that must be rejected. This is because these -isms underlie discrimination, oppression and racism and so they must be unacceptable to a profession seeking to further social humanity. They also underlie the rejection of evidence-informed professional practice on behalf of the humanity which is at the heart of social work.

Conclusion

This chapter explored the senses in which social work can be understood to be a political activity. Consequences flow from this in sometimes covert conflicts and interactions with wider political life and values. Ideas about social work and its practice, explored in Chapters 1–5, and the context of that practice, examined in Chapters 6–8, all incorporate important European and US political philosophies. The global agency, the political and professional context of social work, is complex, difficult to disentangle and hard to practise social work in. Current political contexts and ideas in many countries may not permit social work strategies of challenge and resistance. How, then, can social work globally think about co-production when its work with clients challenges national political philosophies and policy developments?

Action on policy and politics in social work

Social work is open to a range of political ideas that support social humanity and human rights but needs to find ways of rejecting authoritarian, nativist and populist discourses that lead to discrimination, oppression, racism and repudiate evidence-informed practice.

The next chapter ...

... explores the economic and equality contexts of social work.

10

Social work, economics and choice

Social work represents the value of human and social capital and caring

Social work and social service agencies incorporate the economics of their nations and of a globalised world, as well as their political ideas. And, as with the social choices that emerge from political ideas, there are important disagreements about the choices that economic ideas focus on. Social work represents the value of human solidarity and caring as part of a society; that value adds social capital to economic and other resources. Economics is about how any society, people acting as a political and social collective, provides resources for that human solidarity of caring, as well as many other aspects of that society. The question social work asks is: how will this distribution of resources improve social capital and social solidarity?

Of course, people acting on their own, with community and family, use personal and interpersonal resources, help and support as part of collective mutual solidarity for wellbeing. As well as this, Chapter 1 made clear that any human society also provides resources for organised ways of caring and helping. That requires a structure of agencies that includes social work. Chapter 9 explored how social choices about care and help in any society developed a politics as groups came together around the choices that need to be made. Social work as a social structure cannot be divorced from the social choices that the economics of the society makes as it implements those choices. If there is a social work, there must also be an economics of social work. The two are entwined, and because economics connects with political thinking, a society's political economy also links to the politics and policy of social work. If engagement in politics and policy is essential to social work, then engagement in economics is equally so.

I argue in this chapter that one of the reasons why social work is important is because it is essential to maintaining the social objectives and relationships in which the economic system in any society functions. Social work contributes to economic functioning, economic growth and economic and social stability. Neoliberal politics and libertarian economics follow a 'materialist tradition' (Lynch & Lyons, 2009, p 54) that proposes, to the contrary, that social expenditure depends on a strong growing economy, and that social work, alongside other forms of social provision, is a drag on business and the economy; for more discussion, see Chapter 9. It should be minimised, they say, because it is a compulsory expense to the economy that provides the wealth that supports society. But a modern economy is not a separate entity of actions disconnected from wellbeing in society; it contributes to and forms the context of that wellbeing. Similarly, social care and social work provision is inseparable from, and benefits, business and the economy. Economic choices come from the society in which they are made, and social ideas contribute to how a society approaches economics in its human life.

This chapter discusses three issues:

- Social choices in economics that affect inequality and wellbeing.
- Social work concerns with economic choices around production and universalism.
- Social work's economic roles.

Social choice, wellbeing and inequality in economics

Conventional economic values, the human and the social

Economics is a social science concerned with understanding how goods and services are produced, distributed and consumed in society; here, I summarise in a very abbreviated form some aspects of it that are relevant to social work, drawing on Barr (2020), Chang (2014), Sandel (2012) and Sen (2017).

Conventional economics asserts that an economy aims to improve economic efficiency, producing and distributing goods and services in ways that achieve the greatest benefits to both consumers and producers. That requires value judgements, based on ideas about morality, about what would benefit consumers and producers. Most economic opinions value utility, assuming that people are self-interested, seeking the most benefits they can achieve for themselves, and what benefits the greatest number measured by the rational evaluation of monetary benefits of any actions. Because this conventional economics is about individuals, it takes up the individualism of social Darwinism, which I have argued particularly in Chapter 1 but throughout this book is inimical to human social life and also to social work. Ultimately, conventional economics is about the political economy, collective political and social judgements on the balance of benefits between two interest groups in the economic system of any society: producers and consumers. Schwartz (2022) identifies three important issues in global political economy which provide the context for how economics works in society: issues about how countries seek to dominate others, issues about how companies (including giant globalised companies) control their activities, and how profits are distributed.

These political and economic issues also raise issues for social work. For example, concerns about war between Russia and Ukraine, a possible invasion of Taiwan by China and civil conflicts in several Middle Eastern countries are current at the time of writing. These have led to distress and poverty, inflation and migration: all are issues affecting individual and social wellbeing, which communities, families and individuals have to deal with in their daily lives. Behind these current concerns lie longer-term issues that affect the people social workers deal with, for example how European colonialism and slavery have led to some traditional societies being dominated by the cultures and economic interests of colonial powers and their settlers. A reaction against such colonial domination and its aftermath led to indigenous practice ideas, which seek social development and contest inequalities among ethnic groups across the world. Similarly, future issues around climate change will also have an impact on different communities, families, individuals and nations in a variety of ways. Present-day social work has to respond to social tensions arising from people's reactions to current political and economic tensions, future risks and historical traumas passed on in community and family relations. That is a crucial contribution of social work to social advancement and wellbeing.

Everyone in a society is both a consumer and a producer. They are part of an economic system, a continuing process, a cycle, of exchange between consumers and producers in which individuals and organisations in social structures decide how resources are allocated and used. Resources are always scarce, and insufficient to meet all the demands on them. One of the things the economy does is to distribute resources among different groups in society. The economy always has mechanisms to manage or regulate the cycle to improve what economic thinking claims is economic efficiency when trying to achieve improved outcomes for everyone.

Economics, markets and wellbeing

One mechanism is the monetary system because money is used as an easily transferable token of value in the cycle of exchanges. Another mechanism is economic markets, systems for exchanging goods for money in the monetary system. The idea of economic markets uses the metaphor of a location with many small traders in market stalls. Buyers can check the goods on different stalls and choose between them; stalls offering good value are successful, make profits and grow in size, but poor value leads to failure. But replicated on a national or global scale, big companies grow up that can control marketing, that is, promotion and misinformation about goods and services, and the production of goods and services, so buyers have little real choice. Emphasising economic markets leads to the concentration of money and power in global big business that exploits people with very little control over their lives (Stiglitz, 2020, pp 47–78). Modern economics values economic growth and that makes corporations important, constantly enlarging and increasingly global. The aim for economic growth is far from being about human wellbeing except in the individualistic, self-interested monetary sense (Davies & Leonard, 2004). These movements are connected to the value given to enterprise, entrepreneurialism, in social agencies, energy and innovation in organisations (see Chapter 6). Consequently, an important but often neglected feature of markets is that they need to be regulated effectively to avoid exploitation, in the same way that the care homes market needs to prevent ill-treatment or neglect. Social work can legitimately ask how well an economic market combats exploitation that damages wellbeing. Many people in current economic systems struggle with precarious jobs. They are often thrown out of work for a while, before finding another precarious job. Events like this disrupt their contributions to community and family, and add economically damaging stress to mental health, social stability and wellbeing. In its functioning, the conventional economy has the potential to damage wellbeing in parallel with being good for individual participants and big corporations. The potential damage and good have to be managed and provided for, and social work is one of the mechanisms that helps conventional economics manage the damage it causes to human and social wellbeing.

Economic values are concerned with the wellbeing of the people within an economic system, that is, ideally improving, maintaining and protecting their emotional, physical and social wellbeing. In this, they seem to have the same aims as social work, but this is expressed in a markedly different way. These are value judgements about moral ideas. People's wellbeing partly derives from working as successful producers, so the availability of work is an important economic value. In economics, the value of work is often measured in money, but other aspects of work are also important; for instance, social support for work, education and skills development, and emotional and social stability through family and community life. People work to contribute to their society in general and to important social groups they are part of, particularly families and local communities. Another aspect of people's wellbeing is their consumption, being able to feed and house themselves, and developing their humanity through successful human and social relationships, education and worthwhile leisure activities. They can do that in their community, education and family, and in their work through their work's intrinsic and monetary values. But to concentrate on money and profit avoids thinking about important non-financial aspects of society, such as mutual caring, and building successful social relationships (Lynch, Baker, Lyons et al, 2009; Sandel, 2012). In thinking about economic choices, liberal and neoliberal views insist that only money can be a rational measure of economic value. This way of thinking prioritises measurement by numbers, rather than the broader forms of, and significantly human, measurement that Lynch and her colleagues and Sandel are discussing.

Economics, equality, money and social justice

Because economics is about the distribution of resources, it raises questions of equality, differences between people and between social groups, and equity, fairness of distribution among people and groups. There are three kinds of wealth, which form capital, the stock of valuables we can draw on to live. Physical wealth is the stock of things people own, such as houses, furniture, computers and cars. Financial wealth is the money in people's pockets or bank accounts, and that held in shares in companies, government bonds and pension schemes being built up. Human wealth comes from education, skills, abilities and talents, while social capital is contained in community and family networks. Income derives from capital. People earn wages according to the social support they have from their community and family and also their education, skills, abilities and talents, interest and other monies from their bank accounts and investments. Physical wealth produces notional income; people who own a house can rent it out to earn income, or do not need to pay rent from other income. Wealth and income can be shared, often in families but possibly also in social institutions such as cooperatives or through philanthropy in communities. Happiness is also an important form of psychological and social wealth (Layard, 2005).

Production increases wealth and income of all sorts, since goods and services increase the number of things of value that can circulate in the economy. For example, cooking a meal at home using talents and learned skills provides energy and happiness for the family through eating the food, sharing the meal and being together. At a different scale of activity, using financial wealth to build a factory and equip it with machinery to make computers increases the value of the raw materials that go to make the product. It allows factory owners to profit when they sell the product to computer stores; in turn, staff use their education and skills to make a profit by marketing and selling the computers to the end users. They might gain happiness by playing games or generating income from using their skills to write books. In yet another cycle, game designers and sellers, and publishers, professors and students will participate in producing pleasure and knowledge. Growth in production and increasing productivity means everyone in all cycles will increase their happiness, income and multiple kinds of wealth. All economic policy seeks economic growth, although this may be problematic if it uses up irreplaceable resources. Human resources are infinitely replaceable through the life cycle of birth and death, and by creating social relations and education; physical resources are less so. There is an argument, therefore, to focus on human and social resources, which can always be grown, rather than on measuring output only in money and physical goods, which are always used up.

The conventional economic approach to equality, focusing as it always does on money, looks at only one aspect of economic value, fairness in the distribution of economic resources, distributive justice. This often leads neoliberal and libertarian commentators to maintain inequalities in the form of differentials in the rewards that people receive from working so that they are incentivised to make economic contributions to society. Watts and Hodgson's (2019) account of social justice (see the discussion in Chapter 5), however, identifies other aspects that may be equally important, illustrating that broadening the range of equalities that social workers work towards can be an important strategy in explaining and justifying social work's approach. Money isn't everything. Fair access to autonomy, citizenship and rights supports people in being able to act freely, and recognising their human rights and values and developing their personal and social identities may be just as important as earning money to the mental and physical health of many people. So is social justice in participation, by increasing spaces for democratic decision-making inclusion in public discourse and social participation. Another form of equality is fairness in the opportunity to be critical, challenging domination and oppressive relations embedded in economic and political structures.

Economics, money and social justice

The economic cycle therefore requires many choices, by individuals and in economic and social institutions creating policy, and these are moral and social choices. Choice involves deciding what will improve or maintain wellbeing for individuals, social groups and society in general. Equality and equity are factors in making many of these choices. Part of the reasons for this is that having economic and human capital generates more of the same, so some people and social groups who have access to fewer resources are disempowered, disabled by exclusion from the more generative aspects of the economic cycle. Looking at the macro-level of the economic cycle, rich social groups gain more from the economic cycle than poor groups, and the economic system doubles down on that to create inequality between different social groups and poverty for many. Stiglitz (2015, pp 286–9) argues that inequality is primarily a product of political and policy decisions to favour inadequately regulated big business for fear of economic disruption. While some economic inequality helps economic growth, and some economic freedoms are essential, extreme inequality and lack of economic regulation hampers economic growth and undermines social relations and stability.

> Increasing inequalities, with top-heavy income distributions, lessen aggregate demand (the rich tend to spend a smaller fraction of their income than the poor), which can slow economic growth. The attempt of monetary authorities to offset these effects can contribute to credit bubbles, and these bubbles in turn lead to economic instability. That is why inequality is often associated with economic instability ... But perhaps the worst dimension of inequality is inequality of opportunity, which is both the cause and the consequence of inequality of outcome, and causes economic inefficiency and reduced development, as large numbers of individuals are not able to live up to their potential. Countries with high inequality tend to invest less in public goods, such as infrastructure, technology, and education, which contribute to long-term economic prosperity and growth. (Stiglitz, 2015, pp 287–8)

In this section, I have suggested that conventional economic thinking focuses too much on the needs of the money economy and its market metaphor, wrongly equating social wellbeing with money and economic production.

Social work, production and universalism in the economy

Critiques of social work's role in the economy come from three directions. Two slightly differing positions, liberal and neoliberal, are individualistic, and the social Darwinist view rejects human interdependence and solidarity as part of social life. Because social work does not directly enhance monetary productivity, it has no value. I look at these critiques first; the third direction comes from a more socialist perspective and I move on to that later.

The liberal/neoliberal view is wrong for three reasons:

- Social work contributes to productivity in the business economy because it contributes to human development, social cohesion and security, reducing social disruption and increasing social resources.
- Social work is part of the economic system, contributing to economic growth and productivity.
- A philosophy that only values economic productivity is immoral, unacceptable because it degrades civilisation and devalues humanity.

Liberal views argue that people should be able to deal with their own difficulties in life, with voluntary help from the families and communities they are part of. In reality, as with Iulia and Karim in Chapter 1, most people struggle to deal with complex difficulties which engage hard-to-manage emotions, such as grief at childlessness, the loss of a loved one, their work, their marriage or other important relationships. That's why social work is important because it represents society helping its citizens with those struggles. A libertarian view (Barr, 2020, pp 22–4) goes further than a liberal or neoliberal position. It argues that the state, and social work as part of it, interferes with the freedom to hold property and pursue an individual's self-interests. Natural rights libertarians, such as Nozick (1974), define freedom as the absence of coercion or restraints to freedom. They argue that the state should be limited to defending the person and their property, correcting past wrongs and enforcing legal contracts, so that people can operate fairly in the market. Taxation for any other purpose is slavery and theft, making individuals work for the state and not for themselves and forcibly reallocating their income and property. Empirical libertarians, such as Hayek (1944, 1960) and Friedman (1962) argue that markets protect freedom, because they are naturally self-regulating, coordinating vast amounts of pieces of information about people's needs and resources. A state and its social work pursuing collective caring goes against nature to a libertarian. This is because it means coercing people into giving up the free enjoyment of their income and resources, in favour of other people's, that is, collective, democratically expressed views about how resources should be distributed. Against this point of view, there are many other freedoms that this view does not think about. People generally want to be free to accept social responsibility for others in difficulties, they want to care and be cared for, love and be loved; this is called 'affective equality' (Lynch, Baker, Lyons et al, 2009; Lynch, 2022).

This belief in economic markets is crucial to libertarians' moral valuation of freedom based on monetary utility. Carney (2021, pp 121–7), a former governor of two central banks, argues that, in a society where markets are too dominant, commodification corrodes social values. He suggests that a purely commercial society demonstrates to everyone that the most important thing to do in life is to make money within a market. Being involved in matters of social value is marked out as less important. Social work, with its concentration on the social aspects of human life, becomes demonstrably worth less, and perhaps worthless, in a market society. Demanding that it be commodified (that is, turned into a series of paid-for alternatives) just adds to that demonstration of worthlessness. To value the social, we also have to value the elements of the social and that includes social work.

The risks of focusing too much on the market weakens all the social constraints on behaviour that might be built into complex modern societies. So, lying, promoting instability and seeking valuable social goods only for yourself, or for your family or your social class are fine if they promote the market. Whereas seen in a different way, financial self-seeking devalues humanity, and it devalues community, family and other social relationships, social values and ultimately social work.

Sandel (2012) draws attention to the moral questions that conventional economic thinking fails to deal with. He argues that, in human behaviour, monetary incentives crowd out moral ones. My grandson is very keen on playing computer games in his leisure time; he can't understand why you would want to read a book rather than do the more exciting thing. Some parents, according to Sandel (2012, pp 60–1), pay their children to read books rather than look at their mobile phone. This treats reading as something that needs compensation, rather than having intrinsic value which the child needs to learn about so that they make the choice to read. Every attempt to incentivise socially useful behaviour with money gives in to this risk. The aim of educating people to behave sensibly to promote social objectives gets lost in the assumption that people are educated in order to earn more money. Social pedagogy, with its community-based informal social education model, proclaims the importance of the social rather than economic purposes of education, and rejects economic incentivisation as the basis of educational and social progress.

Case example: picking up children from day centres

Gneezy and Rustichini (2000) studied how fines worked when they were used to get people to comply with social norms. They found it was better to get people to learn socially useful behaviour. Day centres explicitly decided to fine parents for inconveniencing staff by picking their children up late. They found that late pickups increased, because the fine was regarded by well-heeled parents as a fee, which removed the social stigma of being late, covering the cost of teachers' inconvenience and allowing parents to optimise their own time. Thus, a market approach to managing selfish behaviour demonstrated clearly that selfishness is priced into markets.

Carney (2021) also suggests that the focus on markets for every purpose, even providing social work and similar services, means that some people are forced to buy or sell in a market, and the pressure to participate in the market means that inequalities arise in how the market affects people. A social work example is where disabled or older people are forced to buy private sector care services, rather than participate in public sector provision, or employ a personal assistant through direct payments in self-directed care systems. People in poverty because of their disability or need then tend to get less good private provision than those who can afford to pay over the odds for more congenial care or wider choice. And public provision is devalued.

Also, putting a price on service that is provided as a matter of social relationships corrodes its value. People stop valuing mothers' care for their children, or families' care for disabled or older people, or voluntary work in the community. Because it does not have to be paid for, it appears to have no value. Certainly, such care is not evaluated fully if it is only evaluated according to monetary value. Thus, personal care or, going further, civic or community engagement are worthless because they are not paid for. Yet they are essential to developing human capital in a society, essential to running any society. Taking caring and helping out of a moral or social arena alters its ethical character. Seeing helping behaviour as something that needs to be priced takes away its moral and social value. In this way, emphasising markets and quasi-markets in what would otherwise be human relationships taints their social value.

The socialist critique of social work's role in the economy favours universal social responses that devalue personalised helping responses. This is also wrong, but in a different way from neoliberal economics, for two reasons:

* Social progress cannot be completely achieved by general interventions in the economy. The generality of such interventions makes them inadequate to deal with the complexity of human need and fails to achieve co-production, genuine engagement and participation with service users.
* Human beings need and want to receive responsive personal care and help (Lynch, Baker, Lyons et al, 2009), if it is appropriate for their needs, and other human beings want to provide it.

The view from the left is to pursue primarily collective and universal interventions, such as insurance and financial benefits or benefits in kind such as education and healthcare. This is because they have a broad effect, are non-stigmatising and treat everyone equally. Universal provision also takes responsibility for social distress; it avoids individualising or privatising the response to collective social failings. It also avoids possibly paternalistic discretion in decision making in individualising professions such as European/US problem-solving social work.

But general purpose services always become inflexible and bureaucratic, lacking personal responses, because dealing with the complex effects of social stresses requires dealing in a human way with individual personal consequences. Concern with individuality through interpersonal caring and professions such as social work is not Darwinist individualisation, but human responsiveness. Countries that only offer individualised help limit the flexibility of the collective possibilities for individuality in responding to a need that social work offers.

Many economic systems see commodified, monetised social work only as a way of imposing political objectives through individualised help. Doing this misses out the education approach of social pedagogy, the collective approaches of community work and social development, social work's engagement with the creative traditional ideas of indigenous models of practice and the importance of empowering advocacy and co-production in giving people agency and voice. Also, the availability of social work offers important services that enhance people's security and the social functioning of any society. Examples are safeguarding children and adults, adoption and foster care, assessment and service provision for people at difficult phases of their lifecourse and the end of life, and people with disabilities, those who are mentally ill and older people.

Alternative understandings of economics

Liberal, libertarian and neoliberal ideas are widely touted, but not universally accepted. They are not only about economic matters, not inevitable products of some iron law of economic interaction, but primarily implement particular moral and political views. Chang (2014) puts forward a number of criticisms, as follows.

Liberal economics assumes individualism, the social Darwinist view that economic decisions, like all decisions, are self-generated by individuals. Most economic decisions are made, however, by governments and by companies' managers in their own financial and organisational interests, not free-thinking owners and shareholders. Employees also have very little freedom of action as individuals. Economic rationalism, assuming that economic decisions are based on objective financial information, is vitiated by complexities in collecting and understanding information. They are also compromised by value judgements, such as the exclusion of caring and domestic work, often done unpaid by women, from the calculations.

Another problem is that liberalism, by concentrating on productivity, neglects the effective use of natural planetary resources. It fails to think about the value of what is produced and waste that comes from growth and production. Is manufacturing and marketing unhealthy food as valuable as contributing, through counselling, social pedagogy and social work, to people's healthy personal relationships, for example? By being concerned only with profit and productivity when it thinks about work, the international financial system also neglects the work's health and social value; having employment keeps people healthy and engaged in relationships within society. But the economic system creates cycles in which unemployment is used to manage economic change, demanding a system that devalues human and social objectives. During economic downturns people are thrown out of work to maintain the productivity and profits of businesses, another form of waste. The system encourages the creation of insecure jobs which mean that businesses can be organised flexibly, but workers and their families suffer from insecurity, and sometimes consequential family relationship and mental health problems, waste again, which has to be repaired using social capital, including the skills of commitment of social workers. Social structures in society bear the cost of those problems, not the businesses that create them.

Chang (2014, pp 277–319) suggests that another issue arises with the banking and financial systems. Traditionally, these allowed people to save their money securely, gaining interest payments, with the bank earning income by lending the money they collected to people who needed it. In some cases, they needed it to start and run businesses to help the economy and its productivity. Also, people borrowed from the bank to overcome temporary difficulties in their lives. Increasingly, though, banks make more profit by dreaming up complicated ways of organising international flows of finance for big businesses and governments. This makes the international financial system very powerful, but more unstable and liable to crises, and this in turn leads to periods of insecurity for ordinary people and disrupts financial flows in the economy. But because large profits are made through unnecessary financial manipulation, organisations in the financial system resist regulation to prevent these disruptions.

Similar effects come from inequality and poverty. Liberal economics argues that people need an incentive to work, even though the evidence is that employment, and the social ties that result from it, is very much valued by most people. Following from the incentive argument, liberal economics argues that generous returns to business and political leaders incentivise them to make the economy more effective. This then leads to higher levels of inequality in the economy. But inequality is, as discussed earlier in this chapter, damaging to the economy, morally unacceptable and unnecessary for economic growth. First, most of what economically successful people earn comes from luck and the support of their family and social milieu, not from their work effort; Rishi Sunak, former UK prime minister, and Donald Trump, former US president, started out by gaining their riches through marriage and inheritance, respectively. Second, if there are too many inequalities in a society, it cannot function as a community in which people feel valued and can participate. Third, inequality undermines democracy, because the rich buy political influence and the poor cannot. Fourth, equal societies can grow more successfully than unequal ones. There is evidence, for example in 1980s Japan, South Korea and Taiwan, that countries with low inequalities can grow successfully. Finland, a very equal country, grew much faster than the very unequal US from 1960–2010 (Chang, 2014, p 322).

Economic growth assumptions and monetisation

One of the important criticisms of conventional economic thinking is the importance given to economic growth as the major foundation for any economy's performance, and therefore, according to the 'materialist tradition' for paying the costs of its social provision. According to this view, wealth has to be created before it can be shared. Economic growth is usually measured internationally by the gross domestic product (GDP) of a country; this figure adds up all the value of everything produced in an economy. If GDP increases in a year, the economy has grown, increased in size, and so there is more money available in that economy, and the people who are part of the economy are richer. The liberal argument, therefore, is that economic growth benefits all parts of the economy.

The evidence, however, is that wealth does not trickle down from economic successes, if it is left to the market. It has to be planned for and organised and that requires government to decide to redistribute riches, of income or of wealth. Since the 1980s, there has been growing inequality because a high proportion of income and wealth has been passed upwards to the rich, but investment from them has stagnated. The relative size of the economy of many countries has increased but not most people's share of that wealth (Chang, 2010, pp 137–47). Part of the reason is that unregulated markets can be manipulated by the people who manage the organisations within them (Chang, 2010, pp 148–56). In social agencies, managers cannot annexe a high proportion of the income, because their income is controlled by donors to third sector organisations and voters for public organisations. But in business organisations, managers set the rewards for employees, not the owners of the business, the shareholders. US managers, particularly, are overpriced compared with historical comparators and other countries (Chang, 2010, pp 148–9). In globalised companies, this has increased income and wealth going to the rich more widely. The increasing size of global companies makes them more cautious and controlling and less entrepreneurial, while smaller companies and economies are often more entrepreneurial, but have less control of the global market.

Marketisation is an element of libertarian and neoliberal thinking, in which services provided in the public sector of the economy are moved towards competing in a market system of provision, without necessarily privatising them by shifting them into private companies. Quasi-markets organise public service to gain the claimed benefits of cost-restraint and quality improvement provided by competition between providers in a market in the 'little stalls on the street' market metaphor (Le Grand & Bartlett, 1993). Mechanisms are established to mimic purchasing and providing in a market, and to regulate the market processes. The UK social care system was established as a quasi-market during the mid-1990s, including care management, and self-directed care (see Chapter 4). Another possibility is 'market testing', to see whether outcomes and service costs are equivalent to those in a private company. All these arrangements provide alternatives to public provision, but the result is not necessarily an economic market. Market competition may lead to fragmentation of provision among competing providers, and driving prices down through competition may lead to poorly understood reductions in quality.

One objection to the priority that economic thinking gives to economic growth is that it ignores the social, all the issues in society that social work is concerned with. The emphasis on economic growth monetises everything. I have already discussed how damaging this is to social relations. The only thing that is valued is more money, and people being happier, healthier or having better social relations is not counted. It also emphasises commercial activity and the production of physical goods rather than social progress or stability, or the social cohesion that comes from caring activities (Lynch, Baker, Lyons et al, 2009).

There are some answers to this sort of criticism from social work's point of view. First, since, as we have seen, social work is part of the economy, it is important to understand that it is also part of the GDP, so growth in social work is growth that will be measured in GDP statistics. More and better social work is more productive and contributes to a better GDP. Second, including social provision in the GDP does not mean exploiting the social work workforce. GDP rises if there are increases in productivity, but most increases in productivity come from improvements in education and technology. As a result, better social work education making social workers more effective in their work, and better computerisation of social care services means improved productivity. Better social work education means practitioners are better able to prevent children being abused or help mentally ill people make more of their lives. Clunky computer programs in social work replaced by useful information and communication technology means social work contributes better to the economy. More sensitive caring in care homes or community settings means an improved economy.

Carney (2021, p 128) argues that the value of altruism, caring, generosity and solidarity are not, like commodities and money, in fixed supply, not depleted by use. Rather they are enhanced by being used in community and social relationships. Caring and social concern experienced now lead people to offer caring and social concern in the future. Caring bought with money stops when the money runs out.

Poverty and social exclusion

Poverty is lack of access to the resources to participate equally in the economic cycle and, therefore, in society. I say 'therefore' because human societies all incorporate economic cycles, so not being significant economically implies social exclusion. Poverty is difficult to measure and to understand, because it is more than lack of money and affects not only individuals but also their communities, families and social groups and networks, and this varies over time during individuals' and families' lifetimes. For example, a baby cannot produce but must consume although also contributing happiness to parents and possibilities for the future: money does not measure the value of that happiness and future productivity. Another example, an older person, who may not be able to produce because of increasing disability and ill-health, must still consume, but may contribute to family and community relationships in general or by grandparent care, and by providing social opportunities for others to care, or they may have contributed in the past. Some people may not be productive, judged by financial measures, therefore, but are nevertheless social contributors.

Poverty has been widespread throughout history, and globally one in five people still live in absolute poverty, and one in six people in rich countries live in relative poverty, that is poverty compared with what is considered a decent standard of living in their country. Since poverty rates vary a great deal, it must be possible for unequal countries to intervene to improve poverty, since this has been successfully achieved in many Nordic countries (Chang, 2014, pp 317–43).

Two broad explanations of poverty are as follows:

- Structural explanations see poverty as the product of the way societies are organised, so that poverty derives from external or environmental factors. These may be economic factors, such as the stage of the economic cycle, the cost of living, labour market conditions, or the consequences of the political philosophy that underlies important political decisions. There may also be events affecting a large area and its population, such as disasters, floods, fires, storms, affecting a community, or affecting a family. Social provision to combat these broad factors in any society may be inadequate or increase precariousness of lifestyle for individuals and families.
- Individual theories explain poverty as the product of individuals, families and perhaps communities, the outcome of their choices and actions. This was often the assumption of the social systems of the nineteenth century from which social work emerged, but was rejected by the political changes leading to welfare states.

Social work has always had a close connection with poverty. Early on, it sought to alleviate the individual and social consequences of financial impoverishment. Social development now focuses on poverty alleviation as an important aim (Patel, 2015). Important social provision to deal with poverty may not involve social work in many countries, but often leads social work to contribute to helping, control, social justice and support social work actions. Broader social provision includes providing both private and public insurance against disability, sickness and unemployment, and financial benefits to smooth consumption. Examples are family allowances and other benefits targeted at the costs of childrearing and retirement. These benefits shift income within the life cycle from stages of life where people have surplus income, during periods of employment for example, to periods when they cannot cover costs of living, during childrearing and retirement. They also shift income between social groups, from people with surplus income to people in various forms of poverty. Education, healthcare and housing may also be subsidised or provided free of charge.

Martinussen (1997), examining social development strategies, discussed the interaction of cycles of economic poverty interacting with political poverty. Economic poverty leaves people with little purchasing power, with the consequences that they are poorly nourished, have poor standards of housing and poor health together with poor education, so that people in poverty have erratic involvement and low productivity in the economic system, and their low income is perpetuated. Their poverty excludes them from many social relationships; they are divided from people with more resources, have little access to, and low power within, decision-making processes in society, leading to a poor understanding of options that might be available to them. Consequently, people in poverty have difficulty in organising themselves and so become politically passive, losing more influence. Poverty alleviation, as the most important social development strategy, involves practices that increase people's engagement with communities and networks important to them, so that they can reduce their political poverty and begin to have an influence by responding to economic poverty.

Enhancing capability

An alternative approach to economics, Sen's (1993) capability approach, is another perspective that questions traditional economic approaches to value. In this view, developing human capabilities and wellbeing, not financial outcomes, should be at the centre of economic output. This approach to social work emphasises European-style social education and social pedagogy, rather than the Anglophone social assistance, care and treatment approach.

Den Braber (2013) argues that the capability approach is consistent with social work values: actions should be evaluated according to the extent to which they expand people's freedom to enjoy being and doing what they most value. This would imply investment in social education and improvements, and evaluation and research should focus on the extent to which an organization or policy improves human capabilities rather than increasing economic production. Den Braber's example is youth unemployment: if young people's contributions are devalued by commercial and industrial production priorities, the risk of alienation and social unrest rises, leading to poor productivity. Valuing and improving social capabilities through positive social education thus contributes both to human development and also to economic productivity.

This also has implications for management processes, both generally and also in social care and social work services. If the main purpose of management is control on behalf of economic and political drivers, it fails to develop the contribution and skills of devalued workers, and alienates both employees and service users. More productive management, and more effective social work and social care services aim to facilitate the development of effective practice and objectives defined by groups of practitioners listening to and working with clients and carers building on self-defined values and objectives.

Hendriks and van Ewijk's (2017) study of Moroccan and Turkish Islamic women social workers in the Netherlands uses capability ideas to illustrate the same point applied to migrant workers with different spiritual values from the dominant Christian and secular ethos of Dutch society. Their Islamic spiritual identity was important to them, but there were conflicts between the cultural expectations of their home environment and former country, on the one hand, and those of their adopted country, on the other. For example, although both Dutch and Islamic values emphasised gender equality, the values of their former country and family privileged men's interests. In social situations, they experienced these clashes of values as sometimes constraints and sometimes aspirations which gave them objectives, opportunities and resources to bring together some elements of their identity and reduce the impact of other parts of the values that influenced them. Sen's capabilities approach suggests that social workers helping with such issues would aim to increase the opportunities for choice and decision making for both the practitioner and the client. Similarly, their agencies and managers should be facilitating transparent choices to enable practitioners to practise flexibly.

Making moral and social choices

Because economics deals with individual and collective choices, I have noted in this account that it inevitably reflects the values of the people making the choices, their moral views. Liberal views of economics assume that individuals will make rational economic choices according to self-interest. But broad policy choices are made collectively through public debate about evidence and information, and enshrined in collective decision-making processes, such as voting in elections. Sen (2017, pp 39–40) illustrated this by his studies of famines. He observed that famines never occur in countries, poor or rich, which have multiparty democracies with regular elections and a free press. This is because famines do not directly affect the wellbeing of dictators and the ruling classes in undemocratic countries unless their rule is threatened. Famines are preventable, with only a small proportion of the food and income and the population affected, so stopping them from becoming troublesome is actually quite easy economically and cheap for political action to achieve. Thus, facing public criticism and regular encounters with the electorate means that urgent action to deal with famines in such societies is always taken and the economic consequences are dealt with. Sen considers this to be evidence that people are not invariably and completely self-centred; they take account of others' misery and social distress in making their decisions. Democrats and the owners of a free press know that they do and take account of it.

When people make economic decisions, therefore, they make social as well as individual choices, based on their moral ideals, and they balance the individual with the social. Monetised economic thinking, based on individualised, social Darwinist ideas, on the other hand, puts forward a populist economics claiming to speak on behalf of ordinary people, but not representing their true values.

Social work's economic roles

Social work makes important contributions to any economy. First, it enables an economy to tackle the social determinants of need that arise from inequality. In the next section, I use the example of the global struggle to confront the social determinants of health as an example. Social provision often gives priority to political and social autonomy and freedom and to healthcare because, without these, human beings cannot respond to the challenges of achieving wellbeing and survival. But these great priorities are unachievable without the contribution of many aspects of social provision, including social care and social work (Doyal & Gough, 1991). Gough (2017) argues, regarding the economic and social risks of climate change, that poverty and exclusion from opportunities to build worthwhile lives are a threat multiplier. Fail to achieve greater equality, fail to secure health and social wellbeing, and it becomes harder to tackle the serious threats to the environment. Second, social work is part of and contributes to any economy, so it has the potential to enhance that economy; it is neither a separate aspect of society nor a drag on business and the economy.

Social determinants of health and of need for social care and social work

An important area of social progress globally, and in European countries and the UK, is preventive public health. It exemplifies how social factors that social workers work with are directly relevant to important social policy objectives and to reducing inequalities. Although administrative boundaries mean that social work is sometimes seen as separate and less important than healthcare or housing its practice is directly implicated in everything that societies seek to undertake in these areas. This is true of the individualistic problem-centred work of European/US social work and of the practice of social pedagogy and social development, as well as the insights of critical and indigenous practice.

Issues about the social determinants of ill-health particularly affect social work service users. This refers to worldwide and British research (WHO, 2008; Marmot Review, 2010) suggesting that there is a social gradient of health inequalities in which richer people who are more in control of their lives and work are healthier for longer than poorer people. The poorer you are, the more likely it is that you will suffer from more disabling serious health problems in later life.

A WHO analysis of these determinants (Solar & Irwin, 2010, p 6) divides them into three categories.

- Socioeconomic and political context:
  - governance
  - macroeconomic policies
  - social policies for the labour market, housing and land
  - public policies for education, health and social protection
  - culture and societal values
- Socioeconomic position:
  - social class, gender, ethnicity and race
  - education, occupation, income
- Social cohesion and social capital, interacting with the health system, affected by:
  - material circumstances, living and working conditions, food availability
  - behaviours and biological factors
  - psychosocial factors

In combination, these are found to influence equity in health and wellbeing. Comparing the social determinants of health with the analysis of social work practice in this book indicates that preventive healthcare globally and locally corresponds directly with the issues that social workers deal with in all aspects of their practice. Social work practice, therefore, is relevant to many of the actions proposed to respond to these issues. Pursuing social cohesion and social capital through social work is crucial to responding to inequalities in health in any population. Policies on work, housing and land supply, education, health and social protection are all relevant to good social work as well as to social progress in public policy.

A subsequently published scoping review of the literature on barriers to equity and access to healthcare (De Paz, Valentine, Hosseinpoor et al, 2017) lists a range of social barriers to universal access to health. Among them are:

- Cross-sectoral platforms for a participatory approach to public service provision.
- Robustness of anti-discrimination, minority and migrant inclusion policies and legislation on the right to health.
- Women's empowerment and gender equality legislation, advocacy and social initiatives.

Again, the responses to economic inequalities that lead directly to adverse health consequences are directly relevant to social work aims and practice.

Social care and social work contribute to the economy

Social care and social work are not a drag on the economy, as libertarian or neoliberal opinion sometimes claim; they are part of and contribute to the economy. In the same way that they are integral to achieving important social policy objectives such as removing barriers to equity in healthcare, they are also relevant to all aspects of the economy because they are part of the economy.

As an example of the kind of evidence available, this section summarises a study of the role of adult social care in the UK economy. Although it covers the whole UK, it also compares the economic value of social care and social work in the four national economies, England, Northern Ireland, Scotland and Wales (ICF Consulting, 2018). Such studies indicate that, in any country, social work and social services are a substantial part of the economy.

The study found that in 2016 adult social care was provided on 45,000 sites, mostly residential care facilities. A further 72,000 individuals received direct payments enabling them to receive services in their home and employ personal assistants to help them. About 1.6 million people (1.2 million full-time equivalents [FTEs]) were employed, mostly in providing domiciliary care, plus 151,300 jobs (69,500 FTEs) created by people employing personal assistants. This represented 6 per cent of the total employment in the UK. The gross value added (GVA) to the economy was £24.3 billion, mostly in domiciliary care (£7.6 billion, 31 per cent), representing 1.4 per cent of the GVA by employment in the UK. The average level of productivity (GVA per FTE) was £19,700; the average earnings of employees was £17,300, so their work contributed more than they were paid.

All that work had indirect effects on the economy because the services bought goods and services to do their work. This contributed about 603,500 jobs (424,800 FTE) and £10.8 billion GVA to the economy. It also had 'induced' effects because people directly and indirectly employed in adult social care contributed about 215,300 jobs (176,100 FTE) and £11.1 billion of GVA to the economy, for example from shopping.

Totalling it all up, the direct, indirect and induced value of adult social care to the UK economy was about 2.6 million jobs (1.8 million FTE) and £46.2 billion. Since the study, the size of the workforce has increased: in 2021/22, the adult social care sector contributed 1.79 million jobs, with 1.5 million working in adult social care, more than in the UK National Health Service (Skills for Care, 2022).

Similar information is not available for children's social care and social work, but 2021 statistics identified 32,502 child and family social workers in England employed by local government, and 5,977 agency workers (Department for Education, 2022). Many more will have been employed in residential and other social care settings. In addition, social workers and other social care staff were employed in private and third sector agencies, working in the Education Welfare Service and youth offending. While the children's social care and social work sector is smaller, it adds to the picture of a substantial contribution to and participation in the economy. As with adult social care, there are also indirect and induced effects on the whole economy.

Conclusion

This chapter has focused on the economic value of social care and social work, as part of the political economy. There are different views about how we should see the role of the economy in the political structures and the choices that any society has to make. Concentrating on the market and money economies devalues humanity and degrades the importance of the social in political decision making. I have argued throughout this book that social work represents the organised contribution of the human and social in local, regional, national and international society. We need to value the human and social capital that emerges from our society and understand how social care and social work make their own contributions as part of the commitment to human and social value.

Action on an economic position for social work

Economics should measure and value, not monetised growth and profit, but human solidarity and social capital for people in every social group, and should recognise social work's economic contribution to human potential and economic growth.

The next chapters ...

... explore what people and societies expect from social provision and social work, now (Chapter 11) and in the future (Chapter 12).

11

Views of social work

One challenge to social work is other people's views of it, particularly the views of the public and service users. After the expansion of Western social work in mid-twentieth-century welfare states, there was criticism that it was self-regarding, that its own analysis of its practice and its work made it self-evidently a good thing. It failed to develop a realistic critical self-examination. This critique had several elements:

- Public views of social provision were mixed and perhaps hostile. Neoliberal economic and political values devalued public social provision and gave greater salience to ideas about risk (see Chapters 9–10). So, was social work worthwhile? Did it really prevent or solve social problems? Or was social work simply a target of political views devaluing social provision?
- Did people using the services find it useful in meeting their needs? This led to more self-examination and, particularly, the development of the critical streams of thought discussed in Chapter 5. Social policy analysis of perceptions of social provision also emerged: were welfare states really worthwhile?
- Did research show social work to be effective, and for what purposes? 'Yes' is the answer from developing empirical research generally, and particularly consumer and effectiveness research.

This chapter explores some evidence about these issues. There has been a general consumer movement since the mid-twentieth century, which has also informed social care services and social work. Analysis and research about public perceptions of these and other services have demonstrated that broader public views are multifaceted and affected by a wide range of attitudes and factors. Public reaction to the COVID-19 pandemic of 2020–22 is an example of an event, recent at the time of writing, that affected broad attitudes to and perceptions of social provision and also understanding of aspects of social care and social work (Buzelli, Cameron & Gardner, 2022); to some extent, this overtook attitudes generated by previous events and experiences noted in earlier research. Another complexity in research in the UK is the overbearing emphasis of government, political and public interest in the NHS, and the policy of referring to 'health and social care' when there is very little coverage of information about social care. There is minimal coverage of social care, for example, in regular government surveys of public opinion, and social work remains completely absent (Ipsos/MORI, 2017).

Generally, however, over the years social work has built up evaluation and participation, integrated within its services, not only of its outcomes but of its process. While it does not neglect the demands of economic and productive effectiveness, social work wants more for humanity in how its practice affects the people it works with. Research is beginning to confirm the social value of its practice, better understanding and more of it is needed.

The picture of general understanding of public response and service user responses to and understanding of social care and social work, however, remains consistent both in the UK and more globally; I look at some studies in more detail later in this chapter. It suggests that the public is not well-informed about social provision and social work, but in principle regards the social as a valuable element of the range of services available. People understand that the social is important, unlike individualist economics and politics tainted by social Darwinism. Chapter 9 noted that theories of need acknowledge the overwhelming priority given to economic and political freedom and personal autonomy and healthcare, even though these depend substantially on other forms of social provision. While people would avoid social work for themselves, therefore, because receiving attention from social workers is stigmatised, reduces people's self-esteem and risks devaluing them in others' perceptions, they nevertheless value the fact that it is there.

People who have had personal contact with social care and social work are better informed and often positive about the services they received, particularly if it was holistic, involving, practical, respectful and well-informed. People are less likely to be positive when it is part of authoritative actions and involves interfering, surveillance or compulsory acts. This is particularly so when rich and secure people supervise poor and precarious people. Social policy research into public social provision shows that attitudes are also informed by a sense of moral appropriateness; people must be deserving of care and help. Surveys in four European countries (van Oorschot, 2006) found that Europeans have similar views about deservingness: older people are seen as most deserving, closely followed by sick and disabled people; unemployed people are seen as less deserving and immigrants as least deserving of all. Support for setting conditions for receiving welfare benefits is greater in poorer countries, where unemployment is low and where people have less trust in fellow citizens and in state institutions.

In this chapter, I argue that the message of both public and service users' views of social work supports the direction of social work thinking. People value the social humanity of social work's practice. The intrusiveness of official actions is acknowledged as necessary, but it has to be involving and respectful. This reinforces the social work movement towards co-production. The public's moral evaluation of social work, however, suggests that social workers must distinguish between the moral valuation of the aims of their work and the professional requirement of respect and self-determination. Keeping this balance enables social workers to engage in alliance with their clients, families and communities while respecting moral responsibility in the public view of their social role.

Attitudes to welfare states and social service provision

An important context of public views of social care and social work is attitudes to social provision in general, and this is often taken up in studies of retrenchment in European welfare states. The conventional liberal assumption is that self-interest means that people most likely to benefit from welfare spending are more likely to support it, whereas people who are likely to contribute most are less likely to do so. Individuals' ideological positions about the proper relationship between citizens, the state and other institutions, however, also have influence on what people think. Political partisanship, economic individualism and gender role attitudes are also relevant. The general policy climate, discourse about social provision, how issues are framed in political discourse and the economic and social conditions of a particular society affect attitudes (Chung, Taylor-Gooby & Leruth, 2018, p 2).

Case examples: social attitudes and social provision

The following case examples are illustrations of research on social attitudes in various contexts to social provision in general. These sometimes complex attitudes broadly indicate that people favour social provision for citizens in need of help, social development and support.

Experiencing economic pressure

Blekesaune (2013) studied support for redistribution via the tax system in 28 European countries, and found that individuals who experienced economic pressures in their lives and those living in countries experiencing economic pressures were more likely to support redistribution than where there was little experience of economic pressures. This illustrates how experience of social need in families and communities leads people to realise the importance of the social.

Health and scrutiny of welfare benefits

In a comparative study of the effect of German, UK and US unemployment benefits on health status, Rodriguez (2001) found that means-tested benefits, as opposed to contributory benefits received as of right, did not compensate for factors leading to poor health during periods of unemployment. This was because of the stress of stigma arising from the official scrutiny of welfare benefit provisions.

'Work ethic' and welfare benefits

Important commentary by writers such as Lindbeck (1995a, 1995b) have proposed that generous social benefits degrade the 'work ethic' among people who benefit from them, and that damages the economy. The implication is that if a welfare state or social work service helps people to become scroungers on the generosity of others rather than relying on their own efforts to work for an income, they will reduce the productivity of an economy because they take wealth from it, rather than contribute wealth to it. The 'work norms' debate, however, is irrelevant to social work, even if, which is doubtful, it applies to broad social benefits. Social work in most countries is irrelevant to employment, since it mainly deals with social problems among children and families requiring action or vulnerable groups such as disabled, elderly or sick people whose access to employment is in any case minimal. Helping people with the sorts of problems that social work deals with helps them to live more successful lives contributing to the economy and society.

Women's caring labour

Evans (2022) discusses how mothers relying on welfare benefits are stigmatised as 'bad mothers', with benefits seen as undeserved, devaluing their caring labour. Jun's (2022) study showed how single mothers on welfare benefits were stigmatised by the framing of the political discourse in the UK arguing for activating them to move into paid work. The mothers saw themselves as failed workers and citizens, rather than as struggling mothers trying to support their children. They internalised feelings of shame, adversely affecting family and other social relationships.

Legitimation of social provision

Studies in general suggest that the factors that affect people's decisions are complex, and providing or rolling back social provision does not have strong effects either way. As with the case examples on attitudes to mothers' caring roles, and to the health consequences of means-tested rather than contributory unemployment benefits, attitudes to work and their social consequences are important. Corneo (2012) studied attitudes to work in four groups of countries, Anglo-Saxon, Nordic, continental European and Southern European countries covering the period 1981–2008, finding that increases in social expenditure led either to a stronger work ethic or to a minor reduction in commitment to work. Comparing groups of countries with different levels of social expenditure, he found that public belief in hard work and social expenditure were negatively correlated; generous social expenditure led to a stronger belief in hard work. He also studied work ethic at different stages in life and for different levels of income. People with a strong commitment to hard work and who strongly felt that it was humiliating to receive social welfare 'handouts' were often in lower income groups, but so also were some people with less commitment to work. Explanations for this might include that if you are poorly paid, believing in hard work will not increase your income, or some poorly paid people belong to a social group that rejects hard work, preferring to accept a less secure life.

Lynch and Lyons (2009, p 54) draw attention to the 'materialist tradition' of liberal political ideas which defines work as primarily concerned with economic productivity (see Chapter 10) and the 'phenomenological tradition' that I argued for in Chapter 10, of seeing work as being about individual cultivation and self-fulfilment. Materialist views neglect socially valuable work which may not always be economically or psychologically productive, but is socially productive in achieving social cohesion through caring and nurturing. Caring for your child or frail parent at home may be experienced as personally fulfilling, or it may be that it's frustrating and isolating, but it is still recognised as socially valuable.

Social work's aims (see Chapter 2), practice (see Chapters 3–5) and agencies (see Chapters 6–8) are part of this social productivity. But it is not recognised until it is absent: when a child is not cared for, when the economy cannot find enough workers because they are prioritising caring. Lynch, Baker, Lyons et al (2009) therefore argue that, among the equalities that societies must achieve, is affective equality. Caring, love and relationships should be available to everyone, because all human beings need them.

Roosma's (2016) extensive comparative study frames the issue as one of 'social legitimation', suggesting that to be accepted as legitimate, state social provision needs legitimate institutions. These offer:

- substantive justice, for example concerning the goals of social provision, the range of policies and the degree of spending;
- distributional justice, concerning who pays and who benefits;
- procedural justice around efficient implementation and appropriate targeting;
- just outcomes, including intended and unintended consequences.

These arguments are important to social workers, because social work practice concerned with effective social justice can make a difference to the perceived efficiency and fairness of social provision. And arguing for being concerned with fairness and clients' wellbeing also makes a difference. Kootstra and Roosma's (2018) experimental study in the Netherlands and the UK explored public support for welfare sanctions applied to unemployed people who do not want to accept jobs with wages or skill levels lower than their previous jobs. They found that public support for welfare sanctions was high in both countries, more persistent in the UK than in the Netherlands. Arguments that the policy should be opposed, however, reduce support for sanctions more than arguments in favour of it. Moral arguments, considering unemployed people's wellbeing, were more effective than economic arguments about reducing welfare spending and taxation. People with strong political commitment, higher education and men are less likely to change opinions favouring the policy after being confronted with counterarguments.

Studies of attitudes to inequality, which have been increasing in many countries, including the UK, in recent decades, also suggest considerable complexity. For example, some recent research suggests that as inequality increases, there is growing tolerance of inequality (Mijs, 2021). This appears to be because people have come to accept the neoliberal argument that people have gained their riches through meritocratic social policies, the merit of hard successful work, and the losers are to blame for their lack of effort. Chapter 10, on the other hand, noted research showing that extreme inequality damages economic growth and social relations and creates social instability. Mijs (2021) argues that where inequality is greater, poorer and wealthier people have less contact with each other. Because of that, people often do not see the unfairness of the effects and misunderstand the social effects of the inequalities. Bartram (2023), in a later study covering a larger number of countries, refines this analysis. Media presentations of the gap between the worst-off and best-off exaggerate the picture, while in particular localities, people do not experience such wide discrepancies in wealth. They see people in their social circle who make personal economic progress because of merit and hard work, so they continue to accept that merit still brings rewards. If they experienced the whole-society effects of inequality, they would more easily see that merit often does not bring appropriate rewards.

One of the important issues for social workers is whether people are prepared to pay for their own care for long-term conditions, particularly in old age, where, as in the UK, they will substantially have to pay for services themselves. The regular English government survey of attitudes to NHS and social care services (Ipsos/MORI, 2017) suggests that most people do not expect to pay the cost of social care, particularly in old age. This is because they are misled by a general expectation that social care will be paid for, based on the fact that healthcare treatment is paid for out of general taxation.

Complexities in attitude towards social provision, including social work, thus, comes about in many cases because personal social experience does not help people to understand the practical consequences of economic and political policies and the attitudes that inform them. In the case of social work, educated people, who have understood broader evidence about social inequalities and need, are more accepting of the principles underlying social provision. On the other hand, receiving social work help remains stigmatised by more general moralistic views that people should merit social help in some way. Evidence of views about social work, however, is also influenced by personal knowledge. The next section reviews the evidence that people who have experienced it value social work more highly than people who have not, even though in some cases, they disliked the social work actions and decisions affecting themselves.

Views of social work

Client and consumer views

Because general discourse about social provision has an important impact on its legitimacy and in particular on the debate between economic concerns about the 'fiscal crisis of the welfare state', discussed in Chapter 9, this must also be true about discourse around social work and its value. In this section, I explore some of the research published in the twenty-first century about attitudes to social work.

A useful starting point is Penhale & Young's (2015) review of the literature on public and service users' views in England about the conduct and competence of social workers. They found that few members of the public were aware of current regulation or standards of conduct of social workers, although they assumed it was there. An important theme of their views was 'putting the person first', providing support services that enable people to be involved in decision making and achieving their agenda, a view that supports co-production and similar practices. Social workers' personal qualities should include courtesy, integrity, honesty, trustworthiness, openness, respect, compassion, reliability, reassurance, empathy and warmth. Maintaining confidentiality, fairness, awareness of cultural and religious difference and clear communication in English was valued. People wanted practitioners to inspire confidence, be empowering, enable people to make choices, be non-discriminatory, non-judgemental, informal and flexible. They wanted continuity in relationships and service, to get clear, up-to-date, factual and comprehensive information and expert, targeted, holistic and efficient help. All this shows that how the agency organises practice is as important as how social workers practise.

A small focus group study by Research Works (2001), one of the studies covered by Penhale & Young's (2015) review, was undertaken because of concerns about recruitment to social work education and a shortage of qualified social workers. Public perception of social work was found to be unfavourable for two reasons:

- Social workers dealt with intractable situations involving unpleasant issues and disapproved people, in particular child abuse.
- They were seen as hemmed in by large workloads and bureaucratic procedures.

Respondents were not well informed about social care or social work, some working-class participants more so, but some of these were concerned about the intrusiveness of social work actions in people's lives (see Chapter 3). Public perception of social care, as opposed to social work, was that it consisted of mainly practical tasks caring for elderly people, carried out by women. Both social care and social work roles were seen as stressful, difficult and unpleasant, requiring a sense of vocation.

Wiffin (2010), in another study covered in Penhale & Young's (2015) review, contributes to understanding situations where social workers take authoritative action. It was a focus group study of family members receiving child protection services. Service users recognised that individual social workers had a hard job, and 'most had good intentions towards families and were focused on helping their children, but they were less sure they were focused on helping them, as family members' (Wiffin, 2010, p 9). Many experienced poverty throughout their lives and could not get help with this from social work services, despite the historical importance given to this issue in social work thinking. They had often been involved with social workers when they were children, as well as being involved because of their own children. Having to accept social work involvement adversely affected their self-esteem, and they disliked feeling judged. 'This mother felt that having spent years asking for support [for her poverty], she suddenly found herself under the spotlight as an uncaring mother' (Wiffin, 2010, p 22). This suggests that broad responsiveness to need is often appreciated more than targeted help, which is intrusive or controlling.

Another important source of consumer opinion is studies of service user views, and analysis of views of palliative care services (Beresford, Adshead &

Croft, 2007) also part of Penhale & Young's (2015) review, helpfully explores practice in a healthcare setting characterised by a more therapeutic milieu. Here people most valued the personal qualities of practitioners and their relationship with social workers, with elements of friendship, openness and not too much professional distance. Good listening, being facilitated to set your own agenda and pace, and feeling respected and not judged were important aspects of the more valued professional approach. Availability, accessibility, ability to offer time, continuity of support and reliability were important, as were making home visits and being responsive to the needs of the people involved.

The most influential source of user views derives from the mental health service users' or recovery movements, deriving from activist survivor or ex-patient movements of the late twentieth century in the US (Adame & Leitner, 2008). Many Western governments, including Ireland, New Zealand, the UK and the US, developed policies favouring recovery in the twenty-first century (Watts & Higgins, 2017). Recovery perspectives focus on the whole life experiences of people with mental illnesses and social and community reactions to changes in their wellness and illness. The aim is to find ways of accepting and overcoming social disabilities created by the condition (Deegan, 1988). This includes both short-term and longer-term disabling factors in the personal psychological reactions, social life and relationships of people who have experienced mental illness. These areas all form relevant locations for social work practice. Leamy, Bird, Le Boutillier et al's (2011) conceptual review of the literature isolates characteristics of the recovery journey from a wide range of literature. Recovery is an active, individual, gradual and non-linear process of trial and error, a journey in which there are stages and much struggle, multidimensional in the issues tackled. It is a life-changing but not curative process. Supportive and healing environments help recovery but can occur without professional actions. Again, here, how services are provided by the agency is as important as the professional actions of social workers. Tew, Ramon, Slade et al's (2012) literature review of social factors in recovery from mental illness identified the importance of working with families and communities. They suggested this forms a proactive agenda for mental health practice in social work, which is distinctive compared with clinical and medical interpretations of healthcare practice with mentally ill people.

There is a record of studies of social work users supported by the Scottish government. A Scottish survey by a public opinion polling company (Davidson & King, 2005) found that, while social work had a high public profile, its details were poorly understood and views were multifaceted. People were confused about the differences between social work and wider social provision. While they would approach social work services for disabled and older people and families with serious problems, they would themselves approach social workers for help only if there were no alternatives. Using social work was stigmatised particularly for highly personal issues such as problems with children, alcoholism and drug abuse. People recognised that it was difficult to decide whether to take action in difficult situations and social workers were 'damned if they do and damned if they don't'. Well-known, longstanding problems posing dangers to vulnerable others justified official social work action. Particularly among working-class people, social work was seen as a soft option for problematic young people. Prevention by tackling the causes of problems was more important than sorting out difficulties afterwards. Social work was overburdened, asked to deal with too wide a range of problems, and other agencies should take on some services; particularly, advice on benefits and debt should not be a social work matter.

A later Scottish survey (McCulloch & Webb, 2020) also found a positive view of the role and public value of social services. People with lower levels of education were more doubtful and readers of the quality broadsheet newspapers were more positive than people who read the tabloids. People with direct experience of the social services had the most positive views.

Studies in the US have similar findings. LeCroy & Stinson (2004) found in a telephone survey that people had a positive view of social work, although a more positive view was associated with White women with better educational qualifications. They compared it with a study (Condie, Hanson, Lang et al, 1978) carried out in the 1970s and found little change in many attitudes. Social workers were seen as primarily for working-class people in poverty, but valuable in providing support for people in need. In the 2004 study, social workers were seen as broadly useful with various client groups as other professionals such as nurses, psychiatrists and psychologists. They were more important, however, in child protection and domestic violence.

Olin's (2013) review of US research found, as in the British studies, that there was little awareness of social work, and most people had little idea of social workers' responsibilities, associating social work with media stories about taking children away from their parents. Even intending students had little idea of the range of social work activities (Dennison, Poole & Qaqish, 2007). A survey of newspaper coverage found mainly positive material, treating social workers as experts, with reports of innovations and interesting practice (Reid & Misener, 2001), so perhaps consistent efforts to explain would benefit the profession more broadly.

A well-constructed study of service user views of UK mental health social work (Wilberforce, Abendstern, Batool et al, 2020) found that social workers' holistic focus on the 'whole person' beyond immediate mental health symptoms was most valued. Service users also valued continuity and reliability of support, and did not particularly value social workers acting as a broker or link between services. Since policy research suggests this is useful and effective, perhaps this positive research comes from government and policy makers appreciating social work's ability to overcome the negative aspects of marketised public services, while the public view is that they would rather have a coherent service in the first place. Co-production practice, so that service users understood and were involved in activities affecting them, was thought to make the activities more individualised and person-specific.

A study for Social Work England (Hemmington, Graham, Marshall et al, 2021) explored the views of approved mental health professionals and best interests assessors about their roles, including from people with lived experience of receiving these services. Most people in these roles were social workers, but other professions also undertook it. Some service users preferred social workers because they wanted a 'social model' alternative to the predominantly medical view of healthcare professionals, and because of social workers' knowledge of community resources. Mostly, however, because all the professions involved had similar training, any mental health professional was acceptable. Both patients and nearest relatives valued '… good communication, seeing the human side of the work and not just taking a legalistic approach. Information sharing was a key theme …' (Hemmington, Graham, Marshall et al, 2021, p 118).

The regular English government survey of attitudes to the NHS and social care has only weak coverage of social care, but shows that there is a decline in positive perceptions of both the NHS and social care services, with fewer than half having a positive view (Ipsos/MORI, 2017). A survey of attitudes after the COVID-19 pandemic in the early 2020s shows declining positive views about the availability and standard of both NHS and social care, with particularly strong growth in pessimism about social care. This probably reflects public discourse in the media, which made information about concerns more transparent to public perceptions.

Social work is stressful

There is also evidence suggesting that practising social work may be experienced as stressful, but this often derives from failings in employers' taking responsibility for staff support rather than from the intrinsic nature of the work, which offers many satisfactions. In all work situations, general social support in practitioners' personal lives and in their employment, personal psychological and social resilience and specific organisational responses to particular events can reduce stress (Payne, 2008b). This connects with the discussion in Chapter 6 about the extent to which both organisational requirements for social work practice are met by the agencies that are its organisational contexts, and also to which the economic, political and policy objectives are met by practice.

These issues arise from the research about stress in social work. McFadden, Campbell & Taylor's (2015) systematic survey of literature about stress and burnout in child protection social work, for example, found that it was a stressful occupation. Practitioners often experienced job satisfaction and benefited from a positive coping style, good personal development, qualifying and continuing education, constructive agencies, professional supervision and support, and manageable workloads. On the other hand, defensive organisational cultures, poor social support and unmanageable caseloads increased stress. Lloyd, King and Chenoweth's earlier literature review (2002) found that social workers were more likely than other similar professionals to experience stress and burnout. This was because of a tension between their professional philosophy and work demands and how their agency organised their work environment. Good personal supervision, though, protected them to some degree. A South African study, carried out because of a social worker shortage, found high levels of job satisfaction, but high workloads and difficulty in time management made people feel unproductive and led to feelings of stress and burnout (Calitz, Roux & Strydom, 2014).

Social work research

Research on social work faces the same challenges as social work in societies where an agenda of populist political ideas and economic libertarian thinking controls the discourse. A focus on economic productivity leads to a focus on research productivity; focusing on achieving political outcomes that represent the interests of existing sources of political power and economic power in large rich corporations is unlikely to favour the collective social humanity of community-near co-production espoused by social work practice ideals.

Much early social work research was concerned with describing and understanding the aims and methods of the work that social workers sought to pursue. In the US, Richmond's (1922) *What is social case work?* based on analysis of case records of agencies known to her, Kogan & Hunt's (1954) study of change in social work clients, and Hollis's (1968) typology of social casework are examples. From the 1950s, empirical studies of social work outcomes (Meyer, Borgatta & Jones,1965; Goldberg, Mortimer & Williams, 1970) led to a perception that social work methods were ineffective and to a critique (Fischer, 1976) favouring empirically supported psychological therapies in the Western problem-based interpersonal stream of thought about practice, interpreted for social work (Sheldon, 1987; Macdonald et al, 1992).

Deriving from this work, an influential movement, evidence-aware, evidence-based or evidence-informed practice, grew up within the politics of social work theory to argue for an empiricist approach to knowledge. Such a position supports the view that knowledge comes only from human experience and evidence derived from the senses applied in observation and experimentation, together with reflection and rational deduction from that evidence, and is the basis of research knowledge in the natural sciences. Using empirical practice to inform practice in decision making (Gambrill, 2019) and service provision more generally (for example, McLaughlin & Teater, 2017) and claiming relevance internationally and with a range of types of intervention (Thyer & Kazi, 2004) gained widespread support. Empiricism is contested by rationalism, which argues that knowledge can be developed by analysis and debate based on ideas. There has been a critique of evidence-based practice (Gray, Plath & Webb, 2009; Otto, Polutta & Ziegler, 2009) that generalised knowledge cannot be made applicable within every cultural and ethnic group and service situation and is never specific enough to guide practitioners' decision making and actions in everyday situations or policy decisions about service provision, which is more influenced by political policy.

Alongside this, both agencies and governments pursued many experiments and evaluations both in specific services and with specific client groups.

The development of academic, agency and research infrastructure in the UK has also led to an increasingly rich range of research, validating social work practice, including:

- Agencies for dissemination and reporting of research findings in ways that are relevant for practitioners such as the Social Care Institute for Excellence and the (Scottish) Institute for Research and Innovation in Social Services, including government-supported agencies such as, in the UK, the National Institute for Health and Care Excellence.
- Debate about and then development of financial and institutional support through research funders (Shaw, Arksey & Mullender, 2004).
- A wide range of research-focused journals in addition to an increasing range of broadly based academic social work journals.
- Greater opportunities for research in doctoral and other higher education degrees, in addition to smaller-scale dissertations for bachelor's and master's degree qualifying courses.
- A movement for more practitioner research where social workers examine their own agency, clientele or practice (Broad & Fletcher, 1993; Mitchell, Shaw, & Lunt, 2008).
- Research and evaluation studies in agencies to support and provide accountability for their work.
- Almost every day, continuing work in client studies, building on early work by Mayer and Timms (1970; Phillips, 1983), Rees and Wallace (1982) and Sainsbury, Nixon & Phillips (1982).

A similar picture emerged in Europe, the US and other Western countries, and developments in Asian countries. While research infrastructure and attempts by governments to evaluate and support the productivity of universities have led to an institutionalisation of evaluations of academic research, there are question marks about whether the hegemony of Western academic and governmental processes appropriately represents the cultural and traditional social relations in non-Western countries, particularly in Africa, Asia, many American countries and the Pacific region. Undoubtedly, there is more and greater understanding to come.

The financing of research in social work by governments and research funders more broadly is still very weak, compared with, for example, healthcare. Moreover, in the UK and elsewhere, there is a dichotomy between policy research on behalf of the government and organisations acting in the political and policy space and professional healthcare and social work research. Governments are interested in evaluating the services and infrastructure of social provision. They may also have an interest only in representing present policy lines and selecting research outcomes accordingly. This may particularly be so if they seek to press forward a neoliberal and populist economic and political agenda inimical to the human priorities of social work professional thought. In the UK, each country has a research infrastructure, but health comes first and this reflects global research and financing priorities. An example is both the naming and the website of the National Institute for Health and Care Research (www.nihr.ac.uk). Although it includes 'health and care' using the commonplace omnibus policy term, it devalues in priority any social care and social work agenda; nevertheless, it has generated worthwhile and interesting research on social work.

What this account of the development of research in the West illustrates, however, is an increasing commitment to using human intellectual resources to understand and further develop social work. The direction of movement accepts, through its work on client studies, the need for the engagement of people using these services both in research infrastructure and in having an important role in the co-production of social work education and practice.

Conclusion

Do people want social work? Yes, public views of the value of social provision in general and social work suggest that people as citizens mostly expect and want help with social development and social issues in their society, and are broadly happy with social work being available as part of that. Consumers of social work want it to be a humanised provision that meets their needs and priorities, accepting elements of social control as a difficult but necessary aspect of that. By expanding scholarship as evidence of its effectiveness, social work has shown it produces the results society wants. A strong research and consumer base of support for social work always needs to be maintained and improved.

Action on views of social work and research
Research and evaluation generally make clear that social work is effective and wanted by the people it serves. It supports combining the human and the practical and working through co-production. Shared endeavours among agencies and carers are valued. Bringing together the people served and engaging the professionals who help them benefits both the practice and services that provide it.

In the final chapter ...
... I argue that social work has a future because of its humanity and social engagement.

12

Social work's contribution in the future

Driving for social improvement

I started this book by asking whether social work would exist in a utopia, a perfect world. The answer depended, I argued, on your political and social beliefs. In this book, I have argued for cooperative social relations as natural in any human society and reject competition and conflict as the antithesis of a social humanity.

The argument I have put forward is as follows. A human society always involves social relations. Sociality must be integral to any society's existence and improving social relations is essential both for individuals and for society. Anything other is non-human. The social works analysed in Chapter 2 demonstrate that the concern to improve a society's social relations requires social institutions, including a profession committed to pursuing that endeavour. It is not just a personal and political endeavour to improve society, although that is part of social work's aim. But to seek an improved society, you have to back it up with social workers who are knowledgeable and skilled in social relations and committed to improving them.

Social work practice, discussed in Chapters 3–5, demonstrates how social work contributes through its combination of human actions and practice strategies, drawing on streams of thought relevant to the cultural and social traditions of the societies in which any particular social profession operates. Any context for social work, like the organisations and structures discussed in Chapters 6–8, must drive forward policy and practice for social advancement, and an economics and politics of alliance, collaboration and mutuality, not of competition, monetisation and oppression.

Thinking about the future

We look to the future: what will social work need to do to achieve, demonstrate and enhance social relations? I looked at recent futurology: publications about the next thirty years until 2050, by three eminent writers about social and political issues, Mark Carney, Peter Hennessy and Kathleen Lynch. All three challenge whether capitalist societies can be caring societies, especially if they have authoritarian, libertarian economics and politics.

Both Carney and Hennessy start from the economic, political and social failings revealed by the COVID-19 pandemic of 2020–22. Mark Carney (2021) is a former governor of the banks of Canada and England and an economist; when he wrote his book on values for the future he was the UN Special Envoy for climate action and finance. His book focuses on economic and moral values (see Chapter 10) and argues, looking forward, for three main points of change. The first is that change is needed so the economy is simpler and safer for people to participate in. He says it has become too complex and concerned with producing economic returns of little human value. I would say it has become a non-human economic system, because it does not, in its operation, value human social life. In particular, Carney's second point is that it needs to be reformed to promote greater equality and fairness. The economy, political and social systems will also need to respond to climate change, the third point. This analysis of the future connects with social work's aims: simple and safe structures so that people may participate together in a valuable human life of greater fairness and justice that meets the challenges of the current struggles of humanity in their environment.

The unique contribution of social work services and practice explored in this book similarly rejects the burgeoning complexity of corporate priorities solely for monetary returns. The future requires priority to be given to equal and fair human and social returns on economic and political policies and structures. Social work aims for the security of co-production, whereby individuals and organisations join in solidarity to achieve not just economic growth and money for some, but also growth in holistic human and social capital.

Historian and political commentator Peter Hennessy's (2022) book puts flesh on Carney's vision. He writes about the future of care within the history of welfare in the UK. Perhaps surprisingly, social care is at the top of the list of issues that he thought would be important in the period up to 2050, after the COVID-19 pandemic of 2020–22 (p 132); the others are social housing, technical education, digital literacy and climate change. These issues in politics, he argues, are the basis for a consensus of public support.

What is called 'social care' in the UK is regarded almost everywhere else as social work and the services it provides. As I said in Chapter 9, most academic writing on economics and social policy ignores social care and social work in favour of giving importance to education, healthcare, social security, and sometimes housing; serious journalism is the same. Hennessy (2022, pp 132–8) argues that social care, including social work, is important because the Covid pandemic demonstrated the structural failure of social provision built up since the reforms in the 1940s that created a welfare state in the UK. That failure was worldwide, not only in the UK, because the failure of care systems to provide adequately and safely for older people during the pandemic was a global failure, and arose from ageism within economic and political policy making (Payne, 2022). It came from an economic and social system that bakes in injustice to older people particularly but also to many others suffering oppression and poverty. Similarly, Hennessy says, the failures of all kinds of structures and systems of care come from the denial and denigration of state responsibility for care that we see in libertarian economics and politics. Responsibility for caring should be recognised by giving importance to social work and similar elements of human societies. That is so if we understand social work in its broadest organisation and conception, presented in the first two parts of this book. Furthermore, as in the Covid pandemic experience, failures of the structure of social provision in any country lie at the door of inequality. There is arrant denigration of, discrimination against and ignorance and oppression of people who have care needs while living in poverty.

Social housing is Hennessy's (2022, pp 138–41) next area, declining since the 1980s in the UK, that is essential for effective social justice and social provision in the UK. This is true across the world. Safe shelter is essential for human security, whether for families to bring up children, migrants and refugees, older and disabled people, rough sleepers or street children. To help people successfully, social work relies not only on education and healthcare but also on housing.

Technical education and digital literacy to enhance people's capacity to use increasingly sophisticated communication, computer and information technology will be crucial in the next decades for everyone (Hennessy, 2022, pp 142–5). This is also true for social workers; in the next thirty years, presently unimaginable advances in artificial intelligence and digital technology are bound to contribute to social work's effectiveness. I argued in Chapter 9 that social work's economic contribution to societies depends on enhancing its effectiveness. But technology must not trespass on the human. Social work needs to understand and use technology in a human way to contribute to and strengthen the interpersonal, personal and social experience of using technology.

Finally, Hennessy's fifth point (2022, pp 146–51) is combating and mitigating climate change. He notes that we are living in the Anthropocene era, in which the world is being shaped by human activity. Humanity's duty of care to the environment needs to be at the top of our list of priorities. That ought to be so in social work, but while this is being debated, social work has not yet found a way of including the environment in a practical way in its human and social priorities (Payne, 2023).

The work of Kathleen Lynch and her colleagues (Baker, Lynch, Cantillon et al, 2009; Lynch, Baker, Lyons et al, 2009; Lynch, 2022) focuses on achieving equality in social relations that include 'affective equality'; I have cited it frequently throughout this book. Lynch is professor emerita of equality studies at University College Dublin and a commissioner at the Irish Human Rights and Equality Commission. Drawing on philosophy, this whole body of work on affective equality makes clear that providing and receiving care is a primary part of relationships in social life; accessing care, providing it well and receiving it appropriately, is a central aspect of equality. Achieving human rights and social justice inevitably requires caring to be integral to society. In her recent book, like Carney, she argues that economic and political structures and thinking fail to provide for the importance of care in capitalist societies founded on neoliberal thinking. More than this, what I have called the competitive view of society represented in neoliberal thinking rejects human values, the 'core affective, cultural and intellectual values' (Lynch, 2022, p 8). Capitalist societies fail to accord the necessary importance to affective equality as a crucial aspect of social justice. Competition, measurement and meritocracy, all issues in current economic thinking of concern to social work, are ideologies that harm care giving (Lynch, 2022, pp 134–51). To achieve affective equality, it is necessary to move from ideals of individualism towards mutuality, solidarity and a concern for human social capital (Lynch, 2022, pp 115–33). Emotional labour in caring for others with love is distinctive from other human relations, must be given time to be carried out and cannot be monetised or commoditised (Lynch, 2022, pp 57–95). As the arguments I reviewed in Chapter 10 suggested, seeing all kinds of caring activity only in terms of monetary value devalues humanity, the social relations of human beings. And a great deal of economic thinking recognises that; it is an inadequate partial analysis to allow the fiscal and monetary economics to dominate the structures and values that support social relations.

Lynch, Baker, Cantillon et al (2009) further argue that the social sciences also subordinate affective issues in their work. This is primarily because they have given primacy to abstract, rational reasoning and empirical observational science as the basis for intellectual and scientific work. Economics, in particular, has ignored non-monetary work and its value to human societies. Both economics and sociology have focused on the public domains of life where empirical, rational thinking is given priority over affective human relations. It is a constant reproach to social work research and thinking that it adopts this non-human approach to the social in its wish to be part of the development of social science. This is apparent both in the early twentieth century and equally in its concentration on empirical, observational evidence of practice achievement in the early twenty-first century.

This is also true in the law, at least until feminist scholarship began to influence it. Both in the formulation of law through existing political power structures and in the analysis of legal rights. These prioritise the individual and neutrality, objectivity and male power in thinking about problematic issues. Consequently, the law devalues affective and social equalities. This must have an impact on social work practice and thinking, because social work often enforces the law or participates in legal decision making, and its agency context is mostly governmental or official.

Lynch and Walsh (2009, p 40) further argue against affective justice being commodifiable, capable of being measured in monetary terms. They propose that there are three circles of care relations, and this view deals with some of the ambiguities of commentary, research and understanding about caring that I discussed in Chapter 3. 'Love labour', the most interpersonal and affective, is the 'caring' work that communities, families and individuals do with people because of their emotional connections with that person, their mutuality in relationship; a social care worker or social worker may sometimes be working in this circle of caring as part of their practice. Surrounding such work is 'general care work' where there are responsibilities for caring but less interdependency, fewer complex connections between the people involved, perhaps only demonstrating 'basic psychosocial skills' (Chapter 8); much social care and social work is concerned with this circle of care work. Surrounding this, again, is 'solidarity work' (Lynch, 2022, p 25; 'solidary' in the earlier texts), which produces social capital, social relations and social structures that support caring. This might include the informal education of social pedagogy and the collective practices of community work, critical practice and social development. This is also important for indigenous practice, where traditional social structures from devalued cultures assist in building caring practices.

Solidarity work is also an important aspect of the agency contexts discussed in Chapters 6–8. There, I argued that to be effective places for social work practice to be undertaken, social work agencies must provide human social structures as contexts for practice. Some of these ideas connect with Hochschild's (2012 [1983]) discussion of emotional labour which explores how, as work becomes increasingly commodified, successful action requires the worker's emotional engagement to provide successful responsiveness. This is where a social care worker or social worker doing general care work using 'basic psychosocial skills', in the second circle, shifts their practice to become 'love labour', and can be achieved if this practice strategy is valued by the agency context's development of 'solidarity work'. The discussion in Chapter 6, of how attempts were made to make child protection work less proceduralised and the development in UK social work of principal social workers to support good-quality practice are examples of how 'solidarity work' has been taken up in some social work agency developments.

If Lynch's (2022) analysis of the caring actions of human societies is true, it is also relevant to the actions of professions – in particular, professions such as social work whose actions are centred on the human and the social. Lynch is concerned about education, because she argues that cultural and intellectual values that dismiss the affective element of equality required for social justice in all human relations are transmitted through both formal and informal education. The argument of this book is that it is also integral to incorporating social work in any society that there should be a profession that works to develop the cultural and intellectual expertise to improve social relations through human cooperation and solidarity.

It is striking that all three of these writers, none of them directly concerned with social work, but all of them concerned with current and future trends in societies in our human world, have singled out how our societies must give greater value to affective relations, to caring, to social life and relations. This is necessary if humanity is to flourish in the future and reject sciences based on existing unjust power relations.

Failures in political and social responses

Part of the reason that Mark Carney, Peter Hennessy, Kathleen Lynch and other writers have come together in putting forward their arguments for a human and social priority in future societies is the perception that economics has failed current social provision. This is because, in its values, politics and thinking, it neglects the social structures concerned with caring, both interpersonal and social. This strongly emerged in the early 2020s from failings in public services and social responses in the COVID-19 pandemic; it also reflects the increasingly polarised political discourse between authoritarian, libertarian ideas and more social democratic or socialist ideas. This affects social work because it developed most strongly in the welfare states of the mid to late twentieth century, but now seems to have less political and social 'solidarity work' in support of its actions, thinking and practice strategies and tactics.

One of the issues which suggests that greater caring and concern for each other will be important is the growth in populations that will need that solidarity in social life. The UK Office for National Statistics (ONS) draws on international information to provide a context for the growth in ageing in the UK and across the world:

> Population ageing is a global phenomenon. In 2015, there were around 901 million people aged 60 years and over worldwide, representing 12.3% of the global population. By 2030, this will have increased to 1.4 billion or 16.4% and by 2050, it will have increased to 2.1 billion or 21.3% of the global population. The [...] proportion of older people is projected to grow in all regions of the world. By 2050, the developed nations of Europe, Japan and North America will still be amongst the countries with the oldest populations, but China and Latin America notably will also have experienced considerable population ageing. Compared with other EU countries, the UK ranks around the middle in terms of the proportion of older people in its population (those aged 65 years and over and aged 85 years and over), but by 2035, it is projected to fall a few places down the rankings as other European countries such as Switzerland, the Netherlands and Poland age more rapidly. (ONS, 2018)

The World Health Organization identified increases in the prevalence of disability between 2010 and 2021.

> As of 2021, an estimated 1.3 billion people – 16% of the global population – have significant disability [...] A decade ago, approximately 1 billion people had significant disability. This means that within only 10 years, there has been an increase globally of more than 270 million people who now have disability [...] (WHO, 2022, pp 23–6)

There are many complex reasons for this, but the increase in ageing populations, medical treatments and changes in the physical and social environments suggests that these problems will continue to grow. Chapter 10, exploring health inequalities, pointed to evidence that many developments in health problems have social determinants. Growth in populations with health problems and difficulties in caring for disabled and older people are therefore likely to grow. The need for actions to reduce the social determinants of increasing health problems and disability is equally likely to grow with them, both the broad social interventions and preventive social actions of the kind that social work provides.

The 'care gap' is another of Hochschild's (2003) striking concepts. Her analysis concerns how attempts to commercialise, marketise and privatise in the political economy fail to meet the needs of people who need care and care services. Partly, this comes from the demands of family life in increasingly pressurised communities and families. Such demands make it impossible to make time for caring when insecure jobs and long working hours prevent people from providing quality care in many situations. The loss of community social structures such as churches or community centres to support families or localities in difficulties and the reality of population and social changes make it impossible to provide the care people want.

Case example: Michael's ageing care needs

Michael talks about his fears about care, as he approaches 80 years of age. He can feel himself becoming increasingly frail; he has had cataract operations and treatment for age-related macular degeneration, his teeth are deteriorating, and he has increasing problems with walking (he has fallen on several occasions), which probably means he will need artificial hips or knees soon, judging by the experience of several of his friends. He has seen friends his age and younger admitted to care homes and dying. He hopes he can stay at home and be cared for by his wife of nearly fifty years. But he realises that she is, if anything, rather frailer than he is, and he might be caring for her. He has seen the immense level of dependence of some of his friends on cheerful and practical but frankly rather uncongenial workers from various care and nursing services. He knows that friends who became very dependent, able to do very little for themselves, had different paid carers in and out of their houses several times a day. He realises that he or his wife would be on duty 24/7 for the other partner, with little support, perhaps some from their busy children, or from paid carers, most of whom are migrants or refugees from troubled societies. Not enough local people want to do this kind of work. There is a gap between what he wants – shared caring between himself and his wife – and the likely reality. There is not enough caring available to provide the human, loving care he wants. He knows some needs can be eased by an increasing dependency on all sorts of clever gadgets, pressure pads to check that he is still alive and moving around and other smart home monitoring systems, but he doesn't want that either.

All the commentary and evidence suggest that improving social capital, social responsiveness and social caring will be needed over the next few decades. Part of that will be social work and its agencies. Yet social work professions across the world fear that the already minimal 'solidarity work' in support of their practice will continue to be reduced further, along with roles and opportunities for continuing to develop their social contributions. Are we going to allow this to become an inevitability?

Reviewing the progress of social work research in Chapter 11, I found that clients and service users want a structure of social provision that uses human and practical professional actions and involves them in an alliance. Reviewing the progress of thinking about social work organisations and practice in Part II of this book, I found commitment to co-production to achieve the same: human and practical professional actions. Reviewing the agency, political and economic contexts in Chapters 6–8, I found that human and practical professional actions required balancing with policy aims and economic and political thinking. Social work practice needs to operate in contexts that facilitate a social humanity in fair and secure economic, and political structures.

Looking at Michael's care gap, technological skills and more efficient provision can help to meet some care needs, and humanising that effectiveness will be vital for social workers and social care services.

Case example: Eva's old house

Eva, a single parent, lives in a small rural house with her two children and does various paid jobs in the locality, cleaning, serving at local shops and child minding. The house is old, almost falling down and near a river: charming, but last winter it flooded and several people in the local community had to help her clear it up. But it's still not in a good state and she has been told flooding in their area is more likely with climate change. She knows this problem is likely to be repeated, and most local people are in the same position. She is also having difficulty getting the children to school, now they have to travel to the town for secondary education. Local government support for them is limited because of a big project to prevent flooding in their area by changing watercourses further up the river to meet the needs of the urban area nearby.

Eva is experiencing some of the early consequences of climate change; these are long-term issues. Environmental disasters are likely to become more frequent and have consequences for the lives of many, particularly affecting people in poverty like Eva. So far, despite much discussion and dissent, both responses to climate change and practice in disaster situations are not yet well developed in social work (Payne, 2023). Another care gap exists between current provision for the individual and the social changes that society must make to facilitate social citizenship in a new ecological environment. But it will become important; Matthies & Närhi (2017) propose that societies will live through a process of ecosocial transition as social relations respond to ecological conditions. This will involve social work's human focus to facilitate relational changes to achieve social wellbeing (Helne & Hirvilammi, 2017). Their account of a future social work thus calls on social work's unique dual human/social focus and is likely to involve both interpersonal social work and social development practices.

Case example: Jotul's final stages in care

Jotul has been looked after in the care of the local council for his home area. He was a migrant to the UK with his mother after the death of his father in a continuing conflict in his home country, but his mother experienced severe mental illness and was unable to care for him; his relationship with her is minimal. He was in foster care for some time, but conflictual behaviour with other children at school led to his being placed in a local authority boarding school some way away, returning to the foster home for holiday periods. Approaching the age of 16 years, he was able to complete his course at the school for the next two years, but changes in the foster home meant they were unable to accommodate him for holiday periods and he would need accommodation in the area of the school. New home arrangements, however, were unavailable. The social worker, therefore, considered placing him in a small apartment for these two years, enabling him to continue independently afterwards, so retaining some contact out of school hours with friends at school. But he did not have the life experience or financial resources to be independent in an apartment and achieve a secure, good quality of life.

Jotul's position is another care gap, this time between the care available in any community and the particular needs of a young person in care. Many communities, families and individuals are unlikely to be able to meet their own needs in the aftermath of extensive climate disasters, political conflicts and social change in the coming decades. Greater migration is probable from the areas affected to more economically developed countries with ageing populations because their citizens live longer and have fewer children. There is often, however, political resistance to migration because of a lack of social acceptance of increases in migration, which would be economically and politically sensible because it would rebalance resources and help with declining economic growth in developed economies (Bloom & Zucker, 2023). As with ecosocial transitions because of climate change, it is likely that collaboration and partnership between countries and communities, solidarity rather than conflict, will be needed in the future. This also is a potential direction for social work's unique human/social contribution (Grandi, 2023). Cooperation and solidarity in co-production with professions such as social work will increasingly have to face global issues to be a vital part of human society in a complex world.

Conclusion: social work's future care agenda

Social work, its aims and identity, its practice and the social infrastructure in which it operates will continue to make its unique contribution to future social agendas.

- It focuses on policy and social structures that build social capital and social relations; policy and those structures support and further the wide range of social provision required for wellbeing in any society.
- It favours cohesion and solidarity in social relations, not competition and conflict.
- Care, love and solidarity are central to a social humanity that builds first on community, family and interpersonal relations and extends them into service provision concerned with the social.
- Social work's practice is a unique contribution of its several streams of thought, calling on and relevant to diverse cultural and social traditions.

- Social work is organised human actions with thoughtful practice strategies. The actions enhance the human capital of individuals' and groups' personal and social resources. The strategies enhance connectedness and relatedness, forming the social capital in the networks of organisations and people in any society.
- True alliances among agencies, professionals and service users in every aspect of social work's education and practice reject the failures of authoritarian and libertarian economic, political and social policies. Policy and practice must provide for a social humanity in community, family and personal lives.

Bibliography

Adame, A.L. & Leitner, L.M. (2008) Breaking out of the mainstream: The evolution of peer support alternatives to the mental health system. *Ethical Human Psychology and Psychiatry. 10:* 146–62.

Akabas, S.H. & Gates, L.B. (2000) A social work role: Promoting employment equity for people with serious and persistent mental illness. *Administration in Social Work, 23*(3–4): 162–84.

Alakeson, V. (2010) International development in self-directed care. *Issue Brief (Commonwealth Fund), 78:* 1–11.

Allen, S.F. & Tracy, E.M. (2004) Revitalizing the role of home visiting by school social workers. *Children and Schools, 26*(4): 197–208.

Ashton, R. (2010) *How to be a social entrepreneur: Make money and change the world.* Chichester: Capstone.

Askeland, G.A. & Payne, M. (2017) *Internationalizing social work education: Insights from notable figures across the globe.* Bristol: Policy Press.

Asquith, S., Clark, C. & Waterhouse, L. (2005) *The role of the social worker in the twenty-first century: A literature review.* Edinburgh: Scottish Executive.

Bagdonas, A. (2001) Practical and academic aspect of social work development in Lithuania. In P. Helppikangas (ed.) *Social work and civil society from an international perspective* (pp. 37–83) Rovaniemi: Lapin Yliopisto.

Bailey, R. (1980) Social workers: Pawns, police or agitators? In M. Brake & R. Bailey (eds) *Radical social work and practice* (pp. 215–27). London: Arnold.

Bailey, R. & Brake, M. (eds) (1975) *Radical social work.* London: Arnold.

Bakalinsky, R. (1980) People vs. profits: Social work in industry. *Social Work, 25*(6): 471–5.

Baker, J., Lynch, K., Cantillon, S. & Walsh J. (2009) *Equality: From theory to action* (2nd edn). Basingstoke: Palgrave Macmillan.

Baker, R. (1976) *The interpersonal process in generic social work.* Bundoora: PIT Press.

Baldwin M. (2011) Resisting the EasyCare model: Building a more radical, community-based, anti-authoritarian social work for the future. In M. Lavalette (ed.) *Radical social work today: Social work at the crossroads* (pp. 187–204). Bristol: Policy Press.

Bandler, B. (1963) The concept of ego-supportive psychotherapy. In H.J. Parad & R.R. Miller (eds) *Ego-oriented casework: Problems and perspectives* (pp. 27–44). New York: Family Service Association of America.

Banks, S. (2004) *Ethics, accountability and the social professions.* Basingstoke: Palgrave Macmillan.

Barclay Report (1982) *Social workers: Their role and tasks.* London: Bedford Square Press.

Barker, R.L. & Briggs, T.L. (1968) *Differential use of manpower: An analysis and demonstration-study*. New York: National Association of Social Workers.

Barker, R.L. & Briggs, T.L. (1969) *Using TEAMS to deliver social services* (Manpower Monograph 1). Syracuse, NY: Syracuse University Department of Social Work.

Barnes, F.M., Brannelly, T., Ward, L. & Ward, N. (eds) (2015) *Ethics of care: Critical advances in international perspective*. Bristol: Policy Press.

Barnes, J. & Connelly, N. (eds) (1978) *Social care research*. London: Bedford Square Press.

Barnes, M. (2012) *Care in everyday life: An ethic of care in practice*. Bristol: Policy Press.

Barr, N. (2020) *The economics of the welfare state* (6th edn). Oxford: Oxford University Press.

Bartnik, E. & Chalmers, R. (2007) It's about more than money: Local area coordination supporting people with disabilities. In S. Hunter & P. Ritchie (eds) *Co-production and personalisation in social care: Changing relationships in the provision of social care* (pp. 19–38). London: Jessica Kingsley.

Bartram, D. (2023) Does belief in meritocracy increase with inequality? A reconsideration for European countries. *British Journal of Sociology*, https://doi.org/10.1111/1468-4446.13042.

Bayley, M.J., Parker, P., Seyd, R. & Tennant, A. (1987) *Practising community care: Developing locally-based services*. Sheffield: Social Services Monographs: Research in Practice.

Bazzi, S., Fiszbein, M. & Gebresilasse, M. (2020) Frontier culture: The roots and persistence of 'rugged individualism' in the United States. *Econometrica*, *88*(6): 2329–68.

Beadle-Brown, J., Murphy, B. & Bradshaw, J. (2017) *Person-centred active support*. Hove: Pavilion.

Beckett, C. & Horner, N. (2016) *Essential theory for social work practice* (2nd edn). London: Sage.

Beddoe, L. (2017) Field, capital and professional identity: Social work in health care. In Webb, S.A. (ed.) *Professional identity and social work* (pp. 122–35) Abingdon: Routledge.

Beder, J. (1998) The home visit, revisited. *Families in Society*, *79*(5): 514–22. https://doi.org/10.1606/1044-3894.718.

Beresford, P. & Croft, S. (1986) *Whose welfare? Private care of public services*. Brighton: Lewis Cohen Centre for Urban Studies.

Beresford, P., Adshead, L. & Croft, S. (2007) *Palliative care, social work, and service users: Making life possible*. London: Jessica Kingsley.

Beresford, P., Branfield, F., Maslen, B., Sartori A. & Shaping Our Lives (2007) Partnership working: Service users and social workers learning and working together. In M. Lymbery & K. Postle (eds) *Social work: A companion to learning* (pp. 215–27). London: Sage.

Betz, H.-G. (2019) Facets of nativism: A heuristic exploration. *Patterns of Prejudice, 53*(2): 111–35. https://doi.org/10.1080/0031322X.2019.1572276.

Bew, J. (2016) *Realpolitik: A history*. Oxford: Oxford University Press.

Biestek, F.P. (1961) *The casework relationship*. London: Allen & Unwin.

Biestek, F.P. & Gehrig, C.C. (1978) *Client self-determination in social work: A fifty-year history*. Chicago, IL: Loyola University Press.

Blekesaune, M. (2013) Economic strain and public support for redistribution: A comparative analysis of 28 European countries. *Journal of Social Policy*, *42*(1): 57–72.

Bloom, D.E. & Zucker, L.M. (2023) Ageing is the real population bomb. *Finance and Development*, *60*(2): 58–61.

Bochel, D. (1976) *Probation and after-care: Its development in England and Wales*.

Boehm, W.W. (1961) Social work: Science and art. *Social Service Review*, *35*(2), 144–52.

Bourdieu, P. (1980) *The logic of practice*. Stanford, CA: Stanford University Press.

Bourdieu, P. (1991) *Language and symbolic power*. Cambridge: Polity.

Bower, M. (2005) Working with families who see help as the problem. In M. Bower (ed.) *Psychoanalytic theory for social work practice: Thinking under fire* (pp. 153–64). Abingdon: Routledge.

Bowers, S. (1949) The nature and definition of social casework. *Social Casework*, *30*(8), 311–17; 369–75; 412–7.

Boyle, D., Clarke, S. & Burns, S. (2006) *Aspects of co-production: The implications for work, health and volunteering*. London: New Economics Foundation

Breakwell, G.M. (1983) *Threatened identities*. Chichester: Wiley.

Breakwell, G.M. (1986) *Coping with threatened identities*. London: Methuen.

Brieland, D., Briggs, T. & Leuenberger, P. (1973) *The team model of social work practice* (Manpower Monograph 5). Syracuse, NY: Syracuse University Department of Social Work.

Briggs, T.L. (1973) Identifying team functional roles and specializations. In D. Brieland, T. Briggs & P. Leuenberger, *The team model of social work practice* (pp. 16–25). Syracuse, NY: Syracuse University School of Social Work.

British Association of Social Workers (1977) *The social work task: A BASW working party report*. Birmingham: British Association of Social Workers.

Broad, B. & Fletcher, C. (eds) (1993) *Practitioner social work research in action*. London: Whiting and Birch.

Browne, T. (2019) Social work roles and healthcare settings. In S. Gehlert & T. Browne (eds) *Handbook of health social work* (3rd edn) (pp. 21–38). San Francisco, CA: Jossey-Bass.

Brubaker, R. (2017) Why populism? *Theory and Society*, *46*, 357–85.

Bruno, A. & Dell'Aversana, G. (2018) 'What shall I pack in my suitcase?' The role of work–integrated learning in sustaining social work students' professional identity. *Social Work Education*, *37*(1): 34–48.

Bulmer, M. (1987) *The social basis of community care*. London: Allen & Unwin.

Burford, G. (2017) *Family group conferencing: New directions in community-centered child and family practice*. Abingdon: Routledge.

Burnham, D. (2012) *The social worker speaks: A history of social workers through the twentieth century*. Farnham: Ashgate.

Buzelli, L., Cameron, G. & Gardner, T. (2022) *Public perceptions of the NHS and social care: Performance, policy and expectations.* London: Health Foundation. www.health.org.uk/publications/long-reads/public-perceptions-performance-policy-and-expectations.

Calitz, T., Roux, A. & Strydom, H. (2014) Factors that affect social workers' job satisfaction, stress and burnout. *Social Work/Maatskaplike Werk, 50*(2): 152–63.

Cameron, C. & Moss, P. (eds) (2011) *Social pedagogy and working with children and young people: Where care and education meet.* London: Jessica Kingsley.

Cameron, C., Petrie, P., Wigfall, V., Kleipoedszus, S. & Jasper, A. (2011) *Final report of the social pedagogy pilot programme: Development and implementation.* London: Thomas Coram Research Unit, Institute of Education, University of London.

Canda, E.R., Furman, L.D. & Canda, H.J. (2019) *Spiritual diversity in social work practice: The heart of helping* (2nd edn). New York: Oxford University Press.

Cannon, M.A. (1939) Recent changes in the philosophy of social workers. In F. Lowry (ed.) *Reading in social casework 1920–1938* (pp. 99–108). New York: Columbia University Press.

Caplan, G. (1974) *Support systems and community mental health: Lectures on concept development.* New York: Behavioral Publications.

Caplan, G. & Killilea, M. (eds) (1976) *Support systems and mutual help: Multidisciplinary explorations.* New York: Grune and Stratton.

Carkhuff, R.R. with Benoit, D. (2019) *The art of helping* (10th edn). Amherst, MA: HRD Press.

Carney, M. (2021) *Value(s): Climate, credit, covid and how we focus on what matters.* London: Collins.

Carpenter, J. & Dickinson, S. (2016) *Interprofessional education and training* (2nd edn). Bristol: Policy Press.

Carr, E.H. (1960) *The new society.* London: Macmillan.

Castells, M. (1997) *The power of identity.* Cambridge, MA: Blackwell.

Chang, H.-J. (2010) *23 things they don't tell you about capitalism.* London: Penguin.

Chang, H.-J. (2014) *Economics: The user's guide.* London: Penguin.

Charfe, L. (2019) Social pedagogical key thinkers. In L. Charfe & A. Gardner, *Social pedagogy and social work* (pp. 18–31). London: Sage.

Charfe, L. & Gardner, A. (2019) *Social pedagogy and social work.* London: Sage.

Cheung, A.B.L. (2002) The politics of new public management: Some experience from reforms in East Asia. In K. McLaughlin, S.P. Osborne & E. Ferlie (eds) *New public management: Current trends and future prospects* (pp. 243–73). London: Routledge.

Chueri, J. (2022) An emerging populist welfare paradigm? How populist radical right-wing parties are reshaping the welfare state. *Scandinavian Political Studies, 45*(4), pp. 383–409.

Chung, H., Taylor-Gooby, P. & Leruth, B. (2018) Political legitimacy and welfare state futures: Introduction. *Social Policy and Administration, 52*(4): 835–46.

Clarke, J. (2004) *Changing welfare changing states: New directions in social policy.* London: Sage.

Clark, M. (2015) Co-production in mental health care. *Mental Health Review Journal, 20*(4): 213–19.

Clarke, J. & Newman, J. (1997) *The managerial state: Power, politics and ideology in the remaking of social welfare.* London: Sage.

Cochrane, A., Clarke, J. & Gewirtz, S. (2001) *Comparing welfare states* (2nd edn). London: Sage.

Cockerill, E. (1953) The interdependence of the professions in helping people. *Social Casework, 34*(9): 371–8.

Collins, J. (1965) *Social casework in a general medical practice.* London: Pitman.

Compton, B.R., Galaway, B. & Cournoyer, B.R. (2005) *Social work processes* (7th edn). Pacific Grove, CA: Brooks/Cole.

Condie, C.D., Hanson, J.A., Lang, N.E., Moss, D.K. & Kane, R.A. (1978) How the public views social work. *Social Work, 23*(1): 47–53.

Cook, L.L. (2020) The home visit in child protection social work: Emotion as resource and risk for professional judgement and practice. *Child and Family Social Work, 25*(1): 18–26.

Cook, L.L. & Zschomler, D. (2020) Virtual home visits during the COVID-19 pandemic: Social workers' perspectives. *Practice, 32*(5): 401–8.

Cooper, J. (1983) *The creation of the British personal social services, 1962–1974.* London: Heinemann.

Corneo, G. (2012) Work norms and the welfare state. *CESifo Economic Studies, 58*(4): 599–625.

Corney, R. (1993) Studies of the effectiveness of counselling in general practice. In R. Corney & R. Jenkins (eds) *Counselling in general practice* (pp. 31–44). London: Routledge.

Corney, R.H. (1982) Health visitors and social workers. In A.W. Clare & R.H. Corney (eds) *Social work and primary health care* (pp. 133–9). London: Academic Press.

Corney, R.H. & Clare, A.W. (1983) The effectiveness of attached social workers in the management of depressed women in general practice. *British Journal of Social Work, 13*(2): 57–74.

Corrigan, P. & Leonard, P. (1978) *Social work practice under capitalism: A Marxist approach.* London: Macmillan.

Crisp, B.R. (ed.) (2017) *Routledge handbook of religion, spirituality and social work.* Abingdon: Routledge.

Cross, S., Hubbard, A. & Munro, E. (2010) *Reclaiming social work: London Borough of Hackney Children and Young People's Services.* London: Human Reliability/ London School of Economics and Political Science, https://secure.toolkitfiles. co.uk/clients/28663/sitedata/files/Eileen-Munro.pdf.

Crow, G. & Marsh, P. (1998) *Family group conferences in child welfare.* Oxford: Blackwell.

D'Aeth, F.G. (1925) *Social administration.* Liverpool: Young.

Dahl, R. (1968) Power as control of behaviour. In S. Lukes (ed.) *Power* (pp. 37–58). Oxford: Blackwell.

Dalrymple, J. & Boylan, J. (2013) *Effective advocacy in social work.* London: Sage.

Daly, M. (2018) Fish in or out of water? A Bourdieusian analysis of the social work professional identity [PhD thesis]. Glasgow: Glasgow Caledonian University.

Daly, M. & Kettle, M. (2017) Making professional identity: Narrative work and fateful moments. In Webb, S.A. (ed.) *Professional identity and social work* (pp. 210–25). Abingdon: Routledge.

Dash, B., Kumar, M., Singh, D.P. & Shukla, S. (eds) (2021) *Indian social work.* Abingdon: Routledge.

Davidson, S. & King, S. (2005) *Public knowledge of and attitudes to social work in Scotland.* Edinburgh: Scottish Executive.

Davies, B. & Challis, D. (1986) *Matching resources to needs in community care: An evaluated demonstration of a long-term care model.* Aldershot: Gower.

Davies, L. & Leonard, P. (eds) (2004) *Social work in a corporate era: Practices of power and resistance.* Aldershot: Ashgate.

Davies, M. (1985) *The essential social worker: A guide to positive practice* (2nd edn). Aldershot: Wildwood House.

Day, J. (2013) *Interprofessional working: An essential guide for health and social care professionals* (2nd edn). Andover: Cengage.

Deegan, P.E. (1988) Recovery: The lived experience of rehabilitation. *Psychosocial Rehabilitation Journal, 11*, pp. 11–19.

Defourny, J. & Kim, S.Y. (2011) Emerging models of social enterprise in Eastern Asia: A cross-country analysis. *Social Enterprise Journal,* 7(1): 86–111.

den Braber, C. (2013) The introduction of the capability approach in social work across a neoliberal Europe. *Journal of Social Intervention: Theory and Practice,* 22(4): 61–77.

Dennison, S.T., Poole, J. & Qaqish, B. (2007) Students' perceptions of social work: Implications for strengthening the image of social work among college students. *Social Work,* 52(4): 350–60.

Dent, M. (2017) Perspectives on professional identity: The changing world of the social worker. In S.A. Webb (ed.) *Professional identity and social work* (pp. 21–34). Abingdon: Routledge.

Department for Education (2022) *Children's social work workforce.* https:// explore–education-statistics.service.gov.uk/find-statistics/children-s-social-work-workforce.

De Paz, C., Valentine, N.B., Hosseinpoor, A.R., Koller, T.S. & Gerecke, M. (2017) *Intersectoral factors influencing equity-oriented progress towards universal health coverage: Results from a scoping review of literature.* Geneva: World Health Organization. www.who.int/publications/i/item/9789241512329.

Desai, M. (2014) *The paradigm of international social development: Ideologies, development systems and policy approaches.* New York: Routledge.

Desai, M. (2015) *Social development in Asia: Diversity and implications.* Jaipur: Rawat.

DH (Department of Health) (1998) *Partnership in action (New opportunities for joint working between health and social services): A decision document.* London: DH.

DH (2002) *Requirements for social work training.* London: DH.

Dominelli, L. (2002) *Anti-oppressive social work theory and practice*. London: Red Globe Press.

Dominelli, L. (2004) *Social work: Theory and practice for a changing profession*. Cambridge: Polity

Dominelli, L. (2012) *Green social work: From environmental crises to environmental justice*. Cambridge: Polity.

Dominelli, L. (2017) *Anti-racist social work* (4th edn). London: Bloomsbury.

Dominelli, L. & McCleod, E. (1989) *Feminist social work*. Basingstoke: Macmillan.

Donzelot, J. (1979) *The policing of families*. London: Hutchinson.

Dowling, B., Powell, M. & Glendinning, C. (2004) Conceptualising successful partnerships. *Health and Social Care in the Community*, *12*(4): 309–17. https://doi.org/10.1111/j.1365-2524.2004.00500.x.

Downie, R.S. (1971) *Roles and values: An introduction to social ethics*. London: Methuen.

Downie, R.S. & Telfer, E. (1969) *Respect for persons*. London: Allen & Unwin.

Doyal, L. & Gough, I. (1991) *A theory of social need*. Basingstoke: Palgrave Macmillan

Dressel, P. (1987) Patriarchy and social welfare work. *Social Problems*, *34*(3), 294–309.

Driessens, K., McLaughlin, H. & van Doorn, L. (2016) The meaningful involvement of service users in social work education: Examples from Belgium and the Netherlands. *Social Work Education*, *35*(7): 739–51.

DuBois, B. & Miley, K.K. (1999) *Social work: An empowering profession* (3rd edn). Boston: Allyn and Bacon.

Duffy, S. (2007) Care management and self-directed support. *Journal of Integrated Care*. *15*(5): 5–14.

Dustin, D. (2007) *The McDonaldization of social work*. Aldershot: Ashgate.

Ekberg, S. (2011) Making arrangements: Remote proposal sequences and attendant structural phenomena in social interaction [PhD thesis]. Adelaide: University of Adelaide https://eprints.qut.edu.au/59058.

England, H. (1986) *Social work as art: Making sense for good practice*. London: Allen and Unwin.

Epstein, I. (1975) The politics of behavior therapy: The new cool-out casework? In H. Jones (ed.) *Towards a new social work* (pp. 138–50). London: Routledge and Kegan Paul.

Esping-Andersen, G. (1990) *The three worlds of welfare capitalism*. London: Polity.

Esquao, S.A. & Strega, S. (2015) *Walking this path together: Anti-racist and anti-oppressive child welfare practice* (2nd edn). Halifax: Fernwood.

Evans, T. (2011) Professionals, managers and discretion: Critiquing street-level bureaucracy. *British Journal of Social Work*, *41*(2), 368–86.

Evans, N. (2022) Coping with gendered welfare stigma: Exploring everyday accounts of stigma and resistance strategies among mothers who claim social security benefits. *Social Policy and Society*, *21*(4): 690–700.

Fargion, S. (2006) Thinking professional social work: Expertise and professional ideologies in social workers' accounts of their practice. *Journal of Social Work*, 6(3): 255–73.

Fargion, S. (2008) Reflections on social work's identity: International themes in Italian practitioners' representation of social work. *International Social Work*, 51(2): 206–19.

Faulks, K (2000) *Citizenship*. London: Routledge.

Fenton, J. (2019) *Social work for lazy radicals: Relationship building, critical thinking and courage in practice*. London: Red Globe.

Ferguson, H. (2004) *Protecting children in time: Child abuse, child protection and the consequences of modernity*. Basingstoke: Palgrave Macmillan.

Ferguson, H. (2011) *Child protection practice*. London: Red Globe.

Ferguson, H. (2016) What social workers do in performing child protection work: Evidence from research into face-to-face practice. *Child and Family Social Work*, 6(3): 283–94. doi:10.1111/cfs.12142.

Ferguson, H. (2018) Making home visits: Creativity and the embodied practices of home visiting in social work and child protection. *Qualitative Social Work*, 17(1): 65–80. doi:10.1177/1473325016656751.

Ferguson, H., Kelly, L. & Pink, S. (2022) Social work and child protection for a post-pandemic world: The re-making of practice during COVID-19 and its renewal beyond it. *Journal of Social Work Practice*, 36(1): 5–24.

Ferguson H., Warwick, L., Cooner, T.S., Leigh, J., Beddoe, E., Disney, T. & Plumridge, G. (2020) The nature and culture of social work with children and families in long-term casework: Findings from a qualitative longitudinal study. *Child and Family Social Work*, 25(3): 694–703. doi:10.1111/cfs.12746.

Ferguson, I. (2000) Identity politics or class struggle? The case of the mental health users' movement. In M. Lavalette & G. Mooney (eds) *Class struggle and social welfare* (pp. 228–44). London: Routledge.

Ferguson, I. & Woodward, R. (2009) *Radical social work in practice: Making a difference*. Bristol: Policy Press.

Fido, J. (1977) The Charity Organisation Society and social casework in London 1869–1900. In A.P. Donajgrodski (ed.) *Social control in nineteenth century Britain* (pp. 76–104). London: Croom Helm.

Filipe, A., Renedo, A. & Marston, C. (2017) The co-production of what? Knowledge, values, and social relations in health care. *PLoS biology*, 15(5): e2001403.

Finch, J. (1989) *Family obligations and social change*. Cambridge: Polity.

Finch, J. & Mason, J. (1993) *Negotiating family obligations*. London: Tavistock/ Routledge.

Fine, M.D. (2007) *A caring society? Care and the dilemmas of human service in the twenty-first century*. Basingstoke: Palgrave Macmillan.

Fischer, J. (1976) *The effectiveness of social casework*. Springfield, IL: Charles C. Thomas.

Fisher, B. & Tronto, J.C. (1991) Toward a feminist theory of care. In E. Abel & M. Nelson (eds) *Circles of care: Work and identity in women's lives* (pp. 35–62). Albany, NY: State University of New York Press.

Fook, J. (2016) *Social work: A critical approach to practice* (3rd edn). London: Sage.

Foren, R. & Bailey, R. (1968) *Authority in social casework*. Oxford: Pergamon.

Frahm, K.A. & Martin, L.L. (2009) From government to governance: Implications for social work administration. *Administration in Social Work*, 33(4): 407–22.

Francis Report (2013) *Report of the mid Staffordshire NHS Foundation Trust public inquiry* (HC 898). London: TSO.

Frank, R. & Muranda, Z. (2016) Social enterprise as the game-changer: Embracing innovation and dynamism in contemporary social work practice in Zimbabwe. *African Journal of Social Work*, 6(1): 30–41.

Fraser, M.W., Lombardi, B.M., Wu, S., de Saxe Zerden, L., Richman, E.L. & Fraher, E.P. (2018) Integrated primary care and social work: A systematic review. *Journal of the Society for Social Work and Research*, 9(2): 175–215.

Freedberg, S. (2009) *Relational theory for social work practice: A feminist perspective*. New York: Routledge.

Freeth, D.S., Hammick, M., Reeves, S., Koppel, I. & Barr, H. (2005) *Effective interprofessional education: Development, delivery, and evaluation*. Chichester: Wiley-Blackwell.

Freire, P. (1970) *Cultural action for freedom*. Harmondsworth: Penguin.

Freire, P. (1972) *Pedagogy of the oppressed*. Harmondsworth: Penguin.

Freire, P. (1974 [1967]) *Education: The practice of freedom*. London: Writers and Readers Publishing Cooperative.

Friedman, M. (1962) *Capitalism and freedom*. Chicago: University of Chicago Press.

Froggett, L. & Chamberlayne, P. (2004) Narratives of social enterprise: From biography to practice and policy critique. *Qualitative Social Work*, 3(1): 61–77.

Gambrill, E. (2019) *Critical thinking and the process of evidence-based practice*. New York: Oxford University Press.

Gardiner, S., Morrison, D. & Robinson, S. (2022) Integrity in public life: Reflections on a duty of candour. *Public Integrity*, 24(2), 217–28.

Garrett, P.M. (2013) Pierre Bourdieu. In M. Gray & S.A. Webb (eds), *Social work theories and methods* (2nd edn) (pp. 36–45). London: Sage.

Garrett, P.M. (2018a) *Social work and social theory: Making connections* (2nd edn). Bristol: Policy Press.

Garrett, P.M. (2018b) *Welfare words: Critical social work and social policy*. London: Sage.

General Medical Council/Nursing and Midwifery Council (2022) *Openness and honesty when things go wrong: The professional duty of candour*. London: GMC/NMC.

Gerth, H.H. & Mills, C.W. (1948) *From Max Weber: Essays in sociology*. London: Routledge and Kegan Paul.

Gilbert, N. (ed.) (1997) *Combatting child abuse: International perspectives and trends.* New York: Oxford University Press.

Gilbert, N., Parton, N. & Skivenes, M. (2011) Changing patterns of response and emerging orientations. In N. Gilbert, N. Parton & M. Skivenes (eds) *Child protection systems: International trends and orientations* (pp. 243–57). New York: Oxford University Press.

Gitterman, A., Knight, C. & Germain, C.B. (2021) *The life model of social work practice: Advances in theory and practice* (4th edn). New York: Columbia University Press.

Glasby, J. & Dickinson, H. (2014) *Partnership working in health and social care: What is integrated care and how can we deliver it?* (2nd edn). Bristol: Policy Press.

Glasius, M. (2018) What authoritarianism is … and is not: A practice perspective. *International Affairs.* 94(3): 515–33.

Glastonbury, B. (1976) *Paying the piper.* Birmingham: BASW Publications.

Gneezy, U. & Rustichini, A. (2000) A fine is a price. *Journal of Legal Studies.* 29(1): 1–17.

Goldberg, E.M. & Connelly, N. (1982) *The effectiveness of social care for the elderly: An overview of recent and current evaluative research.* London: Heinemann.

Goldberg, E.M., with Mortimer, A. & Williams, B.T. (1970) *Helping the aged.* London: Allen & Unwin.

Goldstein, E., Miehls, D. & Ringel, S. (2009) *Advanced clinical social work practice: Relational principles and techniques.* New York: Columbia University Press.

González, A.M. (2018) Practical identity, obligation and sociality. *Journal of Social Philosophy.* 49(4): 610–25.

Gonzalez-Prendes, A.A. & Cassady, C.M. (2019) Cognitive-behavioural therapy and social work practice. In M. Payne & E. Reith-Hall (eds) *Routledge handbook of social work theory* (pp. 193–204). London: Routledge.

Gorman, H. & Postle, K. (2003) *Transforming community care: A distorted vision?* Birmingham: Venture.

Gough, I. (2017) *Heat, greed and human need: Climate change, capitalism and sustainable wellbeing.* Cheltenham: Edward Elgar.

Graham, M. (2002) *Social work and African-centred worldviews.* Birmingham: Venture.

Grandi, F. (2023) Partnerships for refugees. *Finance and Development, 60*(2): 56–7.

Grant, G., Humphreys, S. & McGrath, M. (eds) (1986) *Community mental handicap teams: Theory and practice.* Kidderminster: British Institute for Mental Handicap.

Gray, M., Coates, J. & Hetherington, T. (eds) (2013) *Environmental social work.* Abingdon: Routledge.

Gray, M., Coates, J. & Yellow Bird, M. (eds) (2008) *Indigenous social work around the world: Towards culturally relevant education and practice.* Aldershot: Ashgate.

Gray, M., Healy, K. & Crofts, P. (2003) Social enterprise: Is it the business of social work? *Australian Social Work, 56*(2): 141–54. http://dx.doi.org/10.1046/j.0312-407X.2003.00060.x.

Gray, M., Plath, D. & Webb, S.A. (2009) *Evidence-based social work: A critical stance*. London: Routledge.

Grinker, R.R., MacGregor, H., Selan, K., Klein, A. & Kohrman, J. (1961) The early years of psychiatric social work. *Social Service Review, 35*(2): 111–26.

Gutiérrez, L.M. (1995) Understanding the empowerment process: Does consciousness make a difference? *Social Work Research* 19(4): 229–37.

Gutiérrez, L.M., DeLois, K.A. & GlenMaye, L. (1995) Understanding empowerment practice: Building on practitioner-based knowledge. *Families in Society* 76(8): 534–42.

Guzzetta, C. (1996) The decline of the North American model of social work education. *International Social Work, 39*(3): 301–15.

Habermas, J. (1977) Hannah Arendt's communications concept of power. *Social Research. 44*(1): 3–24.

Habermas, J. (1986 [1971]) *The theory of communicative action: Reason and the rationalization of society, vol. 1: Reason and the rationalization of society*. Cambridge: Polity.

Hackett, M.T. (2010) Challenging social enterprise debates in Bangladesh. *Social Enterprise Journal, 6*(3): 210–24. https://doi.org/10.1108/17508611011088814.

Hadley, R. & Hatch, S. (1981) *Social welfare and the failure of the state*. London: Allen and Unwin.

Hadley, R. & McGrath, M. (eds) (1980) *Going local – Neighbourhood social services*. London: Bedford Square Press.

Hadley, R. & McGrath, M. (1984) *When social services are local: The Normanton experience*. London: Allen and Unwin.

Hadley, R. & Young, K. (1990) *Creating a responsive public service*. Hemel Hempstead: Harvester Wheatsheaf.

Hadley, R., Cooper, M., Dale, P. & Stacey, G. (1987) *A community social worker's handbook*. London: Tavistock.

Hall, P. (1976) *Reforming the welfare: The politics of change in the personal social services*. London: Heinemann.

Hallett, S. (2016) 'An uncomfortable comfortableness': 'Care', child protection and child sexual exploitation. *British Journal of Social Work, 46*(7): 2137–52.

Halmos, P. (1965) *The faith of the counsellors*. London: Constable.

Hammerback, J.C. (1972) Barry Goldwater's rhetoric of rugged individualism. *Quarterly Journal of Speech, 58*(2): 175–83.

Hancock, B.L. & Pelton, L.H. (1989) Home visits: History and functions. *Social Casework, 70*(1): 21–7.

Hardesty, M. (2017) Identity formation, scientific rationality and embodied knowledge in child welfare. In S.A. Webb (ed.) *Professional identity and social work* (pp. 108–21). Abingdon: Routledge.

Harlow, E. (2017) Constructing the social, constructing social work. In Webb, S.A. (ed.) *Professional identity and social work* (pp. 62–75). Abingdon: Routledge.

Harris, J. (1998) Scientific management, bureau-professionalism, new managerialism: The labour process of state social work. *British Journal of Social Work, 28*(6): 839–62.

Harris, J. (2003a) 'Businessology' and social work. *Social Work and Society*, 1(1): 15–18.

Harris, J. (2003b) *The social work business*. London: Routledge.

Harris, J. (2014) (Against) Neoliberal social work. *Critical and Radical Social Work*, 2(1): 7–22.

Harris, J. & Unwin, P. (2009) Performance management in modernised social work. In J. Harris & V. White (eds) *Modernising social work: Critical considerations* (pp. 9–30). Bristol: Policy Press.

Hart, M.A. (2019) Indigenist social work practice. In M. Payne & E. Reith-Hall (eds) *Routledge handbook of social work theory* (pp. 268–81). London: Routledge.

Hatton, K. (2013) *Social pedagogy in the UK*. Lyme Regis: Russell House.

Hayek, F.A. (1944) *The road to serfdom*. London: Routledge.

Hayek, F.A. (1960) *The constitution of liberty*. London Routledge.

Hearn, J., Pösö, T., Smith, C., White, S. & Korpinen, J. (2004) What is child protection? Historical and methodological issues in comparative research on *lastensuojelu*/child protection. *International Journal of Social Welfare*, 13(1): 28–41.

Heisler, E.J. (2018) *The mental health workforce: A primer*. Washington, DC: Congressional research Service. https://fas.org/sgp/crs/misc/R43255.pdf.

Helne, T. & Hirvilammi, T. (2017) The relational conception of wellbeing as a catalyst for the ecosocial transition. In A.-L. Matthies & K. Närhi (eds) (2017) *The ecosocial transition of societies: The contribution of social work and social policy* (pp. 36–53). Abingdon: Routledge.

Hemmington, J., Graham, M., Marshall, A., Brammer, A., Stone, K. & Vicary, S. (2021) *Approved mental health professionals, best interests assessors and people with lived experience: An exploration of professional identities and practice*. Preston: University of Central Lancashire/Sheffield: Sheffield Hallam University.

Henderson, F., Hall, K., Mutongi, A. & Whittam, G. (2019) Social enterprise, social innovation and self-directed care: Lessons from Scotland. *Social Enterprise Journal*. 15(4): 438–56. https://doi.org/10.1108/SEJ12-2018-0080.

Hendriks, P. & van Ewijk, H. (2017) To have voice and choice: Turkish and Moroccan Dutch professionals in social work. *International Social Work*, 60(3): 720–32.

Hennessy, P. (2022) *A duty of care: Britain before and after covid*. London: Allen Lane.

Hetherington, R. (2006) Learning from difference: Comparing child welfare systems. In N. Freymond & C. Cameron (eds) *Towards positive systems of child and family welfare: International comparisons of child protection, family service and community caring systems* (pp 27–50). Toronto: University of Toronto Press.

Hildeng, B. (1995) The Norwegian welfare state: Its aims and organization. In Ø. Tutvedt & L. Young (eds) *Social Work and the Norwegian Welfare State* (pp. 165–98) (Ø.K.S. rapport nr. 95:2). Oslo: NotaBene.

Hill, K., Fogel, S., Plitt Donaldson, L. & Erickson, C. (2017) State definitions of social work practice: Implications for our professional identity. *Journal of Evidence-Informed Social Work*, 14(4): 266–79.

Hindmarsh, J.H. (1992) *Social work oppositions: New graduates' experiences*. Aldershot: Avebury.

Hochschild, A.R. (2003) *The commercialization of intimate life: Notes from home and work.* Berkeley, CA: University of California Press.

Hochschild, A.R. (2012 [1983]) *The managed heart: The commercialization of human feeling.* Berkeley, CA: University of California Press.

Hoefer, R. (2019) *Advocacy practice for social justice* (4th edn). New York: Oxford University Press.

Hohman, M. (2016) *Motivational interviewing in social work practice.* New York: Guilford.

Hollis, F. (1968) *A typology of social casework.* New York: Family Service Association of America.

Hollis, F. & Woods, M.E. (1981) *Casework: A psychosocial therapy* (3rd edn). New York: Random House.

Hollway, W. (2006) *The capacity to care: Gender and ethical subjectivity.* Abingdon: Routledge.

Hooyman, N.R. (1991) Supporting practice in large-scale bureaucracies. In M. Bricker-Jenkins, N.R. Hooyman & N. Gottlieb (eds) *Feminist social work practice in clinical settings* (pp. 251–68). Newbury Park, CA: Sage.

Hornby, S. & Atkins, J. (2000) *Collaborative care: Interprofessional, interagency and interpersonal* (2nd edn). Oxford: Blackwell.

Houston, S. (2013) Jürgen Habermas. In M. Gray & S.A. Webb (eds) *Social work theories and methods* (2nd edn) (pp. 13–24). London: Sage.

Howe, D. (1993) *On being a client: Understanding the process of counselling and psychotherapy.* London: Sage.

Hudson, B. (2002) Interprofessionality in health and social care: The Achilles' heel of partnership? *Journal of Interprofessional Care, 16*(1): 7–17.

Hudson, C.G. (2010) *Complex systems and human behaviour.* Chicago: Lyceum.

Hulgård, L. (2011) Social economy and social enterprise: An emerging alternative to mainstream market economy? *China Journal of Social Work, 4*(3): 201–15.

Humphreys, S., McGrath, M., & Grant, G. (1986) Reflections on an All-Wales Strategy vanguard area. *Journal of the British Institute of Mental Handicap (APEX), 14*(4), 143–47.

Hunter, S. & Ritchie, P. (2007) Introduction: With, not to: Models of co-production in social welfare. In S. Hunter & P. Ritchie (eds) *Co-production and personalisation in social care: Changing relationships in the provision of social care* (pp. 9–18). London: Jessica Kingsley.

Huxley, P., Evans, S., Beresford, P., Davidson, B. & King, S. (2009) The principles and provisions of relationships: Findings from an evaluation of support, time and recovery workers in mental health services in England. *Journal of Social Work, 9*(1): 99–117.

Hyslop, I. (2018) Neoliberalism and social work identity. *European Journal of Social Work, 21*(1): 20–31.

ICF Consulting (2018) *The economic value of the adult social care sector – UK: Final report.* London: ICF Consulting.

Ife, J. (2012) *Human rights and social work: Towards rights-based practice* (3rd edn). Port Melbourne: Cambridge University Press.

IFSW (International Federation of Social Workers) (2014) *Global definition of social work*. Rheinfelden: IFSW.

IFSW (2016) *Constitution of the International Federation of Social Workers*. Rheinfelden: IFSW.

Inter-Agency Standing Committee (2022) *Basic psychosocial skills: A guide for COVID-19 responders*. Geneva: World Health Organization.

Ipsos/MORI (2017) *Public Perceptions of the NHS and Social Care Survey: An ongoing tracking study for the Department of Health, winter 2016 wave*. London: Ipsos/MORI Research Institute.

Irvine, E.E. (1952) The function and use of relationship between client and psychiatric social worker. In E. Younghusband (ed.) (1966). *New developments in casework* (pp. 88–94). London: Allen & Unwin.

Irvine, E.E. (1978) Professional claims and the professional task. In Open University Course Team (eds) *Professional and non-professional roles 1*, Milton Keynes: Open University, pp. 85–113.

James, A.L. (2004) The McDonaldization of social work – or 'Come back, Florence Hollis, all is (or should be) forgiven'. In R. Lovelock, K. Lyons & J. Powell (eds) *Reflecting on social work – discipline and profession* (pp. 27–54). Farnham: Ashgate.

Jaspal, R. & Breakwell, G.M. (eds) (2014) *Identity process theory: Identity, social action and social change*. Cambridge: Cambridge University Press.

Jaspers, S. & Steen, T. (2019) Realizing public values: Enhancement or obstruction? Exploring value tensions and coping strategies in the co-production of social care. *Public Management Review*, 21(4): 606–27.

Jeans, M.S. (1978) *Role analysis in field social work: The development of a new model*. Exeter: Devon Social Services Department.

Jones, H.D. (1994) *Social workers, or social educators? The international context for developing social care*. London: National Institute for Social Work.

Jordan, B. (1979) *Helping in social work*. London: Routledge and Kegan Paul.

Jordan, B. with Jordan, C. (2000) *Social work and the third way: Tough love as social policy*. London: Sage.

Jun, M. (2022) Stigma and shame attached to claiming social assistance benefits: Understanding the detrimental impact on UK lone mothers' social relationships. *Journal of Family Studies*, 28(1): 199–215.

Kane, R.A. (1975) *Interprofessional teamwork* (Manpower Monograph 8). Syracuse, New York: Syracuse University School of Social Work.

Karls, J.M. & O'Keefe, M.E. (eds) (1994) *Person-in-environment system: The PIE classification system for social functioning problems*. Washington, DC: NASW Press.

Kautilya (1992) *The Arthashastra*. L.M. Ranganathan (ed.). New Delhi: Penguin.

Kautto, M. (2001) *Diversity among welfare states: Comparative studies on welfare state adjustment in Nordic countries* (Stakes Research Report 118). Helsinki: National Research and Development Centre for Welfare and Health.

Kearney, J. (2004) 'Knowing how to go on': Towards situated practice and emergent theory in social work. In R. Lovelock, K. Lyons & J. Powell (eds) *Reflecting on social work – discipline and profession* (pp. 163–80). Farnham: Ashgate.

Keddell, E. & Stanley, T. (2017) Risk work in the formation of the 'professional' in child protection social work. In S.A. Webb (ed.) *Professional identity and social work* (pp. 94–107). Abingdon: Routledge.

Kendall, K. (2002) *Council on Social Work Education: Its antecedents and the first twenty years.* Alexandria, VA: Council on Social Work Education.

Kenny, K., Haugh, H. & Fotaki, M. (2020) Organizational form and pro-social fantasy in social enterprise creation. *Human Relations, 73*(1): 94–123.

Khoshnood, K., Raymond, N.A. & Howarth, C.N. (2023) *Russia's systematic program for the re-education and adoption of Ukraine's children.* New Haven, CT: Humanitarian Research Laboratory, Yale School of Public Health.

Keith-Lucas, A. (1972) *Giving and taking help.* Chapel Hill, NC: University of North Carolina Press.

Kidneigh, J.C. (1950) Social work administration: An area of social work practice? *Social Work Journal,* 57, 61–79.

Kitchener, M., Kirkpatrick, I. & Whipp, R. (2000) Supervising professional work under new public management: Evidence from an 'invisible trade'. *British Journal of Management, 11*(3): 213–26.

Kleibl, T., Lutz, R., Noyoo, N., Bunk, B., Dittman, A. & Seepamore, B. (eds) (2020) *The Routledge handbook of postcolonial social work.* Abingdon: Routledge.

Kogan, L.S. & Hunt, J.M. (1954) Two year study of casework uses. *Social Casework, 35*(2): 52–7.

Kootstra, A. & Roosma, F. (2018) Changing public support for welfare sanctioning in Britain and the Netherlands: A persuasion experiment. *Social Policy and Administration, 52*(4): 847–61.

Kornbeck, J. & Jensen, N.R. (eds) (2009) *The diversity of social pedagogy in Europe.* Bremen: Europäischer Hochschulverlag.

Kramer, R.M. & Specht, H. (1969, 1975, 1983) *Readings in community organization practice* (1st, 2nd & 3rd edns). Englewood Cliffs, NJ: Prentice-Hall.

Kravetz, D. & Jones, L.E. (1991) Supporting practice in feminist service agencies. In M. Bricker-Jenkins, N.R. Hooyman & N. Gottlieb (eds) *Feminist social work practice in clinical settings* (pp. 233–49). Newbury Park, CA: Sage.

Kreitzer, L. (2012) *Social work in Africa: Exploring culturally relevant education and practice in Ghana.* Calgary: University of Calgary Press.

Kropotkin, P. (2022 [1902]) *Mutual aid: A factor of evolution.* London: Penguin Classics.

Kummitha, R.K.R. (2016) *Social entrepreneurship: Working towards greater inclusiveness.* New Delhi: Sage.

Kurzman, P.A. (2000) Bakalinsky's conundrum: Should social workers practice in the world of work. *Administration in Social Work, 23*(3/4): 157–61.

Langan, M. & Lee, P. (eds) (1989) *Radical social work today.* London: Unwin Hyman.

Lawler, J. & Bilson, A. (2010) *Social work management and leadership: Managing complexity with creativity.* Abingdon: Routledge.

Layard, R. (2005) *Happiness: Lessons from a new science.* London: Allen Lane.

Leah, C. (2017) Approved mental health professionals: Negotiating dialogic identities as hybrid professionals [EdD thesis]. Manchester: University of Manchester School of Environment, Education and Development.

Leamy, M., Bird, V., Le Boutillier, C., Williams, J. & Slade, M. (2011) Conceptual framework for personal recovery in mental health: Systematic review and narrative synthesis. *British Journal of Psychiatry, 199*: 445–52.

LeCroy, C.W. & Stinson, E.L. (2004) The public's perception of social work: Is it what we think it is? *Social Work, 49*(2): 164–74.

Lee, J.A.B. (2001) *The empowerment approach to social work practice: Building the beloved community* (2nd edn). New York: Columbia University Press.

Le Grand, J. (2007) *Consistent care matters: Exploring the potential of social work practices.* London: Department for Education and Skills.

Le Grand, J. & Bartlett, W. (eds) (1993) *Quasi-markets and social policy.* Basingstoke: Macmillan.

Leigh, J. (2017) Credible performances: Affect and professional identity. In S.A. Webb (ed.) *Professional identity and social work* (pp. 197–210). Abingdon: Routledge.

Leigh, J., Morriss, L. & Morriss, M. (2020) Making visible an invisible trade: Exploring the everyday experiences of doing social work and being a social worker. *Qualitative Social Work, 19*(2): 267–83.

Lévesque, M., Negura, L., Gaucher, C. & Molgat, M. (2019) Social representation of social work in the Canadian healthcare setting: Negotiating a professional identity. *British Journal of Social Work, 49*(8): 2245–65.

Lewis, J. (2002) The boundary between health and social care for older people. In B. Bytheway, V. Bacigalupo, J. Bornat, J., Johnson & S. Spurr (eds) *Understanding care, welfare and community: A reader* (pp. 313–20). London: Routledge.

Lewis, J. & Glennerster, H. (1996) *Implementing the New Community Care.* Buckingham: Open University Press.

Lindbeck, A. (1995a) Hazardous welfare-state dynamics. *American Economic Review, 85,* 9–15.

Lindbeck, A. (1995b) Welfare state disincentives with endogenous habits and norms. *Scandinavian Journal of Economics, 97*: 477–94.

Lipsky, M. (1980) *Street-level bureaucracy: The dilemmas of individuals in public service,* New York: Russell Sage Foundation.

Lloyd, C., King, R. & Chenoweth, L. (2002) Social work, stress and burnout: A review. *Journal of Mental Health, 11*(3): 255–65.

Loch, C.S. (1883) *How to help in cases of distress: A handy reference book for almoners, almsgivers, and others.* London: Longmans, Green.

Lonsdale, S., Webb, A. & Briggs, T.L. (eds) (1980) *Teamwork in the personal social services and health care: British and American perspectives.* London: Croom Helm.

Lorenz, W. (2005) Social work and the Bologna process. *Social Work and Society, 3*(2): 224–35.

Loxley, A. (1997) *Collaboration in health and welfare: Working with difference.* London: Jessica Kingsley.

Lubove, R. (1965) *The professional altruist: The emergence of social work as a career 1880–1930*. Cambridge, MA: Harvard University Press.

Lukes, S. (2005) *Power: A radical view* (2nd edn). Basingstoke: Palgrave Macmillan.

Lurie, H.L. (1935) Re-examination of child welfare functions in family and foster care agencies. In: F. Lowry (ed.) (1939) *Readings in social case work 1920–1938: Selected reprints for the case work practitioner* (pp. 611–9). New York: Columbia University Press.

Lymbery, M. & Postle, K. (2015) *Social work and the transformation of adult social care: Perpetuating a distorted vision?* Bristol: Policy Press.

Lynch, K. (2022) *Care and capitalism: Why affective justice matters for social justice.* Cambridge: Polity.

Lynch, K. & Lyons, M. (2009) Love labouring: Nurturing rationalities and relational identities. In K. Lynch, J. Baker, M. Lyons et al. *Affective equality: Love, care and injustice* (pp. 54–77). Basingstoke: Palgrave Macmillan.

Lynch, K. & Walsh J. (2009) Love, care and solidarity: What is and is not commodifiable. In K. Lynch, J. Baker, M. Lyons et al. *Affective equality: Love, care and injustice* (pp. 39–53). Basingstoke: Palgrave Macmillan.

Lynch, K., Baker, J., Cantillon, S. & Walsh, J. (2009) Which equalities matter? The place of affective equality in egalitarian thinking. In K. Lynch, J. Baker, M. Lyons et al. *Affective equality: Love, care and injustice* (pp. 12–34). Basingstoke: Palgrave Macmillan.

Lynch, K., Baker, J., Lyons, M. with Cantillon, S., Walsh, J., Feely, M., Hanlon, N. & O'Brien, M. (2009) *Affective equality: Love, care and injustice.* Basingstoke: Palgrave Macmillan.

Lynch, K., Kalaitzake, V. & Crean, M. (2020) Care and affective relations: Social justice and sociology. *Sociological Review, 69*(1), 53–71.

MacAlister, J. (2022) *The independent review of children's social care: Final report.* London: Independent Review of Children's Social Care.

Macdonald, G., Sheldon, B., with Gillespie, J. (1992) Contemporary studies of the effectiveness of social work. *British Journal of Social Work, 22*(6): 615–43.

Mackay, T. & Zufferey, C. (2015) 'A who doing a what?' Identity, practice and social work education. *Journal of Social Work, 15*(6): 644–61.

MacLehose, A. (2011) A Foucauldian analysis of 'troubled families' [PhD thesis]. London: University of East London https://repository.uel.ac.uk.

Mafile'o, T. & Vakalahi, H.F.O. (2018) Indigenous social work across borders: Expanding social work in the South Pacific. *International Social Work, 61*(4): 537–52.

Mafile'o, T.A. (2004) Exploring Tongan social work: *Fakafekau'aki* (connecting) and *fakat-kilalo* (humility). *Qualitative Social Work, 3*(3): 239–57.

Mantell, A., Simpson, G.K., Vungkhanching, M., Jones, K.F., Strandberg, T. & Simonson, P. (2018) Social work-generated evidence in traumatic brain injury from 1975 to 2014: A systematic scoping review. *Health & Social Care in the Community, 26*(4): 433–48.

Margolis, E. & Laurence, S. (2013) In defense of nativism. *Philosophical Studies, 165*: 693–718.

Marmot Review (2010) *Fair society, healthy lives: Strategic review of health inequalities in England post-2010.* London: Marmot Review.

Marsh, P. & Doel, M. (2005) *The task-centred book.* London: Routledge.

Marshall, T.H. (1949) Citizenship and social class. In S. Lazar (ed.) (2013) *The anthropology of citizenship: A reader* (pp. 52–60). Chichester: Wiley.

Marshall, T.H. & Bottomore, T.B. (1992) *Citizenship and social class.* London: Pluto.

Martinussen, J. (1997) *Society, state and market: A complete guide to competing theories of development.* London: Zed Books.

Matthies, A.-L. & Närhi, K. (eds) (2017) *The ecosocial transition of societies: The contribution of social work and social policy.* Abingdon: Routledge.

Mayer, J.E., & Timms, N. (1970) *The client speaks: Working class impressions of casework.* London: Routledge and Kegan Paul.

Mayeroff, M. (1971) *On caring.* New York: Harper and Row.

McBeath, G.B. & Webb, S.A. (1997) Community care: A unity of state and care? Some political and philosophical considerations. In R. Hugman, M. Peelo & K. Soothill (eds) *Concepts of care: Developments in health and social welfare* (pp. 36–51). London: Arnold.

McCold, P. & Wachtel, B. (2012) *Restorative policing experiment: The Bethlehem Pennsylvania Police Family Group Conferencing Project.* Eugene, OR: Wipf and Stock.

McCulloch, T. & Webb, S. (2020) What the public think about social services: A report from Scotland. *British Journal of Social Work, 50*(4): 1146–66.

McDermott, F.E. (ed.) (1975) *Self-determination in social work: A collection of essays on self-determination and related concepts by philosophers and social work theorists.* London: Routledge and Kegan Paul.

McFadden, P., Campbell, A. & Taylor, B. (2015) Resilience and burnout in child protection social work: Individual and organisational themes from a systematic literature review. *British Journal of Social Work, 45*(5): 1546–63.

McGregor, J., Mercer, S.W. & Harris, F.M. (2018) Health benefits of primary care social work for adults with complex health and social needs: A systematic review. *Health & Social Care in the Community, 26*(1): 1–13.

McKinnon, J. & Alston, M. (eds) (2016) *Ecological social work: Towards sustainability.* London: Palgrave Macmillan.

McLaughlin, H. & Teater, B. (2017) *Evidence-informed practice for social workers.* London: Sage.

Meyer, H.J., Borgatta, E.F. & Jones, W.C. (1965) *Girls at Vocational High: An experiment in social work intervention.* New York: Russell Sage Foundation.

Midgley, J. (1995) *Social development: The developmental perspective in social welfare.* London: Sage.

Midgley, M. & Conley, A. (eds) (2010) *Social work and social development: Theories and skills for developmental social work.* New York: Oxford University Press.

Mijs, J.J.B. (2021) The paradox of inequality: Income inequality and belief in meritocracy go hand in hand. *Socio-Economic Review, 19*(1): 7–35

Miller, W. & Rollnick, S. (2013) *Motivational interviewing: Helping people change* (3rd edn). New York: Guilford.

Milner, J. (2001) *Women and social work: Narrative approaches*. Basingstoke: Palgrave.

Milner, J., Myers, S. & O'Byrne, P. (2015) *Assessment in social work* (4th edn). London: Palgrave.

Mishra, R. (1990) *The welfare state in capitalist society: Policies of retrenchment and maintenance in Europe, North America and Australia*. Hemel Hempstead: Harvester Wheatsheaf.

Mitchell, F., Shaw, I.F. & Lunt, N. (2008) *Practitioner research in social services: A literature review*. Glasgow: Institute for Research and Innovation in Social Services.

Mitendorf, A. (2020) Professional social work narratives in a young, complex neoliberal society [PhD thesis]. Tallinn: Tallinn University Dissertations in Social Sciences.

Mitendorf, A. & van Ewijk, H. (2018) Between multi-layered normativity and path finding in professional social work: The case of the individual and neo-liberal Estonian society. *British Journal of Social Work*, 48(7): 1892–909.

Moffitt, B. (2020) *Populism*. Cambridge: Polity.

Montgomery, J. (2006) Legal issues of multiprofessional teamwork. In Speck, P. (ed.) *Teamwork in palliative care: Fulfilling or frustrating*. Oxford: Oxford University Press.

Mullaly, B. & Dupré, M. (2019) *The new structural social work: Ideology, theory, and practice* (4th edn). Don Mills: Oxford University Press.

Mullaly, B. & West, J. (2018) *Challenging oppression and confronting privilege: A critical approach to anti-oppressive and anti-privilege theory and practice* (3rd edn). Don Mills: Oxford University Press.

Munro, E. (2010) *The Munro review of child protection, Part 1: A systems analysis*. London: Department for Education. https://asscts.publishing.service.gov.uk/government/uploads/system/uploads/attachment_data/file/624949/TheMunroReview-Part_one.pdf.

Munro, E. (2011) *The Munro review of child protection, Final report: A child-centred system* (Cm 8062). London: TSO. https://assets.publishing.service.gov.uk/government/uploads/system/uploads/attachment_data/file/175391/Munro-Review.pdf.

Muzicant, A. & Peled, E. (2018) Home visits in social work: From disembodiment to embodied presence. *British Journal of Social Work*, 48(3): 826–42.

Navrátil, P. & Bajer, P. (2018) Social construction of social work identity in the processes of its institutionalisation. *Annals of Social Sciences and Management Studies*, 1(3): doi: 10.19080/ASM.2018.01.555563.

Needleman, J. (2017) Nursing skill mix and patient outcomes. *British Medical Journal Quality and Safety*, 26: 525–8.

Newman, J. (2002) The new public management, modernization and institutional change: Disruptions, disjunctures and dilemmas. In K. McLaughlin, S.P. Osborne & E. Ferlie (eds) *New public management: Current trends and future prospects* (pp. 77–92). London: Routledge.

Newth, G. (2021) Populism and nativism in contemporary regionalist and nationalist politics: A minimalist framework for ideologically opposed parties. *Politics*, 44(1), 3–24. https://doi.org/10.1177/0263395721995016.

Nicholls, A. (2006) Introduction. In A. Nicholls (ed.) *Social entrepreneurship: New models of sustainable social change* (pp. 1–35). Oxford: Oxford University Press.

Nokes, P. (2013 [1976]) *The professional task in welfare practice.* London: Routledge and Kegan Paul.

Norton, M. (2023) *Co-production in mental health: Implementing policy in practice.* Abingdon: Routledge.

Nozick, R. (1974) *Anarchy, state and utopia.* Oxford: Blackwell.

O'Brien, M. & Penna, S. (1998) *Theorising welfare: Enlightenment and modern society.* London: Sage.

O'Connor, J. (2017 [1973]) *The fiscal crisis of the state* (with a new introduction by the author). Abingdon: Routledge.

Offer, J. (2006) *An intellectual history of British social policy: Idealism versus non-idealism.* Bristol: Policy Press.

Oham, C. & Macdonald, D. (eds) (2016) *Leading and managing a social enterprise in health and social care.* London: Community Training Partners.

Olin, J. (2013) The public and the profession's perception of social work. *Columbia Social Work Review*, 11(1): 92–102.

Oliver, C. (2017) *Strengths-based child protection: Firm, fair and friendly.* Toronto: University of Toronto Press.

ONS (Office for National Statistics) (2018) *Living longer: How our population is changing and why it matters.* www.ons.gov.uk/peoplepopulationandcommunity/ birthsdeathsandmarriages/ageing/articles/livinglongerhowourpopulationisch angingandwhyitmatters/2018-08-13#how-is-the-uk-population-changing.

ONS (2023) *Care homes and estimating the self-funding population, England: 2021 to 2022.* www.ons.gov.uk/peoplepopulationandcommunity/healthandsocialcare/ socialcare/articles/carehomesandestimatingtheselffundingpopulationengland/ 2021to2022#care-homes-for-working-age-adults.

Ostrom, E. (1996) Crossing the great divide: Coproduction, synergy, and development. *World Development*, 24(6): 1073–87.

Otto, H.-U., Polutta, A. & Ziegler H. (eds) (2009) *Evidence-based practice – Modernising the knowledge base of social work?* Opladen: Barbara Budrich.

Parker, G. & Lawton, D. (1994) *Different types of care, different types of carer: Evidence from the General Household Survey.* London: HMSO.

Parker, R.A. (1988) An historical background. In I. Sinclair, I. (ed.) *Residential care: The research reviewed.* London: HMSO.

Parker, R., Ward, H., Jackson, S., Aldgate, J. & Wedge, P. (eds) (1991) *Looking after children—Assessing outcomes in child care.* London: HMSO.

Parton, N. (ed.) (1996) *Social theory, social change and social work.* London: Routledge.

Parton, N. (2014) *The politics of child protection: Contemporary development and future directions.* Basingstoke: Palgrave Macmillan.

Parton, N. & O'Byrne, P. (2000) *Constructive social work: Towards a new practice.* Basingstoke: Macmillan.

Patel, L. (2015) *Social welfare and social development* (2nd edn). Cape Town: Oxford University Press.

Payne, M. (1993) *Linkages: Effective networking in social care.* London: Whiting and Birch.

Payne, M. (1995a) Partnership between organisations in social work education. *Issues in Social Work Education, 14*(1): 53–70.

Payne, M. (1995b) *Social work and community care.* Basingstoke: Macmillan.

Payne, M. (1996) *What is professional social work?* Birmingham: Venture.

Payne, M. (1997a) Care management and social work. In J. Bornat, J. Johnson, C. Pereira, D. Pilgrim & F. Williams (eds) *Community care: A reader* (pp. 277–86). Basingstoke: Macmillan.

Payne, M. (1997b) Government guidance in the construction of the social work profession. In R. Adams (ed.) *Crisis in the human services: National and international issues* (pp. 381–90). Hull: University of Lincoln and Humberside.

Payne, M. (2000) The politics of case management in social work. *International Journal of Social Welfare, 9*(1): 82–91.

Payne, M. (2002) The politics of systems theory within social work. *Journal of Social Work* 2(3): 269–92.

Payne, M. (2005) *The origins of social work: Continuity and change.* Basingstoke: Palgrave Macmillan.

Payne, M. (2006) *What is professional social work?* (2nd edn) Bristol: Policy Press.

Payne, M. (2008a) Research and audit in palliative care. In N. Hartley & M. Payne (eds). *The creative arts in palliative care* (pp. 66–80). London: Jessica Kingsley.

Payne, M. (2008b) Staff support. In M. Lloyd-Williams (ed.) *Psychosocial issues in palliative care* (2nd edn) (pp. 232–52). Oxford: Oxford University Press.

Payne, M. (2009) Dictionary definitions of social work. Unpublished paper. www.scribd.com/doc/14979297/Dictionary-Definitions-of-Social-Work

Payne, M. (2012) Political and organisational contexts of social work internationally. In K. Lyons, N. Huegler, M.C. Hokenstad & M. Pawar (eds). *Handbook of international social work* (pp. 121–35). London: Sage.

Payne, M. (2014a) European social works and their identities. *ERIS Web Journal.* 2/2014: 2–14. https://periodika.osu.cz/eris/dok/2014-02/1-payne-european-social-work-and-their-identities.pdf.

Payne, M. (2014b) Social care and social justice. In M. Reisch (ed.) *The Routledge international handbook of social justice* (pp. 398–408). Abingdon: Routledge.

Payne, M. (2017) *Older citizens and end-of-life care: Social work practice strategies for adults in later life.* Abingdon: Routledge.

Payne, M. (2021) *Modern social work theory* (5th edn). London: Bloomsbury.

Payne, M. (2022) Ageism, older people and COVID-19. In P. Fronek & K.S. Rotabi-Casares (eds) *Social work in health emergencies* (pp. 201–15). Abingdon: Routledge.

Payne, M. (2023) Critical eco practice: How should it develop in social work practice thinking? *Czech and Slovak Social Work*, *23*(4): 4–17.

Payne, M. & Askeland, G.A. (2008) *Globalization and international social work: Postmodern change and challenge*. Aldershot: Ashgate.

Pease, B. & Fook, J. (1999) *Transforming social work practice: Postmodern critical perspectives*. London: Routledge.

Penhale, B. & Young, J. (2015) *A review of the literature concerning what the public and users of social work services in England think about the conduct and competence of social workers*. Norwich: UEA Consulting.

Penketh, L. & Pratt A. (2000) The 'two souls of socialism': The labour movement and unemployment during the 1920s and 1930s. In M. Lavalette & G. Mooney (eds) *Class struggle and social welfare* (pp. 117–38). London: Routledge.

Perlman, H.H. (1957) *Social casework: A problem-solving process*. Chicago, IL: University of Chicago Press.

Perlmutter, F.D. (2006) Ensuring social work administration. *Administration in Social Work*, *30*(2): 3–10.

Petch, A., Cook, A. & Miller, E. (2013) Partnership working and outcomes: Do health and social care partnerships deliver for users and carers? *Health and Social Care in the Community*, *21*(6): 623–33. https://doi.org/10.1111/hsc.12050

Phillips, D. (1983) Mayer and Timms revisited: The evolution of client studies. In M.I. Fisher (ed.) *Speaking of clients* (pp. 8–23). Sheffield: Joint Unit for Social Services Research.

Pink, S., Ferguson, H. & Kelly, L. (2020) Child protection social work in COVID-19: Reflections on home visits and digital intimacy. *Anthropology in Action*, *27*(3): 27–30.

Pinker, R. (1982) An alternative view. In Barclay report. *Social workers: Their role and tasks* (App. B, 236–62). London: National Institute for Social Work.

Pithouse, A. (2019 [1984]) *Social work: The social organisation of an invisible trade* (2nd edn). Abingdon: Routledge.

Pollitt, C. (1993) *Managerialism and the public services: Cuts or cultural change in the 1990s?* Oxford: Blackwell.

Pollitt, C. (2002) The new public management in international perspective: An analysis of impacts and effects. In K. McLaughlin, S.P. Osborne & E. Ferlie (eds) *New public management: Current trends and future prospects* (pp. 274–92). London: Routledge.

Popple, K. (2015) *Analysing community work: Theory and practice* (2nd edn). Maidenhead: Open University Press.

Postle, K. (2001) The social work side is disappearing. I guess it started with us being called care managers. *Practice*, *13*(1): 3–18.

Postle, K. (2002) Working between 'the idea and the reality': Ambiguities and tensions in care managers' work. *British Journal of Social Work*, *32*(3): 335–51.

Powell, J.L. (2013) Michel Foucault. In M. Gray & S.A. Webb (eds) *Social work theories and methods* (2nd edn) (pp. 46–62). London: Sage.

Pritchard, C. & Taylor, R. (1978) *Social work: Reform or revolution?* London Routledge and Kegan Paul.

Prochaska, J.O. & DiClemente, C.C. (1983) Stages and processes of self-change of smoking: Toward an integrative model of change. *Journal of Consulting and Clinical Psychology, 51*, pp. 390–5.

Prochaska, J.O., DiClemente, C.C. & Norcross, J.C. (1994) *Changing for good.* New York: Avon Books.

Puig de la Bellacasa, M. (2017) *Matters of care: Speculative ethics in more than human worlds.* Minneapolis, MN: University of Minnesota Press.

Pulla, V.R., Das, T.K. & Nikku, B.R. (2020) Indigenous or blended model for South Asian social work? *Space and Culture, India, 8*(1): 40–58.

Ramon, S., Moshe Grodofsky, M., Allegri, E. & Rafaelic, A. (2019) Service users' involvement in social work education: Focus on social change projects. *Social Work Education, 38*(1): 89–102.

Rapp, C.A. & Goscha, R.J. (2012) *The strengths model: A recovery-oriented approach to mental health services* (3rd edn). New York: Oxford University Press.

Realpe, A. & Wallace, L.M. (2010) *What is co-production?* London: Health Foundation.

Rees, S. & Wallace, A. (1982) *Verdicts on social work.* London: Arnold.

Reid, W.J. & Epstein, L. (1972) *Task-centered casework.* New York: Columbia University Press.

Reid, W.J. & Misener, E. (2001) Social work in the press: A cross-national study. *International Journal of Social Welfare, 10*(3): 194–201.

Reisch, M. (1998) The sociopolitical context and social work method, 1890–1950. *Social Service Review, 72*(2): 161–81.

Richmond, M.E. (1922) *What is social case work? An introductory description.* New York: Russell Sage Foundation.

Richmond, M.E. (1965 [1917]) *Social diagnosis.* New York: Free Press.

Riggall, S. (2012) *Using counselling skills in social work.* London: Sage.

Ritzer, G. (1996) *The McDonaldization of society – An investigation into the changing character of contemporary social life.* Thousand Oaks, CA: Pine Forge.

Robb, M., Montgomery, H. & Thomson, R. (eds) (2019) *Critical practice with children and young people* (2nd edn). Bristol: Policy Press.

Robinson, K. & Webber, M. (2013) Models and effectiveness of service user and carer involvement in social work education: A literature review. *British Journal of Social Work, 43*(5): 925–44.

Robinson, V.P. (1930) *A changing psychology in social case work.* Chapel Hill, NC: University of North Carolina Press.

Rodriguez, E. (2001) Keeping the unemployed healthy: The effect of means-tested and entitlement benefits in Britain, Germany, and the United States. *American Journal of Public Health, 91*(9): 1403–11.

Rogowski, S. (2013) *Critical social work with children and families: Theory, context and practice.* Bristol Policy Press.

Rojek, C., Peacock, G. & Collins, S. (1988) *Social work and received ideas*. London: Routledge.

Ronen, T. & Freeman, A. (eds) (2007) *Cognitive behavior therapy in clinical social work practice*. New York: Springer.

Roosma, F. (2016) A multidimensional perspective on the social legitimacy of welfare states in Europe [PhD thesis]. Tilberg: Tilberg University.

Roscoe, K.D. & Pithouse, A. (2018) Discourse, identity and socialisation: A textual analysis of the 'accounts' of student social workers. *Critical and Radical Social Work*, 6(3): 345–62.

Rosenhaft, E. (1994) The historical development of German social policy. In J. Clasen & R. Freeman (eds) *Social policy in Germany* (pp. 21–41). Hemel Hempstead: Harvester Wheatsheaf.

Ruch, G., Turney, D. & Ward, A. (eds) (2018) *Relationship-based social work: Getting to the heart of practice* (2nd edn). London: Jessica Kingsley.

Rüesch, P., Graf, J., Meyer, P.C., Rössler, W. & Hell, D. (2004) Occupation, social support and quality of life in persons with schizophrenic or affective disorders. *Social Psychiatry and Psychiatric Epidemiology*, 39: 686–94.

Russell, B. (1938) The forms of power. In S. Lukes (ed.) *Power* (pp. 19–27). Oxford: Blackwell.

Ryan, J.J. (1963) Social work executive: Generalist or specialist? *Social Work*, 8(2): 26–33.

Sainsbury, E.E., Nixon, S. & Phillips, D. (1982) *Social work in focus: Clients' and social workers' perceptions in long-term social work*. London: Routledge and Kegan Paul..

Salomon, A. (1937) *Education for Social work. A sociological interpretation based on an international survey* (edited by ICSSW). Zurich: Verlag für Recht und Gesellschaft.

Samuels, R. (2002) Nativism in cognitive science. *Mind and Language*, 17(3): 233–65.

Sandel, M.J. (2012) *What money can't buy: The moral limits of markets*. London: Allen Lane.

Sanders, D.S. (1982) The developmental perspective in social work. In D.S. Sanders (ed.) *The developmental perspective in social work* (pp. 379–87). Honolulu: University of Hawaii, School of Social Work.

Sands, R.G. & Nuccio, K. (1992) Postmodern feminist theory and social work. *Social Work*, 37(6): 489–94.

Satka, M. (1995) *Making social citizenship: Conceptual practices from the Finnish Poor Law to professional social work*. Jyväskylä: SoPhi.

Satyamurti, C. (1979) Care and control in local authority social work. In N. Parry, M. Rustin & C. Satyamurti (eds). *Social work, welfare and the state* (pp 87–103). London: Edward Arnold.

Schriver, J.M. (1987) Harry Lurie's critique: Person and environment in early casework practice, *Social Service Review*, 61(3): 514–32.

Schwartz, H.M. (2022) What's missing when we think about Global Political Economy? *Global Political Economy*, 1(1): 155–72.

SCIE (Social Care Institute for Excellence) (2020) *Taking self-directed support back to its roots*. London: SCIE.

SCIE (2022) *Coproduction: What is it and how to do it*. London: SCIE.

Scora, D. (2005) Engaging respondents in situations of alleged child abuse. In Compton, B.R., Galaway, B. & Cournoyer, B.R. *Social work processes* (p. 171). Belmont, CA: Brooks/Cole.

Seebohm Report (1968) *Report of the committee on local authority and allied personal services* (Cmnd 3703). London: HMSO.

Seligman, M. (2017 [2002]) *Authentic happiness: Using the new positive psychology to realize your potential for lasting fulfilment*. London: Brearley.

Sen, A. (1993) Capability and well-being. In A. Sen & M. Nussbaum (eds). The quality of life (pp 30–53). Oxford: Clarendon Press.

Sen, A. (2017) *Collective choice and social welfare* (expanded edn). London: Penguin.

Sevenhuijsen, S. (1998) *Citizenship and the ethics of care: Feminist considerations on justice, morality and politics*. London: Routledge.

Shakespeare, T. (2000) *Help*. Birmingham: Venture.

Shaw, I., Arksey, H. & Mullender, A. (2004) *ESRC research, social work and social care*. London: Social Care Institute for Excellence.

Sheldon, B. (1987) Implementing findings from social work effectiveness research. *British Journal of Social Work*, *17*(6): 573–86.

Shennan, G. (2019) *Solution-focused practice: Effective communication to facilitate change* (2nd edn). Basingstoke: Palgrave Macmillan.

Sipilä, J. (ed.) (1997) *Social care services: The key to the Scandinavian welfare model* (pp. 27–50). Aldershot: Ashgate.

Sipilä, J., with Andersson, M., Hammarqvist, S.-E., Nordlander, L. Rauhala, P.L., Thomsen, K. & Nielsen, H.W. (1997) A multitude of universal public services – how and why did four Scandinavian countries get their social care service model? In J. Sipilä (ed.) *Social care services: The key to the Scandinavian welfare model* (pp. 27–50). Aldershot: Ashgate.

Skills for Care (2022) *Headline social worker information: Social workers employed by local authorities in the adult social care sector*. Leeds: Skills for Care. www.skillsforcare.org.uk/Adult-Social-Care-Workforce-Data/Workforce-intelligence/documents/Social-Worker-Headline-Stats-Feb-2022.pdf.

Slusser, M.M., Garcia, L.I., Reed, C.-R. & McGinnis, P.Q. (2019) *Foundations of interprofessional collaborative practice in health care*. St Louis, MO: Elsevier.

Social Work England (2019) *Professional standards*. London: Social Work England. www.socialworkengland.org.uk/media/1640/1227_socialworkengland_standards_prof_standards_final-aw.pdf.

Social Work Task Force (2009) *Building a safe, confident future: The final report of the Social Work Task Force*. London: Department for Children, Schools and Families.

Solar, O. & Irwin, A. (2010) *A conceptual framework for action on the social determinants of health* (Social Determinants of Health Discussion Paper 2: Policy and practice). Geneva: World Health Organization. www.who.int/publications/i/item/9789241500852.

Solomon, B.B. (1976) *Black empowerment: Social work in oppressed communities.* New York: Columbia University Press.

Spitzer, H., Twikirize, J.M. & Wairire, G.G. (eds) (2014) *Professional social work in East Africa: Towards social development, poverty reduction and gender equality.* Kampala: Fountain.

Stajduhar, K.I., Giesbrecht, M., Mollison, A., Dosani, N. & McNeil, R. (2020) Caregiving at the margins: An ethnographic exploration of family caregivers experiences providing care for structurally vulnerable populations at the end-of-life. *Palliative Medicine, 34*(7): 946–53.

Starkey, P. (2000a) *Families and social workers: The work of Family Service Units 1940–1985.* Liverpool: Liverpool University Press.

Starkey, P. (2000b) The feckless mother: Women, poverty and social workers in wartime and post-war England. *Women's History Review, 9*(3): 539–57.

Staub-Bernasconi, S. (2011) Human rights and social work: Philosophical and ethical reflections on a possible dialogue between East Asia and the West. *Ethics and Social Welfare, 5*(4): 331–47.

Staub-Bernasconi, S. (2016) Social work and human rights—linking two traditions of human rights in social work. *Journal of Human Rights and Social Work, 1*: 40–9.

Staub-Bernasconi, S. (2017) The problem with 'social problems' as domain of social work: A critical approach to the Melbourne 'global definition of social work' of 2014 and constructivist theories of social problems. *European Journal of Social Work, 20*(6), 958–71.

Stephens, P. (2013) *Social pedagogy: Heart and head.* Bremen: Europäischer Hochschulverlag.

Stepney, P. (2018) Community social work. In N. Thompson & P. Stepney (eds) *Social work theory and methods: The essentials* (pp. 227–39). New York: Routledge.

Stepney, P. & Davis, P. (2018) Cognitive behavioural therapy. In N. Thompson & P. Stepney (eds) *Social work theory and methods: The essentials* (pp. 78–93). New York: Routledge.

Stiglitz, J.E. (2015) *The great divide.* London: Penguin.

Stiglitz, J.E. (2020) *People, power and profits: Progressive capitalism for an age of discontent.* London: Penguin.

Streatfeild Committee on the Business of the Criminal Courts (1961) *Report of the Inter-Departmental Committee on the Business of the Criminal Courts* (Cmnd 1289). London: HMSO.

Studt, E. (1959) Worker–client authority relationships in social work. In E. Younghusband (ed.) (1966) *New developments in casework* (pp. 167–83). London: Allen & Unwin.

Sullivan, E. (2000) An examination of identity in the professional context of social work, leading to the introduction of a systemic model of identity [PhD thesis]. Royal Holloway and Bedford New College, University of London.

Tamm, T. (2010) Professional identity and self-concept of Estonian social workers [PhD thesis]. Tampere: University of Tampere.

Tan, N.T., Chan, S., Mehta, K. & Androff, D. (eds) (2017) *Transforming society: Strategies for social development from Singapore, Asia and around the world*. Abingdon: Routledge.

Tanner, D., Littlechild, R., Duffy, J. & Hayes, D. (2017) 'Making it real': Evaluating the impact of service user and carer involvement in social work education. *British Journal of Social Work, 47*(2): 467–86.

Teare, R.J. & McPheeters, H.L. (1970) *Manpower utilization in social welfare: A report based on a symposium on manpower utilization in social welfare services*. Atlanta, GA: Social welfare Manpower Project, Southern Regional Education Board.

ten Hoeve, Y., Jansen, G. & Roodbol, P. (2014) The nursing profession: Public image, self-concept and professional identity. A discussion paper. *Journal of Advanced Nursing, 70*(2): 295–309.

Tew, J., Ramon, S., Slade, M., Bird, V., Melton, J. & Le Boutillier, C. (2012) Social factors and recovery from mental health difficulties: A review of the evidence. *British Journal of Social Work, 42*(3): 443–40.

Thompson, N. (2016) *Anti-discriminatory practice* (6th edn). London: Palgrave.

Thyer, B.A. & Kazi, M.A.F. (eds) (2004) *International perspectives on evidence based practice in social work*. Birmingham: Venture.

Timmins, N. (1996) *The five giants: A biography of the welfare state*. London: Fontana.

Timms, N. (1964a) *Psychiatric Social Work in Britain (1939–1962)*. London: Routledge and Kegan Paul.

Timms, N. (1964b) *Social casework: Principles and practice*. London: Routledge and Kegan Paul.

Tolson, E.R., Reid, W. & Garvin, C.D. (2003) *Generalist practice: A task-centered approach* (2nd edn). New York: Columbia University Press.

Trevillion, S. (1999) *Networking and community partnership* (2nd edn). Aldershot: Arena.

Tronto, J.C. (1993) *Moral boundaries: A political argument for an ethic of care*. New York: Routledge.

Twikirize, J.M. & Spitzer, H. (eds) (2019) *Social work practice in Africa: Indigenous and innovative approaches*. Kampala: Fountain.

UNICEF (1989) *Convention of the Rights of the Child text*. www.unicef.org/child-rights-convention/convention-text.

United Nations Permanent Forum on Indigenous Issues (n.d.) *Who are indigenous peoples?* www.un.org/esa/socdev/unpfii/documents/5session_factsheet1.pdf

van Oorschot, W. (2006) Making the difference in social Europe: Deservingness perceptions among citizens of European welfare states. *Journal of European Social Policy, 16*(1): 23–42.

Venugopal, R. (2015) Neoliberalism as concept. *Economy and Society, 44*(2): 165–87.

Wachtel, T. (2017 [2000]) Restorative practices with high-risk youth. In G. Burford & P. Hudson (eds) Family group conferencing: New directions in community-centered child and family practice (pp. 86–92). Abingdon: Routledge.

Wall, T. (2023) 'Heartbreaking': Private care homes accused of failing UK children due to closures. *The Guardian* 30 April. www.theguardian.com/society/2023/apr/30/heartbreaking-private-care-homes-accused-of-failing-uk-children-due-to-closures.

Walsh, F. (2016) *Strengthening family resilience* (3rd edn). New York: Guilford.

Walton, R.G. & El Nasr, M.M.A. (1988) Indigenization and authentization in terms of social work in Egypt. *International Social Work*, *31*(2): 135–44.

Wang, E.L. (2022) From state partnership to social entrepreneurship: A top-down approach to social enterprise in China. *Asian Social Work and Policy Review*, *16*(2): 152–64.

Warham, J. (1975) *An introduction to administration for social workers* (2nd edn). London: Routledge and Kegan Paul.

Watts, L. & Hodgson, D. (2019) *Social justice theory and practice for social work: Critical and philosophical perspectives*. Cham: Springer.

Watts, M. & Higgins, A. (2017) *Narratives of recovery from mental illness: The role of peer support*. London: Routledge.

Webb, A., Vincent, J., Wistow, G. & Wray, K. (1991) Developmental social care: Experimental community mental handicap teams in Nottinghamshire. *British Journal of Social Work*, *21*(5): 491–513.

Webb, S.A. (2017) Matters of professional identity and social work. In Webb, S.A. (ed.) *Professional identity and social work* (pp. 1–18). Abingdon: Routledge.

Webb, S.A. (2020) *The Routledge handbook of critical social work*. Abingdon: Routledge.

Webb, S.A. (2022) *The Routledge handbook of international critical social work: New perspectives and agendas*. Abingdon: Routledge.

Weber, M. (1978) *Economy and society*. (G. Roth & C. Wittich, eds). Berkeley, CA: California University Press.

Weerakoon, C. & McMurray, A. (2021) Social entrepreneurship perspective of social innovation. In C. Weerakoon & A. McMurray (eds) *Theoretical and practical approaches to social innovation* (pp. 66–97). Hershey, PA: IGI. https://doi.org/10.4018/978-1-7998-4588-1.ch004.

Weick, K.E. (2007). Drop your tools: On reconfiguring management education. *Journal of Management Education*, *31*(1): 5–16.

Weinstein, J. (2011) *Case Con* and radical social work in the 1970s: The impatient revolutionaries. In M. Lavalette (ed.) *Radical social work today: Social work at the crossroads* (pp. 11–25). Bristol: Policy Press.

Westrum, R. (1993) Thinking by groups, organizations, and networks: A sociologist's view of the social psychology of science and technology. In W. Shadish & S. Fuller (eds) *The social psychology of science* (pp. 329–42). New York: Guilford.

Wheeler, J.M. (2017a) How do social work students develop their professional identity? [DEd thesis]. Plymouth: Plymouth Institute of Education.

Wheeler, J. (2017b) Shaping identity? The professional socialisation of social work students. In Webb, S.A. (ed.) *Professional identity and social work* (pp. 183–96). Abingdon: Routledge.

White, V. (2006) *The state of feminist social work*. Abingdon: Routledge.

Whittington, C. (2016a) The promised liberation of adult social work under England's 2014 Care Act: Genuine prospect or false prospectus? *British Journal of Social Work*, *46*(7): 1942–61. https://doi.org/10.1093/bjsw/bcw155

Whittington, C. (2016b) Another step towards the promised liberation of adult social work under England's 2014 Care Act? The implications of revised statutory guidance and the politics of liberation. *British Journal of Social Work*, *46*(7): 1962–80, https://doi.org/10.1093/bjsw/bcw155.

Wiffin, J. (2010) *Family perspectives on safeguarding and on relationships with children's services*. London: Office of the Children's Commissioner for England.

Wilberforce, M., Abendstern, M., Batool, S., Boland, J., Challis, D., Christian, J. et al (2020) What do service users want from mental health social work? A best–worst scaling analysis. *British Journal of Social Work*, *50*(5): 1324–44.

Wiles, F. (2013) 'Not easily put into a box': Constructing professional identity. *Social Work Education*, *32*(7): 854–66.

Wilson, T. & Wilson D.J. (1982) *The political economy of the welfare state*. London: Allen & Unwin.

Winter, K. & Cree, V.E. (2016) Social work home visits to children and families in the UK: A Foucauldian perspective. *British Journal of Social Work*, *46*(5): 1175–90.

Wongboonsin, J., Merighi, J.R., Walker, P.F. & Drawz, P.E. (2021) Travel arrangements in chronic hemodialysis patients: A qualitative study. *Hemodialysis International*, *25*(1): 113–22.

World Bank (2022) *The World Bank in social protection*. www.worldbank.org/en/topic/socialprotection.

WHO (World Health Organization) (2008) *Closing the gap in a generation: Health equity through action on the social determinants of health*. Geneva: WHO.

WHO (2018) *Mental health atlas, 2017*. Geneva: WHO.

WHO (2022) *Global report on health equity for persons with disabilities*. Geneva: WHO.

Wuenschel, P.C. (2006) The diminishing role of social work administrators in social service agencies: Issues for consideration. *Administration in Social Work*, *30*(4): 5–18.

Yang, H. & Yi, H. (2023) Frontiers of policy process research in China. *Review of Policy Research*. doi: 10.1111/ropr.12558.

Yates, P. (2018) 'Siblings as better together': Social worker decision making in cases involving sibling sexual behaviour. *British Journal of Social Work*, *48*(1): 176–94, https://doi.org/10.1093/bjsw/bcx018.

Yelaja, S.A. (ed.) (1971) *Authority and social work: Concept and use*. Toronto: University of Toronto Press.

Yelloly, M. (1980) *Social work theory and psychoanalysis*. Wokingham: Van Nostrand Reinhold.

Young, A.F. & Ashton, E.T. (1956) *British social work in the nineteenth century*. London: Routledge and Kegan Paul.

Younge, G. & Henley, J. (2003) Wimps, weasels and monkeys – the US media view of 'perfidious France'. *The Guardian*, 11 February. www.theguardian.com/world/2003/feb/11/pressandpublishing.usa.

Younghusband, E. (1959) *Report of the Working Party on Social Workers in the Local Authority Health and Welfare Services* [the Younghusband Report], London: HMSO.

Younghusband, E. (1981) *The newest profession: A short history of social work*. Sutton: Community Care, IPC Press.

Zhang, J. (2013) A grounded theory analysis of hospital-based Chinese midwives' professional identity construction [PhD thesis]. Edinburgh: University of Edinburgh.

Zuchowski, I. & McLennan, S. (2023) A systematic review of social work in general practice: Opportunities and challenges. *Journal of Evidence-Based Social Work*, *20*(5): 686–726.

Index

References to figures are in *italics*, tables in **bold**

assessment 66–9
Australia 36
authoritarianism 126, 153, 156–9
authority and power in social work
    112–14

B
Bagdonas, A. 112
Bailey, R. 57
Bakalinsky, R. 101
Baldwin, M. 145–6
Bangladesh 105
banking and financial systems 170–1
Barclay Report (1982) 21, 53, 125
Barnes, J. 22
Bartram, D. 185–6
Beckett, C. 58
Beddoe, L. 37
behaviour management 57–8
Belgium 140
benefits, welfare 109, 150, 153, 169, 174,
    182–94
Benoit, D. 54
bereavement care 108
best interest assessors 189–90
Betz, H.-G. 153–4
Bew, J. 114
Biestek, F.P. 73, 74
Bilson, A. 122–3
Blekesaune, M. 183
Boehm, W.W. 65–6
Bottomore, T.B. 149
Bourdieu, P. 85
Bower, M. 54
Bowers, S. 65
British Association of Social Workers
    133
Brubaker, R. 154
bureau-professional roles 122, 144, 146
bureaucracy 99–100, 123, 146

C
Canada 37–8, 71
capability approach 175–6
Caplan, G. 62

Care Act 2014 119
care and caring 46–50
    and affective equality 6–7, 48, 167,
      185, 197–9
    care and social care 46–7
    care gap 201–3
    defining 48
    economic value of 169
    ethics of care 49–50, 68
    future of 196–7
    interpersonal and collective caring
      46–7
    and social productivity 184–5
    see also social care
care gap 201–3
care management 68, 119–20, 121, 147,
    172
Care Quality Commission 157
Carkhuff, R.R. 54
Carney, M. 167, 168, 173, 195–6
Carpenter, J. 136
Castells, M. 26, 33
Chamberlayne, P. 105–6
Chang, H.-J. 170–1
change 51–3, 79–80
chaos theory 52
charitable organisations
    currently 102–4, 115, 116
    historically 57, 66–7, 70, 78–9,
      147
children's social care 21–2
    advocacy 92–3
    client and consumer views 187
    economic contribution of social work
      179
    management style 123
    networks and relationships 75
    proceduralisation 117–19
    professional identity 38
    safeguarding 70–3, 93–4, 117–19, 123,
      140, 187, 190
    sexual exploitation 140
    and social control 57–8
    socialisation 84
    stress and burnout 190
    structural social work 86
China 105, 126

www.ingramcontent.com/pod-product-compliance
Lightning Source LLC
Chambersburg PA
CBHW080556030426
42336CB00019B/3213